The Sins of Men

An American Revolutionary War Drama

Danny J Bradbury

D1518225

Copyright © 2023 by Danny J Bradbury

All rights reserved.

No part of this publication may be reproduced, distributed, or transmitted in any form or by any means, including photocopying, recording, or other electronic or mechanical methods, without the prior written permission of the publisher, except as permitted by U.S. copyright law. For permission requests, contact Danny J. Bradbury.

The story, all names, characters, and incidents portrayed in this production are fictitious. No identification with actual persons (living or deceased), places, buildings, and products is intended or should be inferred.

Book cover designed by Getcovers.

1st edition 2023

To my father Eldon who taught me his love for the Navy and sailing on the open seas.

I would also like to thank Deborah Crews for proofreading and giving me great feedback.

Chapter 1

Peter Beale

The Street Urchin

I felt a sudden shaking that startled me out of my deep sleep. My eyes opened to see the dark outline of my mum's face. She looked directly into my eyes and, in her cockney accent, "Pe'er my boy, you need 'o steer clear of 'ha' crowd of hooligans' ha' you run 'he stree's wi'h. I couldn'' bear 'o lose you." She then hugged me tightly. I looked around the bleak room that we called home and saw the early morning rays start to creep in through the smoke-stained window.

"I'll be safe, mum." I loved my mum. I was only ten, but my heart ached to see her wear herself away trying to take care of us. I watched as she walked out the door to make a living doing other people's laundry. I quietly dressed, careful not to wake my siblings. The only sounds I heard were the raspy snores from one of my brothers and the crackling of a fire that heated up a small pot of gruel, our breakfast. My stomach growled. I passed on eating, knowing there would be more for my six brothers and sisters. I felt indestructible, but in the back of my mind, I was troubled by her words.

"Where are you off 'o Pe'er?" I turned back and saw my older sister Sarah. "Mind your business. I shall re'urn wi'h more food. Go back 'o sleep." She laid her head back on the bed. I muttered under my breath, "I'll be back."

I felt the chill of the early spring day as I walked through the narrow, filthy streets surrounding High Street. We lived in an area filled with squalid, poorly built homes among the thriving brothels and ale houses. I tried to breathe in through my mouth but couldn't avoid the stench from open sewers and accumulated trash. The noxious odor crept into every crevice. My eyes started burning from the smoke that billowed from the various dwellings' fires. It hung like low-lying clouds and made it hard to breathe.

I was stopped in my tracks by the all-too-common sight of a dead body. I dared not go too close, but my curiosity was intense, and I needed a better look. I swiveled my head around to make sure no one could see what I was doing and crept up to the body. It was a man lying on his side facing the wall. I had an overpowering urge to look at his face. Without taking my eyes off the body, I reached down and picked up a wooden spoon. I trembled as I jabbed the spoon into the man's back. I jumped back when the corpse belched, and a horrid-smelling gas attacked me. Then I noticed movement under his jacket. I was frozen. Suddenly, several rats began scurrying in all directions. I screamed, threw down the spoon, and ran.

After distancing from the body, I slowed down, catching my breath. No one paid attention to me as I was small for my age. This was probably due to my not eating regularly. I picked up my pace. I couldn't wait to see what my mates had planned for the day. As I rounded the corner, I saw three rough-looking lads sitting on empty crates behind one of the pubs. I instantly smiled, "Hello ma'es, how goes i'?"

The largest boy hopped off his perch. He was tall and thin in his early teens. He had an air about him that I was captivated by. He reached out and put me in a headlock. "How are you, young Pe'er?" He released me, and I turned my attention to the other boys. "James, Wally. How goes?" The brothers nodded at me. Each was barefoot and wore tattered clothes. My nostrils curled being near them.

I looked back at the leader, Andrew. "Wha' 's 'he plan?" I saw his expression change. He was now all business. "We have 'o be more careful. Yesterday was a close call. Pe'er, you were nearly caugh'."

"We made mistakes 'ryin 'o rob 'he bu'cher." He glared at the brothers. They shrank from his stare. "Wha' did you lads do wrong?"

They looked at each other, and James spoke first. "We go' distrac'ed and did no' make sure i' was safe for Pe'er."

Andrew put his hands on his hips, "We will no' make 'ha' error again. Poor Pe'er almos' los' his head."

I snickered and thought about how close that butcher's knife came to take off my head. My family could have used that meat. We rarely had any.

Andrew continued, "Today, we shall find a rich mark on 'he stree' an' pick his pocke'. We will go 'o 'he marke', and once I selec' 'he 'arge' you 'wo shall distrac' him." He pointed to the brothers. He then turned toward me, "Pe'er i' is your 'ask 'o relieve 'he gen'leman of his coin purse."

While we did this successfully several times, I still had doubts. Then I thought back to that small room crowded with starving children for whom I felt responsible. That erased any objections. We followed Andrew back to High Street and mingled with the crowd in the marketplace. It was an open-air market filled with vendors selling their wares. It was a popular spot for our gang to execute our crimes. I looked around for a place to get a better view. I craned my neck and spotted a stack of boxes leaning against a wall. I weaved through the crowd, climbed on the boxes, and spotted Andrew. He turned toward me and made eye contact. He jerked his head toward a fat naval officer. The mark. I kept my eye on the man, who seemed to be alone. He took uneven steps as he flowed with the crowd. Drunk. Without losing sight of the large man, I jumped and got in behind him.

I didn't have long to wait. There was a loud shout, which I heard above the noise from the crowd. As the shoppers gathered around the source of the noise, I approached the man. He was dressed in a dark blue frock coat trimmed gold with rows of ornate buttons. There were golden epaulets on each shoulder. He wore a white powdered wig under his elaborate hat, also trimmed in gold. I knew I had only one shot at reaching into his jacket and taking his purse. I smiled at the ruckus the brothers were making and eased closely to my mark. As I was sure he was distracted, I plunged my arm under his coat. As I felt around for the bag of coins, the man suddenly turned in my direction. I saw the shocked look on his face as he clamped down on my arm. "What are you up to, boy?"

My eyes darted around, looking for a possible escape. As the grip tightened around my arm, the officer called out, "Guards, I am being robbed!" I ignored the pain in my arm as I watched three armed men in red coats run toward me. I scanned for the other gang members and saw the brothers melt into the crowd. While the armed men grabbed me and carried me off, I caught a glimpse of Andrew, who looked at me and shook his head. He turned and made his escape. I never saw him again.

Chapter 2

Peter Beale

Prison

I cried out, "Le' me go. I have done no'hin wrong!" One of the guards hit me on the side of my head with the butt of his rifle. "Shut your mouth, you street urchin." I nearly passed out from the pain and felt the grip from the soldiers tighten. I looked at the man who struck me. "Where are you 'akin me?"

He glanced down. "We are taking you to see the magistrate."

I wasn't sure what that meant, but it didn't sound good. I struggled to free myself from my captors.

"Stop what you're doing, or I shall strike you harder!"

I cowered and stopped moving. I tried to shake the fog from my head and looked around to determine where I was. I noticed a large crowd had gathered around us, and someone shouted, "S'rin him up!" I saw the masts of ships tied up at the pier and knew where I was. *They were taking me to prison.*

My heart sank when I saw the black metal gates at the entrance of Portsmouth's old prison. The structure looked like a castle made of limestone worn down by the elements over its many years of operation. It stood two stories high and was streaked with moss growing in the crevices. One of the soldiers laughed and said, "This will be your new home, lad."

I had never been in prison, but I knew the rumors that once you were locked up, you never left. The guards put me down and pushed me through the open doors. I was whisked into a damp, cold room and came face to face with the magistrate. The man sat behind a large desk and wore a white powdered wig and a black flowing robe. He looked down at me. "What have we here?"

"This boy was caught trying to rob Captain Nigel Thomas of his Majesty's Royal Navy."

"Is that so? What say you, young man?"

I knew I was in trouble and blurted out, "I' 's a lie!"

"You are an impudent lad. What is your name?"

I couldn't make eye contact and looked down at my feet. "Pe'er Beale, gov'ner."

"Well, Master Beale, we don't look too kindly on our royal officers being robbed. You shall serve a ninety-day term here at the prison. What say you?" He partially stood, placing his hands on the desk and glaring down at me.

"I don" understand. Wha' 's 'o happen 'o me?"

"You are to be locked away here for the next ninety days," he said, motioning with his arm.

I nearly collapsed. *How would I survive?* "Who will 'ell my mum where I am?"

"That's not my concern. Take the boy away."

I felt myself being lifted and yanked out of the office. As I tried not to panic, I was dragged toward an iron gate leading to a courtyard in the center of the castle-like building. This couldn't be happening; I needed my mum. I watched in disbelief as a short, stubby man with a large ring full of keys ambled over to the gate and unlocked it. He turned to look at me while he swung it open. I was tossed into the courtyard, and the gate swung shut. I scampered to my feet and grabbed the bars. "Wha' do I do now?"

The man with the keys whispered, "Survive," and walked away.

I stood there for a few minutes, afraid to turn around. I was overcome by being watched, and I slowly swiveled my head. I gasped when I saw the courtyard was packed with desperate-looking men and boys. There were hundreds of them, primarily dressed in rags. Many were covered in sores. They looked like skeletons covered with skin. Some of them staggered in my direction. I looked for someplace to run and hide when an older man with a long white beard called out to me. "Boy, come this way." He motioned his arms toward himself.

I couldn't move. As the others came closer, someone called out. "We shall take care of you, pretty lad."

That broke my paralysis, and I ran to the bearded man.

"Why are you here, boy?"

I looked to make sure the others weren't behind me. "I 'ried 'o rob a gen'leman."

"You will need to do something about that accent. How long are you to serve here?"

"Nine'y days."

He shook his head. "How old are you?"

"I'm 'en, sir."

"Listen to me if you want to live. Trust no one and be on your guard at all times. Do you have any money? I could only shake my head no. "My name is Percy. I will look after you, but I will need you to do things for me when I ask you."

I didn't know what he meant, but what else could I do?

He started to walk away, and I followed him. He asked over his shoulder, "What do I call you?"

"Pe'er."

"Very well, Peter. Let's get you a place to sleep, and I will show you around. Remember, trust no one."

Then why should I trust you?

Chapter 3

Peter Beale

Caught in the Act

"Keep up, boy!"

I picked up my pace. I stared straight ahead and didn't make eye contact with the other prisoners. Percy led me to an area of the yard inhabited by other boys my age. It was an area in the corner against the stone wall. It was partially covered by a wooden overhang, only providing limited protection from the elements. The stone floor was covered with moldy straw used for bedding. The smell was overpowering. The odor of human waste mixed with rotting bodies was worse than anything I dealt with on High Street.

There were ten of them huddled in the corner. They barely had anything to wear and were filthy. Other than their age, we had another thing in common – they looked starving. Each boy looked up at me, and I could see the hopelessness in their eyes.

"Lads, this is our newest member, Peter. Make him feel at home. I need to take care of some business." He turned and walked away.

One of the boys stood up and walked over to where I was standing. He sized me up and said, "Hello, fresh mea'. They call me Rand. Bes' you learn from all us lads. We stick 'oge'her and look ou' for one ano'her."

"Wha' did Percy mean when he 'old me I would have 'o do 'hings for him?"

In a hushed tone, Rand looked around and said, "You stay away from him if you can. He has us do his dir'y work. He won" pro'ec' you if you ge' caugh' breaking the rules."

Over the next few weeks, I learned what to do to survive. The trick was to get enough food to stay alive. We were fed twice daily, and the guards didn't care if everyone got an equal share. The morning meal was maggot-filled gruel. I learned from the other boys to use my size as an advantage. I would line up early for my first ration and then sneak back into the line with the hundreds of other prisoners to get another bowl. We tried to look after each other, and when one of us was too sick, we would make sure they got their share. There were still days that I didn't eat.

I took Rand's advice to heart and avoided Percy as much as possible. I wasn't always successful. One morning, while minding my business, I daydreamed about getting out. My thoughts drifted to what I would do differently when I got released.

"Peter, where have you been?"

I was startled out of my daydream and cringed at the sound of his voice.

"I need you to do something for me."

I looked at him, waiting for more.

"I've been informed that a new shipment of tobacco is to be received this very day. You are to revert to your old ways and nick some of that supply for me. Use a couple of the other lads to help you, but get it done."

I don't know how he got his information, but I learned to avoid crossing him. I just nodded my head.

"Good lad."

I noticed that the prisoners were sometimes given tobacco rations for good behavior. Since this happened rarely, tobacco was a commodity that could be killed over, used for trade, and valued. I gathered up Rand and another street urchin named Niles.

"Percy wan's us 'o steal some 'obacco from a load 'ha' will be delivered 'oday." I knew by the look on Rand's face that this would be dangerous.

"'I' will be heavily guarded. How do we ge' away wi'h i'?"

I shrugged my shoulders. "You and Niles will cause a ruckus, and I will sneak in and grab as much as I can and ge' los' in 'he crowd." Doing something like this was why I was here in the first place, but I knew I needed to satisfy Percy.

We positioned ourselves as close to the front gate as possible, anticipating the load to be delivered. We didn't have long to wait. A lone wagon was drawn by two large oxen heading to the gate. I counted five armed prison guards around the wagon. Once the wagon was inside the gate, it would be moved to a storage room at the rear of the courtyard. We would have only a few minutes to make our move. It helped that the other prisoners saw what was coming and started to crowd around the entrance.

The guards started yelling, "Get back, you scum!" as they pointed their muskets toward the mass of men.

It was time to make our move. I looked at Rand and slightly nodded my head. Both boys ran in front of the oxen and started fighting. Two of the guards ran to break up the fight. Seeing the melee incited the other prisoners, they closed in on the wagon. This forced the other three guards to deal with them. This was my chance. I scampered toward the rear of the wagon and dove underneath. I looked around to make sure no one saw me. Then, I climbed up the side of the wagon, facing the inner wall of the prison.

I knew I had only a few seconds, so I grabbed two sacks filled with dried tobacco and tossed them on the ground behind the wagon. Now, the tricky part. I was on my hands and knees as I dragged the sacks toward the wall.

The bags were heavier than I thought. I was startled by the sound of one of the muskets being fired. I could see from where I was the crowd of prisoners started to back away. There was the shape of one man lying on the ground. His blood flowed out on the stones. I was scared out of my wits and nearly panicked. I looked around to see the guards were still distracted by the other inmates. My only chance was to take one bag and leave the other behind. I wrestled the bag from under the wagon to the wall. I took a deep breath and started to crawl along the wall away from the gate.

The guard's attention was still focused on the inmates, which was the distraction I needed. When I got to the oxen, I took my chance and stood up, grasped the bag of tobacco, and sprinted for the crowd. Just as I reached the mass of men, I saw one of the older criminals look at me. He started to yell, "The boy has a bag of tobacco!" He reached for the treasure. I mouthed, "No."

The next thing I knew, I was being grabbed by multiple arms. I felt the sting of several punches landing on my head and upper body. The bag was snatched from my grip. Then I heard the thunder of another musket being fired.

I was thrown to the ground and lay there as the crowd broke up. I swiped at the blood flowing from my nose when I was picked up by one of the guards.

"Look at all the problems you started."

He dragged me over to the row of solitary confinement cells. He then threw me in and shut and locked the door.

Chapter 4

Peter Beale

The Navy Comes Calling

I was locked away in the "hole" for a week. Time stood still for me, and I would curl myself into a ball and cry for my mum every night. The worst part was the darkness. I couldn't see my own hands in front of my face. After a while, I started to hallucinate. I swore others were locked in that cell as I heard their voices. I have seen much death in my young lifetime, but I don't believe in ghosts. It was a blessing that I couldn't see the bread I was fed. It moved when I took a bite.

When I was released, the guard told me ninety more days were added to my sentence. I never asked for any of this. *Was my life not meant to mean anything?* It was daunting to deal with so much at my age. After that, I made a promise to stay away from Percy and the lost boys. This proved to be a difficult task as it was a small prison. I needed someone to protect me, but who could I trust?

Staying clear of Percy's little kingdom, I made my way to the area of the yard that housed the oldest criminals. I ignored the lewd comments from the mass of men that I moved through searching for a protector. Life on the street and in this place had made me less trusting, but I was still a ten-year-old. I scanned the island of empty faces and spied a solitary man in a corner hemmed in by two wall sections. I could see that he was staring at me.

"Sir, can I speak wi'h you?"

He patted the floor beside him, "Come have a seat, lad."

Something in his light-blue eyes told me I would be safe, but it was still difficult for me to trust. I hesitated and then dutifully sat down.

"What do you need?"

"I need someplace where I can be safe."

He smirked, "There is no place safe here. What's your name, boy?

"Pe'er."

"You need to learn the King's English. I know who you are. I saw you try to steal that tobacco. Stupid thing to do. Why should I help you?"

I hung my head. "I am a small boy, and no one will 'ake pi'y on me."

"You're smart to get away from Percy and his gang. What makes you think I can help you?"

"You have a kind face, and no one bo'hers you."

He laughed. "It wasn't always that way. I'm an educated man and was convicted for a crime I didn't do." He waved a hand in the direction of the yard. "This crowd didn't take kindly to me at first."

"'How long have you been here?"

"More than ten years. I will never be set free." He slapped one of his knees. "I will help you, lad, but you must promise to let me teach you to speak properly. Can you read?"

"No, sir. Wha' is your name?"

"Thomas."

***

Over the next few weeks, I stayed close to Thomas. We were left alone, and I often wondered why but didn't ask. He was strict about me learning to lose my accent. I didn't see the problem. It was all I knew. I tried because

I wanted to please him. He also started to teach me to read from his bible. He told me how important it was to be educated if I ever wanted to make it in this life. He was a patient man. I could have been a better student.

There was only one run-in with Percy's gang. I was standing in line for the evening meal. It was the usual; moldy bread and watery soup. I could feel a presence close to me. Before I could turn, I heard a whisper in my ear.

"Where have you been Pe'er? We have missed you."

It was Rand. I sucked in a breath of stale air. My eyes darted around, looking for other signs of danger. "I have moved on 'o o'her more sui'able arrangemen's."

"Sui'able arrangemen's is i'. Are you now a fancy boy?"

"Wha' do you wan', Rand?"

I could feel his breath on the back of my neck. "Percy needs you back, and i've been sen' 'o collec' you."

Before I could respond, I heard Thomas say, "What have we here? One of Percy's slaves doing his master's bidding?"

I turned and saw Rand's shocked look. Before I knew it, he had taken off and was lost in the crowd waiting for their supper.

I had to work hard every day to survive in prison. I heard tales of what some men did to small boys, but I didn't experience that horror. I couldn't believe what I heard. Along with trying to endure my fate, my time in prison was also dull. Any distraction was usually welcome. It was a scorching day. Thomas and I sat in the shade, working on my reading lesson. We both heard a commotion going on at the front gate. I stood with the other inmates around me to see what was happening. I had to push through the crowd to get a better view. A line of armed soldiers entered the courtyard, led by a young-looking man giving orders. His voice carried throughout the prison yard.

"You men, we are recruiting for the King's Navy. England is at war with the French, and we need good men to assist with the fight."

Someone from the crowd yelled out, "We are always at war with the French."

There was a chorus of laughs from the convicts.

The young officer did not appear to see the humor and turned to the line of soldiers and barked. "Spread out and find me good replacements this time."

I turned around to find Thomas. He had worked his way through the crowd and stood next to me.

"Wha' do 'hey wan'?"

He had a troubled look on his face. "They are impressing men to serve the crown in the navy."

"Why are 'hey here?"

He grabbed me by the collar and started to lead me away. "They are not looking for volunteers. They are here to take men and boys away for service."

"Where are you 'akin me?"

"I'm too old, but we must hide you from those soldiers."

I stared at the soldiers while they walked through the crowd. It looked like they were randomly grabbing younger-looking men, but no boys. I turned to look at Thomas as he continued to drag me away. There was a look of determination on his face. *Do I need to be worried?*

When we were as far as we could go, Thomas pointed and said, "Sit down behind those crates."

I did as I was told but kept watching the unfolding scene. Some of the selected prisoners called out, while others remained stoic. I could feel the tension in the air. I saw the prison guards watching at the top of the walls. They were laughing at the misery that was imposed on the prisoners.

Thomas noticed that I was poking my head above the crate and hissed, "Get down, you fool!"

As I slumped down, I heard Thomas talking to one of the soldiers.

"Old man, where is that boy that was with you?"

"There are no boys here."

"Now, why do you want to lie to me, old man?" The soldier was wearing a bright red uniform and carried a large musket. He pushed past Thomas and looked behind the crate where I was trying to hide. "There you are, lad." He turned and called out. "Lieutenant Pressley, come see what I found."

I stood up and watched the young officer take long strides in my direction. I couldn't take my eyes off him until I saw Thomas step in front of the lieutenant out of the corner of my eye.

"You don't need that boy. He is too young."

"Get out of my way, old man!"

When Thomas didn't move, a soldier struck him on the head with the musket. I watched as my protector crumpled to the ground with a nasty wound on his forehead.

Pressley smiled while he stared at me up and down. "Take that young boy; he should be pleasing to the captain."

The soldier obeyed the order and grabbed me. "Be a good lad and come with us."

I started to panic and tried to escape from the soldier's grip. He only tightened his hold. My eyes pleaded with the other prisoners to step in and help. It was hopeless. I cried out, "Sir, I am bu' a boy. Who will 'ell my mum where I am 'o go?"

The soldier continued to drag me through the crowded prison yard and said, "Shut up, lad, we will be your momma now."

Twenty-five of us were selected. We were led out of the prison and lined up on the street outside. I was in denial, and as I stared at the others, they were equally shocked by the events of the day.

The young officer stood facing us with his arms crossed. He had the smug look of someone who knew he had all the power. When the soldiers controlled us, he said, "Men, by order of King George, we will now take you to your new home. Any of you trying to escape will be shot on sight by one of the soldiers surrounding you." He let that statement hang in the air for a few seconds and then commanded, "Move them out!"

We were slowly paraded through the streets of Portsmouth down toward the docks. I saw a crowd had gathered to watch the spectacle. There was a look of sympathy on the citizens' faces. This must have been a joint event around here, but I knew nothing about it. The only sounds were the orders of the soldiers and the ha-ha-ha of seagulls who floated above us.

As we neared the docks, the odor of rot and briny water from the harbor overpowered me. I took a couple steps out of line and strained my neck to get a good look at the ship. I had seen the British naval ships come and go all my life. I was always curious about the men who sailed on them and what they experienced. I never had been aboard one of them. The closer we got to the ship, the better look I got. She wasn't imposing and looked old and worn. The soldiers halted us near the stern.

As I stood in place, I shifted my weight from one leg to another, considering what was to happen to me. I saw movement going on out of the corner of my eye and focused on all the activity around the pier. It appeared that provisions were being loaded aboard. I wondered if the ship was preparing to go to sea. I was hypnotized by the bustle on the swarming pier. The man beside me told no one in particular, "My God, look at all the ships."

I looked down the length of the pier and counted the masts of twenty ships. This was bigger than anything I had ever been involved in. My pulse quickened, and sweat formed on my upper lip. *Why was I here?* I started to panic. It was only a few blocks from home, and I badly wanted to see my mum before I left.

I thought, *"Surely they wouldn't miss a small boy like me."* I instinctively decided to try to escape before it was too late. I quickly jerked my head to each side, and when I thought it was safe, I darted toward the crowd surrounding the line of impressed men. Just as I thought I would make it, there was a tug on my jacket, and I was violently slammed to the ground, hitting my head. Trying to regain my senses, I looked up into the angry eyes of one of the soldiers.

"Where do you think you're going?" he asked, lifting me off the ground. "You pull another stunt like that; you could find yourself in front of a whip."

I began sobbing uncontrollably. My life had never been extraordinary, and I never thought I had much to live for, but now it was hopeless.

"Quit your crying boy. Get a hold of yourself."

I slowly got control over my emotions. My shoulders slumped as I was shoved back into line. I surrendered to my fate and followed the other men up the gangplank onto the ship.

When we were all aboard, they crowded us onto the main deck. The ship looked much more minor. I could feel the gentle motion of the tide move the boat. There was a maze of activity going on around us. I watched an old, grizzled-looking man with large, muscled arms stand before us.

"My name is Harris, and I am the master-at-arms. My duties include being in charge of discipline and order, among other things. Welcome to His Majesty's Ship the Progress."

Harris narrowed his eyes and crossed his arms across his chest while scanning the "new" crewmen. "I told them to bring me real men to serve on this ship, and they brought me this pathetic group."

He let that sink in and continued, "You men will all be given your assignments, and your training will start today. A word of warning to each of you, I will not tolerate any transgressions, and you will be punished severely if you don't obey all orders that are given to you. We will be setting off soon and are sailing off to fight the French. You all would be wise to learn your new roles quickly."

I watched as other crewmen stepped up after Harris was finished and started barking orders at us. We were divided into groups based on the duties that we would be responsible for performing. We were told we were considered "landsmen" since we had little or no experience on a ship. Most of the new crewmen were sent to the ship's boatswain, who was responsible for the maintenance and upkeep of the boat. As I watched, others were ordered to report to the gunner responsible for the armaments, and the rest went to the carpenter accountable for repairs.

Everyone was assigned a duty except for me. I fought the urge to start crying again when I noticed an overweight man with a ragged beard and a stain-soaked shirt amble toward me. The man towered over me. He looked at me approvingly, "Boy, you will be the captain's new cabin boy. Captain Auger will take a shine to you, as he likes them young. My name is Adams, and I'm the ship's cook. I will be doing your training. Follow me."

My mind was cluttered with everything the fat and disgusting man told me. I dutifully followed him below decks to the galley. As I stepped down the ladder, I took in a gasp of noxious air as I got my first look at the cramped quarters. *How could so many men live down here?*

Adams turned, saw me looking around, and ordered, "Quit lollygagging and follow me!"

I hurried down the ladder and caught up with the cook. When we got to the ship's galley, Adams showed me around. "The galley is located at the forward part of the ship."

My eyes widened as I stood in front of the galley stove. This was the first time I had seen something like it. The cook chuckled when he saw my expression.

"It's made of thick sheet iron and contains several ovens and a large heating area for pots and kettles." He pointed to the deck. "The fire for the stove is self-contained since the fire on a wooden ship is one of the greatest threats to its safety. The stove rests on legs and is placed in a sandbox capped with bricks to prevent burning the timbers below." His head then jerked up. "Smoke from the stove is directed through that copper piping and funneled up through a chimney that goes to the weather deck."

I was already overwhelmed. Adams gave me the uniform I would wear when serving the captain and other officers. Then, the old cook gave me a hammock and showed me where I would be sleeping near the galley.

After the tour, the cook ordered me to assist with the stores. I followed his gaze to the chain of men passing crates down the ladder.

"Wha' do I do?"

The old cook sighed, "You help them carry crates below to the storage hold."

When I didn't move, he kicked my back end, sending me flying toward the ladder. The other sailors laughed at my misfortune. I was humiliated and picked myself off the deck.

One of the sailors beckoned me. "Come here, lad, help me with this heavy crate."

"Wha' 's in i'?

He looked sideways at me and grunted. "This one has cheese."

I helped him pass the crate to another sailor. "Wha' else are 'hey bringing on?"

"All manner of food and drink. There's beef, pork, freshwater, bread, butter, oatmeal, flour, lard, beer, and rum."

Just then, I heard what sounded like animals. "Wha' was 'ha'?"

The sailor, whose name I learned later was Jonsey, laughed. "That would be cattle, pigs and chickens."

"Where do we pu' 'hem?"

"There are pens below where they are kept until they get butchered to feed the crew."

We worked for the rest of the morning stowing the provisions. The whole time I worked, I couldn't figure out why the young lieutenant and the fat old cook thought I would be pleasing to the captain.

Chapter 5

Captain Auger

Getting Underway

This was my favorite time sitting alone in my cabin. I couldn't help but think of the power I possessed. Being the captain of a ship was like being a God. I look around at the mementos scattered around the cramped space. They belay the rewards of my ambitions and lust for command. I should have someone clean up this mess. It didn't seem important to me. I never married. Didn't see the need to. Maybe I would have been more domesticated had I done so. There is an urgency to seal my legacy before it's too late. I'm interrupted by a gentle knock on my cabin door. "Enter."

"Captain Auger, sir. The new recruits have been brought aboard."

I stood up from behind my desk. "Very well, Mr. Crittenden. I will be out in a minute."

My executive officer Ambrose Crittenden looks for more, then turns and shuts the door behind him. He is handsome and high born. *He'll probably take my command some day.* I walk over to the window of my cabin and stare out in the harbor at all the activity. My thoughts drift back to how I got to this point in my life. I have spent most of my forty years at sea serving the crown. It's a long way from growing up poor near the shipyards of Deptford on the river Thames. My only desire was the desperate need to escape the poverty and abuse I suffered. I ran away to join the navy. I was nine. I worked hard to get to my present station as captain of the Progress. Nothing has ever been given to me and it has shaped my outlook on life. I hate all aristocrats who have been pampered and catered to. It is my goal in life to prove them all wrong about me.

I grab my top coat and head for the quarterdeck. We are faced with another war with the French. This time it concerns our common goals of expanding power to the new world. So once again into the breach. This time I will push this crew until I can earn a coveted command and admiral stripes. I know that the crew hates me and I use that power to control and bend them to my will. It is how I was taught.

As I stare down from the quarterdeck at our new "recruits", I have my doubts. It is an old custom born from the need to man the ships. I know from experience that many will fail or try to escape the first chance they get. I would rather have a crew who wants to be here and serve. I feel the familiar stirring when I think about the new cabin boy. That idiot Pressley assured me that I would be "very pleased". That's for later.

"Captain, the provisions have been stowed and we are ready to get underway."

I look up to see the officer of the deck, Lieutenant Thomas. "Very well, Mr. Thomas. Give the order."

He touched the brim of his hat and went off barking orders to the crew.

I watched without showing any emotion as the mooring lines were cast and the anchor was raised. Inwardly, I enjoyed watching the crew work in unison to get the ship underway. Being the captain of a ship was a lonely job, but I love it so. I move to the railing to watch the ship being manually pulled into the harbor using the ship's capstan with cables connected to mooring buoys. My trained eye sees that the tide and winds are favorable. I smile when I hear the order for the sails to be set and the intricate balancing act of a large man-of-war leaving port begins. The next step is the most dangerous and I try to hide my anxiety from the crew. Since Progress was just one of a sizable fleet leaving Portsmouth, there was always the possibility of ships ramming one another. While I tightly grasp the rail, I turn and watch the helmsman gracefully steer the rudder through the maze of docks and ships and direct the old ship to open sea.

It was marvelous to feel the wind in my face and to breathe fresh air. I tired of being in port with its distractions and filth. I sensed the men on the quarterdeck staring at me. It was time to address the crew. "Mr. Thomas, assemble the crew. It is time to let them know where we are going."

"Aye, Captain." He turned to the master-at-arms, "Mr. Harris, call the crew to assemble."

There were other orders given and I watched as the crew came topside. These men had no idea where we were going. The power I have over them is intoxicating. I took a pose with my hands firmly planted on my hips. I had to move my feet apart to have a more solid footing to combat the gentle rolling of the ocean.

After making the men wait at attention long enough to satiate my ego, I spoke, "Men, as you all know we are at war with France." I point out to the ships surrounding us. "We have been ordered to sail as part of this great fleet to take the battle to the French in the American colonies." I paused, but the crew remained silent.

"It will be our greatest honor to make history and to serve the King. I expect each of you to do your duty. There will be severe punishment for anyone not living up to the high standards that this great ship has set."

I raised my voice and the exertions made my cheeks turn a bright red. I wasn't getting the reaction I expected and started to shake with anger at the crew as they just stood there at attention showing no emotion. My mind raced with thoughts of how I would make them all respect me and pay for their insolence.

Finally controlling myself, I shouted, "God save the King!"

The crew in unison responded with little enthusiasm, "God save the King."

I turned quickly and as I exited the quarterdeck and stated under my breath, "My time is now, and I will make this crew bow down to my wishes."

Chapter 6

Peter Beale

Unspeakable Act

The order came down to go topside to hear the captain give the orders. I watched the other crewmen climb the ladder and I sought out the cook. He saw me linger and yelled out, "Get topside with the others!"

I was overwhelmed at the sight of the other ships in the armada. I could see masts that stretched out to the horizon. Just then the cook grabbed me by the collar and dragged me to line up with the rest of the crew. I stood there not knowing what I should be doing, when I noticed the men around me look up in the direction of the quarterdeck. When my eyes followed theirs, I got my first view of the captain. He looked to be short and frumpy. I could see a frown on his face as he began to speak. I was distracted by my surroundings and the disappearing coast of England, and didn't pay attention to what the man was saying. There was something about "war with France and doing our duty".

After we repeated, "God save the King," I heard the order dismissing us. I walked over to the rail as the others went back to their duties. I wasn't ready to go back to the galley yet. I got my first good look at the ocean and I was mesmerized. I felt the ship rocking from the rising and falling water. It was a cold February day on the North Atlantic Ocean. The water had a deep, dark blue tint to it. I could see good sized waves topped with white foam on the surface. Fortunately, the rocking of the ship, as it sailed through the water, didn't bother me. My jaw became unhinged as I got a better view of the other ships. *How could such a force ever be defeated?* I couldn't imagine what the French navy was like, but would they be ready for all this British might?

While I stood at the railing, another sailor walked up to me.

"Quite a view, isn't it?"

I turned toward the man, who looked like most of the sailors I had seen back in town. The older man had his blond hair tied in a bow behind his head. He wore a tattered uniform and his face showed scars from years at sea. I could smell tobacco on the man and wasn't sure how to respond.

The man said, "My name is Jacobs. You must be the new cabin boy."

I slowly shook my head up and down, "My name is Pe'er. Wha' do you do on 'he ship?"

Jacobs' face remained neutral and he answered, "I'm an old deck hand. I was a boy just like you when I joined the navy so I'm going to give you some good advice."

He stared into my eyes and narrowed his brow. "You need to be very careful, especially around the captain. You need to stand up for yourself and try to make friends that you can trust. Do you understand?"

I continued to look at the man, "Yes sir, I 'hink I understand."

Jacobs patted me on my head and walked away.

As I remained in a haze, I heard the old cook yelling at me.

"There you are! I've been looking everywhere for you. Come with me, it's time to prepare the captain's meal. It's also time for you to meet him."

A shiver ran down my spine, but I dutifully followed the cook back to the galley.

As I helped the cook prepare the captain's evening meal, I couldn't help but think back to what the old sailor told me. I shot a sideway glance at the cook. I won't be able to trust him. *Where would I find friends to protect me?* With the meal prepared, the cook ordered me to change into my "serving uniform". The uniform consisted of a white jacket, half pants and stockings, with buckled shoes that were slightly too large for my feet. The cook stared appraisingly at me in the uniform, "It looks like it fits you well. The last cabin boy was about your size."

The cook grabbed me by my shoulders and stared into my eyes, "You are always to keep this uniform clean, especially in the presence of the captain. Do you understand me, boy?"

I felt that I was in danger, but shook my head yes and continued to listen to the old cook.

"I will show you how to get to the captain's cabin and make the introduction. Captain Auger likes to have his first meal at sea alone. After that he will sometimes dine with the other officers. It is very important that you do exactly what I told you earlier and obey every order that you are given no matter how uncomfortable it makes you."

I only half listened as the cook went on to explain how to serve the captain his meal, then to wait quietly off to the side until he was finished and I was dismissed. I would then clear the dishes and return to the galley.

"You will only speak to the captain or any other officer if you are spoken to first."

Cook Adams directed me to pick up the serving tray and led me to the aft part of the ship to the captain's cabin. With the pitch and roll of the ship, it was challenging to not spill any of the contents on the tray.

Finally reaching the cabin, the cook knocked on the door.

"You may enter."

Upon hearing that voice again, I began to shake and almost dropped the serving tray. Adams gave me a stern look and opened the door. We entered the crowded cabin and I came face to face with Captain Auger. Auger's eyes ogled over me while the cook made introductions.

"Captain, sir, this is your new cabin boy, young Master Beale."

The captain had a sinister look on his face and said, "Master Beale, welcome to the Progress. You may set my dinner on that table." He pointed to a table in the corner of his cabin.

After setting down the serving tray, I stood off to the side and awaited further orders. *Why is he staring at me like that?*

The captain then turned to the cook, "You are dismissed, Mr. Adams."

As the cook left the room, he glared at me and closed the door.

The captain took his seat and began to consume his meal. As he ate, he looked over at me and grinned. My senses were heightened. There was something wrong. My mind told my body to run away before it was too late, but I stayed frozen in place against the bulkhead.

The captain continued to eat and started to ask questions.

"How old are you, boy?"

"I am 'en, sir."

"Very good. Are you from Portsmouth?"

"Yes, sir."

"Tell me about your family."

Not calmed by his questions, I only felt more uneasy. "My fa'her was a sailor, bu' he is dead. My mo'her is a laundress. I have six bro'hers and sis'ers."

"No reason to fear, young man. We will become very acquainted."

Just then the captain rose from the table and faced me. I could see the bulge in his pants and stared at it. He noticed where I was staring.

"See what you've done. We shall need to take care of this situation."

I looked at the captain not understanding what he meant.

He then ordered, "Come here boy and put your hands on the table!"

I did as I was told. The next thing I felt was my britches being tugged and pulled down. I bit down on my tongue and escaped to a different place in my mind during the next few minutes to maintain my sanity.

The captain breathed heavily and stated, "Clean yourself up and then you are excused."

I grabbed a linen napkin that was on the tray and wiped up as much as I could. I pulled up my short pants and seized the tray. As I shuffled towards the door, I couldn't bring myself to look back at him.

As I exited the cabin, the captain said, "I look forward to more of our discussions."

I trembled and carefully closed the door behind me.

The cook met me when I returned to the galley. The slimy older man knew what would happen to me. He took the tray away and noticed blood on my pants. "I told you to keep your uniform clean! Change out of those clothes, we need to prepare to feed the crew."

I was in shock from being violated. I did as I was told, but I vowed right there and then that I would make them all pay.

Chapter 7

Peter Beale

Resigned to His Fate

O ver the next few weeks, I continued to serve the captain in his cabin. The abuse did not take place every time, but I still had to endure the captain's lust way too often. It was a relief when other officers dined with the captain. It meant that I would be left alone. I actually had gotten to know several of the officers and, indeed, came to respect some of them. However, a line existed that could not be crossed between the officer class and a lowly cabin boy. *Did they know what was happening to me*?

The routine of daily life at sea could be tedious. The daily prep went into creating and serving meals to the officers and crew. I welcomed the boredom of my routine when I didn't serve the captain alone. I tried to build up a wall between my emotions and surviving the act. I sensed that the captain started to tire of the need to abuse me when I didn't put up a fight. The toll it took on my soul was irreversible.

I continued to seek out my protector among the crew. There were a few occasions when I would have a chance to meet with the seaman Jacobs. Jacobs showed kindness to me that first day, and he remained friendly. However, there was a barrier between us that I could not understand. Maybe he held the same secret I did and couldn't relive his experiences by befriending me. He wasn't the only one. My shame made it nearly impossible for me to make eye contact. I noticed that most other crewmen would avoid me or give me knowing looks that only deepened my despair. It got so bad that I considered throwing myself overboard and ending it. There was something inside of me that wouldn't allow me to take the easy way out. Life was so unfair.

One day, while in the galley preparing a meal, I gathered the courage to talk to the cook. "Sir, can I ask you a ques'ion?"

The cook rolled his eyes and looked at me disgusted, "What is it, boy?"

I hesitated and asked, "Can you 'ell me wha' happened 'o 'he boy before me?"

He stopped what he was doing and tenderly patted me on the shoulder. "Why do you want to know that?"

"I was jus' curious and hoped you could 'ell me."

He put down the knife he held and turned toward me. "Well, he was a lad about your age. Not a bad sort. I actually got to where I liked him."

I listened intently and hung on the cook's every word, "Where is he now?"

The cook looked down at his feet and replied, "Well, he must not have adapted to life at sea too well. The last time we were out, he jumped overboard and was never seen again."

He then looked up at me, "You need to be strong and learn how to survive. This won't last forever. I promise."

I was taken by the sudden show of empathy from a man I had grown to hate. Still, jumping overboard might be a good idea.

Chapter 8

Peter Beale

The Powder Monkey

I learned of the traditions that sailing ships underwent in the 18th century, a time when maritime exploration was at its peak. This was borne from hundreds of years of experience. I was still treated as an outcast, a common experience for a young crew member in those times, so I would have to overhear other sailors talking about these rituals and legends. Tales of sea monsters and mermaids were the most entertaining. I usually spent between midday meals and supper on the weather deck watching the fleet, a sight that never failed to awe me. Since I was small and insignificant, I would listen from the shadows to the conversations of others. One day, I watched two deck hands, down on their knees, scrub the deck and argue.

"I swear to you that I saw one, clear as day."

"You lie. There are no such things."

I snuck closer to the men to try and hear what they were discussing.

The sailor, making his case, sat back and shoved his mate. "I'm telling you, we were off the coast of Bermuda, and I saw two of them swimming around the ship," he insisted, his voice filled with conviction.

"You're daft! You saw a large fish."

"When one of them came out of the water, I clearly saw a woman's face and even saw her hooters."

The other sailor shook his head and went back to work.

I was young and gullible and would believe almost anything. The yells from the cook made me miss the rest of that conversation.

I was included in the mundane. The cook, a burly man with a booming voice, taught me the importance of a daily schedule, which kept the crew busy. This prevented strife and mischief among the crew. These routines included constant drilling to prepare for the battles to come. Each man was assigned to a quarter's station where they would be responsible for ensuring the ship's safety. I was assigned to the gun deck to act as a powder monkey. My duty was to ensure that each gun station had enough powder to fire their cannon. I was also responsible for bringing water to the gun crews to keep the men and their guns operational. These drills were designed to cover all possibilities and honed the men into a finely tuned team. The drills were taken very seriously, as they should be because the lives of everyone onboard the ship depended on the outcome when faced with a real emergency. As the fleet sailed closer to the new world and war with the French, the frequency of the drills increased.

Each time the ship's drummer beat 'quarters,' a signal that sent a thrill through my veins, I would make my way to the gun deck. The space was cramped, with a low overhead that forced the men to crouch while performing their duties. I, however, fit just right. There were ten cannons lined up on each side of the ship, a formidable sight. On my first trip, I reported to the ship's gunner, Mr. Stansbury, a man whose experience and skill commanded my respect.

"Master Beale, since this is your first time, I want you to stay close to me and learn."

"Yes, sir." I followed him as he walked bent over between the row of guns, his tall, lean figure moving with a grace that belied his age and the cramped space.

"Each gun is manned by a crew of three. The gun captain is responsible for ensuring that his gun is properly loaded, primed, sighted, and ready to fire."

We watched as the gun crews went about their work.

He turned and looked to make sure I was paying attention. "Watch as the gun is pulled back from the outer hull using a series of tackles." He pointed to the overhead above each gun. The men strained to pull the heavy cannon using ropes, their muscles bulging with the effort.

"With the gun pulled back, watch as one man loads the gun with a cartridge of gunpowder followed by a cloth wad."

I was amazed at how quickly each man did his task.

A third man rammed the load into the barrel using a wooden rammer.

"Now watch as the gun captain pierces the cartridge with a pricker placed down the touch hole in the breech of the gun. Once that is done, the cannonball is loaded, followed by another wad to prevent it from rolling out. The load is then rammed again."

I was having trouble keeping up, and I knew it would take me a while to learn.

Mr. Stansbury sensed my confusion by the look on my face.

"You will learn quickly. Now watch as the gun crews move back into the firing position."

The men again struggled to move the cannon. It was starting to get hot in that tight space, and they were sweating heavily.

"The next step is to prime the touch hole using a mixture of fine gunpowder and spirits of wine poured from a priming horn. Then the gun is sighted and aimed by raising or lowering to hit the target."

I followed him back to the front of the compartment.

"The gun captain will pull back the hammer mechanism with a lanyard attached to it. Then they wait for my order to fire."

I watched as all the gun captains raised their hands, showing the guns were ready to fire.

Mr. Stansbury yelled, "Fire!"

There was a tremendous thunderous sound, and the ship shook. I brought my hands up to cover my ears too late. The noise was deafening, and I could feel the vibrations of the ship through my body. I shook my head, trying to stop my ears from ringing. I saw that Mr. Stansbury was laughing at me, his deep, hearty laughter echoing in the confined space.

"Wha' is my job, sir?"

"You will be responsible for bringing water and powder to the crews, as needed, to keep the gun firing."

"'How of'en do 'hey fire 'he guns?"

"The process is repeated to ensure crews can fire quickly enough to defeat the enemy. This serious work could mean the difference between life and death for the ship during a real encounter with a French warship."

We continued to run the drill, and I carried buckets of water and powder until my arms ached. This wasn't the end of my day. I still had to return to the galley to prepare the captain's meal.

Chapter 9

Captain Auger

Date With the Cat-O-Nine Tails

I loved to stare out at the sea. It was powerful and unyielding, like being the captain of a naval warship. I was expecting the knock on my cabin door. "What is it?"

I turned and saw Mr. Crittenden.

"Sir, it's time."

"Quite right. Let's get on with this unpleasantness."

Crittenden looked at me with hopeful eyes. "Have you had time to reconsider?"

"Why would I do that?"

He deflated and followed me out the door to the short ladder up to the quarterdeck. I looked down at the gathered crew and smiled when I saw the offender tied to the main mast. Maintaining discipline was the most critical aspect of thwarting a mutiny. Experience also taught me to show mercy on certain occasions, but not now. I made eye contact with the master-at-arms and ordered, "Get on with it, Mr. Harris.

He nodded and turned toward the accused. "Able seaman Willoughby, you have been charged with theft of food from the officer stores. You are sentenced to receive twelve lashes as ordered by Captain Auger." He briefly glanced in my direction. Harris picked up the cat-o-nine tails. I watched his muscles tense as he tightly grasped the handle. There was stunned silence from the crew as Harris raised the whip over his head and snapped it forward, making contact with Willoughby's shirtless back. There were several gasps when Willoughby let out a scream that could be heard over the piece of leather he was biting down on.

I scanned the faces of the entire crew while the lashes continued. Some of them dared to stare at me. I made a mental note of each of these men. I was pleased to see several crew members nodding their heads with each blow, clearly supporting the punishment. After the last strike from the whip, Mr. Harris looked back at me. I nodded.

"Cut him down."

I watched two crew members cut Willoughby down from the mast. He crumpled to the deck, his back shredded and bleeding. The ship's surgeon came forward to attend to his wounds.

I turned toward Mr. Crittenden. "Excuse the crew."

He dipped his head and yelled out, "You are dismissed. Go back to your duties."

I listened to the chatter from the crew as they dispersed with a smug look on my face. They had to learn the importance of discipline. I returned to my cabin, looking forward to my dinner. I needed to spend time with the cabin boy.

Chapter 10

Peter Beale

Needing a Friend

I stood there in shock from what I had just witnessed. I absently wiped my face. When I looked at my hand, I saw pieces of flesh and blood. I leaned over, and my stomach retched uncontrollably. I knew cruelty, but this was on another level. While I was bent over, I heard a voice.

"How are you, lad?"

I slowly raised my head and saw the concerned face of Charles Tilden. He reached down and helped me to my feet. I rubbed my stomach and blew out a stale breath. "'hanks, ma'e."

"That was hard to watch. The captain can be ruthless."

I let out a smirk. *If you only knew.*

I knew Charles from one of the gun crews. He was a few years older than me. He was rail thin and had a head full of unruly black hair. We rarely talked.

"Can I ask you a ques'ion?"

He looked over his shoulder. "If you make it quick."

"'How long 'have you been on 'he ship?"

I watched him think about it. "It's been at least five years, why?"

I hesitated. "'How have you survived 'ha' long?"

He kept looking over his shoulder. His body language showed me that he was hurrying to go somewhere.

"It's not been easy. I must return to work, but I can be your mate if you need someone to talk to."

I smiled broadly as I watched him walk away. The spectacle of the whipping was mostly forgotten. Then I heard the cook's obnoxious voice yelling for me.

"Beale, where are you? It's time to prepare the captain's dinner."

The cook was in a foul mood. He barked at me. "We are late with the captain's meal! Chop up those vegetables." He pointed to the table we used to prepare the food.

I picked up the knife and had a lovely vision of cutting out the disgusting man's tongue. The officer's meals usually consisted of pies and puddings. Due to their station, the officer's meals included fresher meats and vegetables. As I chopped up the carrots, I looked at the stove and saw that the cook was making the captain's favorite dish; kidney pie. *What is the occasion?*

While I detested the cook, I learned valuable lessons in proper meal preparation and the importance of keeping the crew fed nutritious meals. This helped with morale while providing them the energy to do their jobs.

I chopped the vegetables and mentally went over the menus that we served the crew. Breakfast consisted of oatmeal that would be soaked overnight and heated in the morning. The bland-tasting gruel would usually be sweetened with molasses to add some flavor. The other meals would include salted meats: beef, pork, chicken and fish. The meat would be placed in freshwater vats to remove as much salt as possible before the meat was boiled. Then, we also served a variety of pies and stews. Pease pudding was a thick, pasty pudding made with boiled legumes, split peas, and bacon. Then there was plum duff, another thick pudding that contained raisins or currants. Sea pie was a crew favorite, including layers of meat or fish with vegetables and a crust of biscuits. Lobscouse was a stew that also included meat, vegetables, and hardtack. The crew was also given a daily grog ration, rum mixed with water.

The cook yelled out. "Boy, change into your serving clothes!"

I nearly cut off a finger. I saw him remove the pie from the oven and glare at me.

As I carried the captain's meal balanced on the tray, I wondered what my fate would be today. Lately, he had left me alone. When I got to his cabin, I lifted a leg to help me hold the tray and reached out and knocked.

"Enter."

I took a deep breath and opened the door. Auger was standing in the middle of the room, and the look on his face told me everything I needed to know. It was time to escape from my shell.

Chapter 11

Peter Beale

Confessions

As the days turned into weeks, I continued my duties, and the large fleet sailed toward its ultimate destination. At times, I felt the confines of the ship close in on me. There was nowhere to go to escape other than in my mind. The captain's indulgences continued, but instead of letting them destroy me, I would flee to a safe place in my mind while the act was performed. The safe place usually consisted of picturing myself on one of the exotic islands that the other sailors talked about. I would close my eyes tightly and imagine the warm sun beating down on my face while I gazed at the lush vegetation and the massive coconut trees that lined the beach of the tropical island.

My other outlet was spending time with Charles. We plan to meet when we can be alone at odd times, usually on the gun deck. There seemed to be a distance he held. I sensed that he had issues trusting anyone. This included me.

On the day of our first rendezvous, I was giddy with anticipation. Cook even took notice.

"What are you smiling at, boy?"

I lifted my eyes and shrugged my shoulders. The cook grunted and went back to cleaning the stove. I finished washing out the pots used for dinner. "I'm done wi'h my chores. Can I be dismissed?"

He frowned and raised an eyebrow. "I don't know what you're up to. Get out of here."

I quickly left before he could change his mind. Not to raise any suspicions, I climbed up the ladder to the weather deck. I looked at the calm sea and the setting sun directly before the ship. Other sailors were taking in the sunset, and they ignored me. When I got to the ladder amidship going down to the gun deck, I peeked behind me to ensure I wasn't followed. It was dark in the space, and I let my eyes get accustomed to it while trying to see if Charles was waiting.

"Peter, I'm over here."

I saw him sitting against the bulkhead next to the gun that was his duty station. "Why are you si''in here alone in 'he dark?"

"I like it here. It's quiet, and no one bothers me."

I sat down next to him. "Thank you for mee'in wi'h me. I badly need someone I can 'alk 'o."

He shifted to get a better look at me. "What do you want to talk about?"

I felt nervous and wasn't sure how to start. "You 'old me you have been on 'he ship for five years. How have you survived 'ha' long?"

"I was like you when I first got on the ship. A young boy, forced to escape the abuse from my pa."

I leaned forward, waiting for more, but he became quiet and stared into space. I was curious to know how much I could press him for more. "Did you ge' 'aken like I did?"

He shook his head from side to side. "After I ran away from home, I didn't have anywhere to go until I ran into Captain Auger."

My eyes opened wide. "He brought you on the ship?"

He hung his head and whispered. "He promised to give me a job and protect me."

"Wha' was your job?"

Slowly looking up and meeting my eyes, "Cabin boy."

I jumped back against the cannon. I was speechless.

"I know what he's doing to you."

"Bu' how did you make him stop?"

"I didn't. Auger grew tired of me and got a replacement."

"Why do you stay?"

"I have nowhere to go. I'm ashamed to tell anyone."

"Why did you 'ell me?"

He reached out and grabbed my arm. "I didn't help the new cabin boy, and he took his life. I don't want that to happen to you."

"Don" you ha'e him?"

"I think about killing him every day. I'm waiting for the right time."

We sat there for the rest of the evening until it was time for me to return to the galley.

Chapter 12

Captain Auger

The Siege

From my cabin, I heard the shouts, "Land ho!" This was followed by the scurrying of feet and other shouts. It took three months to sail here. My heart raced with anticipation of what was to come, a mix of excitement and suspense. I controlled myself, knowing that decorum called for me to maintain my emotions in front of the crew. I stepped up to the quarterdeck and could smell the unmistakable aroma of land. Low-hanging clouds covered the entire area. There was a chill in the air, and the sea was rough.

"Captain, the coast of Canada lay off the port beam." Mr. Crittenden stated, pointing toward the land.

I took out my spyglass and focused on the shoreline. The absence of any French ships was a relief. I could make out the outline of a large fortress, its imposing presence a testament to the challenges ahead. *That must be Louisbourg.* Turning my attention to the fleet, I saw the larger men-of-war gathering, their sheer size and power a reassuring sight, and the troop transports were hanging back, a sign of their cautious approach.

"Captain, Victory is signaling to lay anchor. All captains are to report for a meeting with the admiral," the officer of the deck called out.

"Very well, Mr. Fields." I slammed my spyglass shut. "Mr. Crittenden, order the anchor lowered and prepare my jolly-boat."

"Aye, sir."

I sat stoically, watching the activity around HMS Victory while the rowers fought the waves. Fleet Admiral Edward Boscawen's flagship was the largest frigate in the fleet. I couldn't hide the envy of the beautiful and powerful warship. She had sleek lines and a double row of cannons, making her dangerous to any enemy.

The admiral's cabin was filled with the captains from all the frigates. There was some chatter among the other captains, but I could feel the tension while we waited for the admiral to give us our orders. Suddenly, the cabin door burst open, and the admiral entered. We all came to attention.

He had a stern look on his face, a clear indication of the seriousness of the mission. "Be at ease, gentlemen. I know it's cramped here, but I wanted you to hear the orders simultaneously."

I only knew the man in passing. He was another high-born, but there was an air about him that I respected. He was all business.

"Our orders are to capture the Louisbourg fortress. The fort protects the Gulf of St. Lawrence and ultimately the French capital Quebec City." He scanned the room for understanding. "Our scouts report a garrison of 3,500 is manning the fort. We will lay siege with our guns in preparation for landing our soldiers to capture it. We have around 14,000 soldiers at our disposal. We must capture the fort before winter sets in." I listened intently, my mind already formulating strategies. This was the moment I had been waiting for, the opportunity to prove my leadership and secure my place in history.

One of the captains spoke up. "Sir, do we know if a French fleet is in the area?"

"Before setting sail, another British fleet bottled up the French in port back in France. We should only face a few French warships at most."

He scanned the room again for additional questions. "Dismissed. We will start the siege immediately."

My mind was filled with possibilities as I called for the ship's officers to gather in my cabin. This could be my chance to make a name for myself and receive my deserved recognition. I stood staring at the maps I had for the coast of Canada, mainly Nova Scotia, when I heard the door open, and the officers started to filter in. I waited until everyone had assembled. "Gentlemen, we have our orders." I looked at each man's face and saw the determination I expected, a reflection of my own. *Excellent.*

"We start a siege on the Louisbourg fortress." I point to the location on the map.

All the officers leaned forward to see where I pointed.

"Once the admiral has determined that the fort has been destroyed, the army will be sent to capture it. Questions?"

No one spoke up.

"Mr. Crittenden, call the crew to quarters. I will give the order to start the bombardment. Do not disappoint me, gentlemen!"

Chapter 13

Peter Beale

Attacking the French

I was in the galley cleaning up the breakfast dishes when I heard the commotion throughout the ship. "Wha' 's 'happenin?" I asked the cook.

"Sounds like land has been spotted."

The look on my face must have said it all.

"Go on, take a look."

I followed the crowd of sailors who were doing the same thing. I had to push through the throng of men to get a good look. My heart raced as I squinted, trying to make out the coastline. It had been a long time since we left England. Everyone was excited. I heard someone yell.

"Look, there's a fort."

"Where's the French ships?" another called out.

I turned toward the sound of his voice and saw him pointing. I tried to follow his arm but couldn't see it. Then, others joined in and were also pointing. Trying again, I made out the vague shape of a large structure. I was disappointed. I expected it to be grander. I scanned the crowd and didn't see Charles. I had a strong desire to share this moment with him.

"You men get back to work."

I heard the other sailors' groans. As I turned to go back to the galley, other orders were shouted.

"Set the anchor."

"Prepare the captain's jolly boat."

It must be important things happening.

When I got back to the galley, the cook asked. "What did you see?"

I frowned, "No' much. Da ou'line of 'he shore and par' of a for'."

"Let's start making the mid-day meal. It will get busy around here."

A few hours later, the drums ordered us to our quarters. I dashed to the gun deck while dodging the others going to their station. When I got there, I spied Charles standing by his gun. I nodded at him, and he nodded back. Mr. Stansbury was walking among the guns.

"Men, we have been ordered to lay siege to the French fort. Be prepared to fire your guns when I give the order."

I watched as each gun crew went through loading and preparing their cannons. I filled my buckets with water and powder. I stood there waiting for the action to start when I noticed how rough the sea was. I saw the water sloshing in the buckets and clutched the handles. Mr. Stansbury walked by and smiled.

"Hold tight, Master Beale."

I felt the anticipation in the air as we waited for the order. I could hear a commotion above us and wondered what they were doing. I looked at Mr. Stansbury and pleaded for answers.

"The captain is having the deck crew turn the ship toward the starboard side so we can fire broadside at the French fort."

Just then a courier from the quarterdeck yelled down, "Captain gives the order to fire your guns!"

Mr. Stansbury nodded toward the courier and turned back to the gun crews. "Fire!"

There was a thunderous explosion as ten cannons fired at once. The ship tilted to port, and the space was filled with smoke. I rubbed my ears and coughed to clear my lungs. The taste of sulfur from the spent gunpowder was bitter. I saw the crews were already in the process of reloading. It was time to do my job. I dragged the heavy buckets of water to each gun on the starboard side. I saw the determination on the faces of the gunners.

The firing went on for hours. I snuck a look through one of the gun ports. There was so much smoke floating on top of the ocean. It looked like the fog that would envelop Portsmouth. I could hear the distant rumblings of explosions but couldn't see if the fort was damaged.

Mr. Stansbury turned my way. "Beale, go to the galley and get something for the men to eat."

As I scrambled up the ladder, I said, "Aye, sir."

My curiosity got the best of me, and I snuck up to the upper deck. I took my first breath of fresh air in hours and peeked around to look at the fort. The deck crew was busy changing the sails, and all eyes seemed glued toward the shoreline. I darted over to the rail and watched as a breeze moved the blanket of smoke away from the ship. My jaw dropped when I saw the direct hits the French were taking. Then I leaned out and looked fore and aft to see the other boats in the fleet fire their guns.

"Boy, what are you doing up here?"

My joy turned to panic as I saw Mr. Harris standing over me.

"Mr. S'ansbury sen' me 'o ge' ra'ions for 'he gunners."

"Does this look like a galley?

"No, sir." Reluctantly, I started for the galley. I slightly turned to get one more look. *How could anyone survive that?*

The cook was busily preparing biscuits with thin slices of salted ham for the crew when he noticed me and growled, "What are you doing here, boy?"

"Mr. S'ansbury sen' me. I'm 'o bring back some'hing for 'he gunners' o ea'."

He glared at me. My hate for him was burning inside me like an inferno.

He looked around, found a large tray, and began loading it with biscuits. "Take this and come back to get their ration of grog."

I navigated the walkways the best I could, trying not to spill the tray. I couldn't avoid the sailors I passed grabbing handfuls of the biscuits. Half my load was missing by the time I got back to the gun deck. I passed the remainder out and went back for more.

Chapter 14

Captain Auger

Surrender

"Captain, we have been ordered to halt our bombardment in one hour."

I turned and scanned through the maze of ships to spot Victory. I pulled out my spyglass and watched the signal flags sending the admiral's orders. I slammed my telescope shut. Time to send in the army. "Very well, Mr. Crittenden. Give the order."

I considered how tedious the last few weeks had been keeping up the siege. I looked out at the calm sea. Then I looked up at a clear sky, feeling the warmth on my face. Well, the weather is finally cooperating.

As I watched from the quarterdeck, the guns from the British fleet fired off their last rounds. After the guns ceased firing, a hush settled over the water. Gradually, the smoke generated by the cannon fire lifted off the top of the ocean. It ascended into the air to be swept away by the wind. It provided a clear view of the coastline. I walked to the other side of the quarterdeck and watched an endless number of boats, loaded with red-coated soldiers, start their journey to shore. "Where are the French ships?"

"There are no reports of any French fleet, sir."

I was baffled by the French. "Why would they leave their fort unprotect-ed?" The question was rhetorical, and none of my officers answered. "We wait."

We watched as hundreds of jolly boats disgorged their load of soldiers on Canadian soil. I watched in horror as the French opened up a deadly fire on the mass of British soldiers. "We miscalculated and did not completely destroy the fortress."

I felt helpless to do anything. We couldn't risk firing our cannons due to the possibility of hitting our own troops. I needed a distraction from all the carnage. My thoughts drifted off to the joy I felt spending time with young Master Beale. *What was the power he held over me?* I knew the boy hated me. Like I hated my abusers. I told the officer of the deck. "Mr. Jennings, I shall take my meal in my cabin. Let the cook know to have the cabin boy bring it to me."

"Very well, Captain."

I saw the look of disgust on the man's face. Another high-born.

A loud knock on my cabin door startled me from a restless sleep. "What is it?"

"Captain, we have received word that the fort has surrendered, and we are ordered to set sail for the St. Lawrence River."

"Very well. I'll be there in a minute." My brain was foggy, and my bedclothes were drenched in sweat.

The quarterdeck was crowded with the ship's officers. They were all looking toward the land and pointing.

"Captain, the Union Jack was just raised above the fort."

I looked out and saw the British flag flutter over the ruins of the fort.

Mr. Crittenden came to me with his hand extended. "Congratulations, Captain."

I took his hand to shake and saw that he was sincere. "What are the orders, Mr. Crittenden?"

"The admiral has ordered us to weigh anchor and escort the troop ships up the St. Lawrence River to capture Quebec City."

This was terrific news. We could capture the French Canadian capital and end the war here in the new world. "Very well. Give the order. Also, tell the cook to give an extra ration of grog to the crew."

Chapter 15

Peter Beale

The Next Prize

I could hear the yelling coming from topside. I looked at the faces of the Men on the gun deck. Most had blank looks, and a few shrugged their shoulders. Charles looked exhausted. We had only spoken a few times since the siege started. He told me he didn't want the others to know we were friends. He didn't think they would approve. So we had to sneak around to spend time together. I couldn't bring myself to tell him what he meant to me. My emotions were a jumbled mess. I had never experienced the joy I felt when I was around him. This was the reality of life during this time and age, a time of intense conflict and secrecy.

Mr. Stansbury said, "I will go find out what the yelling is all about."

We stood there lost in our thoughts, and when we could fall, the ship started moving. I had to reach out and grab one of the pulley ropes to steady myself.

Mr. Stansbury returned with an update. "Men, the French have surrendered the fort. We are setting sail for the river leading up to the capital. Our next prize." He smiled broadly. "We have been ordered to stand down. The captain has ordered you to receive an extra ration of grog."

There was a muted cheer from the gun crews. They all looked as tired as I felt. Still, it was welcome news after so much toil on our part. I wondered what that meant to sail to capture the capital. Was the war nearly over? Did I miss it all? These thoughts swirled in my head, a mix of hope and anxiety, as I tried to make sense of the situation.

I went back to my duties in the galley, a place where I found solace from the harsh realities of life on the ship. It was nice to have a break from the cook and especially from the captain, except that night when the soldiers landed. My body trembles as I think about that night. The disgusting excuse for a man was rougher than usual. He wanted to talk afterward, which was not normal. He said something that has stuck with me, a cryptic statement that hinted at the darker side of human nature and the reasons behind our actions.

"Beale, it is the sins of men that cause us to do what we do."

I still don't know what he meant, but he left me alone after that, at least for now.

I was always mindful of picking up shards of gossip anytime I was around the crew, my hunger for information a constant companion. My life was shuttled between boredom and terror, a monotonous cycle that left me yearning for something more. I craved information about what was happening, and the cook could have been more forthcoming. I made my everyday escape up to the weather deck and struck gold, a brief respite from the confines of the ship. I stood silently in the early evening, watching the setting sun throw shadows on the tree-lined shore. The ship slowly sailed up the river, and it seemed like we were easy targets. Land was the closest it had been since leaving England. I had a strong urge to jump and swim to shore, a desperate longing for freedom. I didn't know how to swim, which could present a problem, but the desire was overwhelming. While I weighed my options, two sailors, who I recognized as the helmsman and the ship's carpenter, were in a heated discussion, their voices a stark contrast to the calm of the evening.

"I heard it directly from the captain."

"You're daft. There's no way any of us are getting off the ship."

"We need to take on provisions, and Auger told me we were anchoring upstream from here and sending a party ashore to barter with the good citizens of Canada." The helmsman let out a chuckle.

The carpenter smiled and said, "You mean to take what we need."

The helmsman noticed me hiding in the shadows. "What are you up to, boy?"

I was embarrassed at getting caught, so I stood up and walked forward to the forecastle. Charles was supposed to meet with me. It was getting dark, and the only light I could see was a lantern hanging from a post. Its flickering glow cast eerie shadows on the forecastle and decking. I called out, "Charles."

I heard a sound barely above a whisper. "Over here."

I walked toward his voice and spotted him staring out toward land. There was excitement in my voice. "I jus' 'heard 'ha' we will be anchoring 'omarrow and bringing on supplies!"

I could barely see his features.

"You should know better than to listen to rumors."

I let his comment pass. "Do you ever think about escaping?"

He was silent for a few minutes. "I used to think about it. This is my home now." He turned slightly towards me. "I don't have anywhere to go."

"We could go 'oge'her." I said hopefully.

"Forget about it. This is where we are supposed to be." He got up and left me alone.

We did anchor the following day, and some crew were sent ashore to get provisions. I was omitted, and I didn't try to escape. The captain, a strict and unforgiving man, would never let me go. The ship was part of a larger British fleet, engaged in a strategic mission to secure supplies and gain control over the region.

Chapter 16

Captain Auger

Not a Retreat

I felt disgusted as I looked around the crowded cabin at each officer under my command. I got out from behind my desk and steadied my breathing. *It isn't their fault.* "Gentlemen, as you have noticed, the weather is turning on us. Ice has started to form on the river, and we are still a few days away from Quebec. In all his wisdom, the admiral has ordered us to turn around and retreat back into the safer waters of the Atlantic." I knew I had crossed a line, and the reaction on some of the officer's faces backed that up. They knew better than to speak up.

"Unfortunately, we were not able to complete our mission. I'm disappointed we did not earn more glory for ourselves and the crew. It looked like we all but had this war won and now retreat." I hung my head.

"It's not a retreat, Captain. Aren't we just waiting for the weather to improve?"

I looked up to see Lieutenant Jennings' smug face. I threw daggers at him with my eyes. "I suppose that's one way to look at it."

Mr. Crittenden tried to defuse the situation. "What are our orders, Captain?"

Well played, Mr. Crittenden. "We have been ordered to sail to Boston in the American colonies for badly needed repairs. This ship is aged and has not been in drydock for several years. Hopefully, the war won't end before we can return to the fray."

I couldn't bear to look at them any further. "You're dismissed."

Chapter 17

Peter Beale

Boston

I stood on the forecastle as we sailed into Boston Harbor. There was a chill in the air as I looked at the sprawling city built on hilly terrain. This was the first city I had seen since we left England. I was thirteen and had been to sea for over two years. I was resigned to the fact that I would never see home or my mum ever again. I used to hold out hope that I would escape and go back, but I was so ashamed. I convinced myself that it was for the better.

It looked like a busy seaport, with several ship's masts visible in the harbor and at the piers. I listened to members of the crew who had been here before. They spoke longingly of the taverns and brothels they visited. I had no interest in any of that. I also learned that we would anchor in the harbor for a few days, waiting for our turn to go into the drydock in Charlestown.

Just yesterday, I spoke with the cook about our time in Boston. "Do you 'hink 'ha' I would be allowed 'o step foo' on land?" I looked at him hopefully.

He stopped what he was doing and actually softened his features before responding. "No, lad, I don't believe the captain will let you leave the ship."

I started to tear up. "It's so unfair. I didn't ask for any of his."

Cook's expression changed. "Listen, boy, if you survive in this world, you must toughen up. Life isn't always going to be fair."

I shifted my gaze to the cutting table and a knife. He followed my eyes. "You better not be thinking about doing what it looks like."

I stormed away from him. I needed to talk to someone. I went to find Charles.

I thought I knew all the good hiding places on the ship, but it took me an hour to find him. He sat in the manger with the cow, pig, and five chickens. There wasn't a place in the ship's bowels with fresh air, but the smell here was horrific. "Why are you here, Charles?"

I could see that I was disturbing him.

"I came here to be by myself!"

"We're in Boston. Why don" you come up and 'ake a look."

"I've been here before. I don't need to see it again."

He was depressing me more than I already was. "Cook 'old me I can" ge' off 'he ship."

Charles poked out his lower lip. "I didn't get off the last time we were here."

I went over and wiped some of the moldy straw away and sat down next to him. I put my head in my hands. "I can" 'ake i' any longer. I have 'o escape. I won" las'."

He put a hand on my shoulder. I felt the warmth of his touch, and it moved me. I turned to look at him. My heart was bursting. "Come with me," he said.

He took his hand away. "They won't let you."

We sat there in silence for a while.

I felt the ship start to move. I hadn't heard any rumors about going anywhere. We had been anchored in the Boston harbor for two weeks. I ran up the ladder to the weather deck. I saw that the sails had been unfurled and were catching the wind. I turned toward the shoreline, which was getting closer. I needed to know what was happening. I spied a familiar face and went in his direction. "Mr. Jacobs. Where are we going?"

He turned at the sound of my voice. "Young Master Beale. We are going into the drydock over in Charlestown." He threw a thumb over his shoulder.

I craned my neck to get a better view. "Why do we need 'o go 'here?

He smiled at me. "Over time, the ship's hull must be repaired and re-sealed to prevent leaks. We must also scrape off the barnacles attached to the ship's bottom."

My eyes were wide with wonder as the crew tied the sails and took on lines from the shore.

We both watched as the ship neared the drydock area, using lines attached to the capstan to tug it toward the structure. Then, two substantial sea gates were opened. I looked at Jacobs.

"The ship will get pulled into the drydock, and the gates will be closed. Then the seawater will be drained, and the ship will rest on a wooden cradle."

"'How many 'imes have you done 'his?"

"This is the fourth time for me."

We both had to brace ourselves when the ship stopped suddenly. "We're there. Now they drain the water."

Jacobs turned my way as we felt the ship slowly settle on the cradle. "Have you taken my advice and found a friend?"

I nodded at him. "Yes, sir."

"Good. Don't let the bastards win." He said while walking away.

I watched all the activities going on around the drydock with fascination. Then I looked out at the city that lay beyond. My depression returned. I could only look out and imagine what it would be like to set my feet on shore.

Chapter 18

Peter Beale

The Fire

A loud crashing noise woke me from my slumber. It was dark, and I felt the confines of my hammock. Maybe I was dreaming. Then I heard shouts. I was suddenly paralyzed with fear. *Were we being attacked?*

Then someone at the top of the ladder yelled, "Fire!"

That broke my motionless state, and I scrambled out of the hammock. I climbed the ladder with the other sailors. When I got topside, I witnessed a scene straight out of the worst parts of the Bible. It looked like the entire city of Boston was engulfed in flames. The fire had taken on a life of its own, flashing bright red, orange, and yellow hues and reaching into the night sky. It made the whole area glow. There were interspersed sounds of explosions and an ungodly howling as the fire destroyed everything it came into contact with.

I watched the chaos on the ship as the crew raced to defend the vessel from the fire. The wind suddenly shifted, and a mass of smoke drifted toward us. My eyes teared from the searing heat, and my lungs burned.

Calls rang out. "We need volunteers to go to Boston to fight the fire!"

I couldn't see where the orders came from, but some crew heeded the call and raced down the gangplank into the night.

I stood there looking around. My adrenaline kicked in. This was my chance. I thought about trying to find Charles. No time. I didn't bother going below and getting my possessions. I turned and ran off the ship onto shore. The glow from the fire across the harbor was the only light. I crouched down, waiting to see if I was followed. A fit of coughing overtook me, and I doubled over. Stupid! I wiped the spittle from my mouth, got up, and ran into the darkness.

I went as far as my legs could carry me. I had to rest and get some fresh air. I bent over, not knowing where I was. I started to inhale air into my aching lungs. I turned my head to see if I was still alone. All I saw was the glow of Boston being destroyed.

I started walking. My mind told me to keep running as fast as possible, but I forced myself to be calm enough to decide what to do next. As I walked, I started to notice how cold it was. I'm not dressed for this. I began to shiver from the cold air and the shock I experienced.

I shuffled further down the street I was on. I noticed lovely homes the further I got away from the drydock. To my amazement, I could see people come out of their houses. They stared and pointed at the fire. As more of a crowd gathered, one of the townspeople noticed me.

"You, young man, do you know what is happening?"

I looked around, wondering who the man was speaking to. I then pointed to myself and raised my shoulders.

The man was animated. He was tall and had piercing eyes lit up by the fire. "Yes, you."

With a weak voice, I responded, "'here is a large fire burning in Bos'on, sir."

The man asked, "Were you involved in the fire? Why are you out here on this cold evening?"

I didn't know I would be questioned. *Would they turn me in if I told them the truth?* Thinking quickly, I replied, "I am all alone and have nowhere 'o go."

The man's wife, standing next to him, noticed how pathetic I looked. She turned to her husband and said, "John, look at this poor boy. We need to take him into our home to get warmed up."

I watched as John furrowed his brow, looked at his wife, and then back at me. He sighed and said, "Come on, boy, let's get you warmed up."

I reluctantly followed the couple into their home. My mouth dropped open as I looked around the house. It was the nicest home I had ever been in. The lower level was spacious, with furniture, rugs, paintings, and nick-knacks. A roaring fire in the fireplace warmed every corner of the main room. The wife grabbed me and led me to the fire, where I sat down to heat my frozen body.

The woman, who was short and somewhat plump and looked to be in her forties, sat next to me. She said, "My name is Amanda. What is your name?"

"Pe'er."

"Can you tell me why you were out on a night like this?"

I stared into the fire as if in a trance and replied, "Mum, I was 'aken from my home and have found myself here."

Standing off to the side, listening to the conversation, John must have detected my thick cockney accent. "What do you mean when you say you were taken from your home?"

I snapped out of my trance. "Some sailors 'ook me and made me go on 'heir ship."

"Son, did you come here from England?"

"Paw'smou'h."

Both man and wife looked at each other. John looked back at me, "Are the sailors looking for you now?"

I was exhausted and still bewildered, "I don" 'hink so. They were all concerned abou' 'he fire."

We sat silently for a few minutes when Amanda said, "Let's get you to bed, and we can talk about this more in the morning."

She led me upstairs to a spare bedroom and tucked me into bed. It was the first real bed I had slept on in over two years.

I opened my eyes wider to better view the darkened room. My body swayed from a gentle rocking motion. At the muffled sounds of men yelling, I cocked my head, but they sounded far away. I cringed and wrinkled my nose at the sour odor of rotting wood and the unmistakable stench of urine. Where am I? I spread out my arms and ran them over a surface that had to be wood. My fingers were cold and wet. Reluctantly, I tried to stand on shaking legs. Every instinct told me I needed to escape. Suddenly, footsteps approached. The loud screech of rusting hinges made me jump back as I turned toward the sound. As light entered the room, I saw the outline of a man.

"There you are, boy. Time to go see the captain."

I put my fist in my mouth to muffle a scream. Panic overtook me, and I sprinted away from the man. I ran faster, not caring where I was going, knowing only evil was waiting for me in the form of the captain. I ran endlessly but could sense the man was right behind me. In the distance, I spied a bright light, and just when I thought I would reach it, a hand clasped me firmly on the shoulder.

I awoke to the sound of my own screams. Soaking in sweat, I sat up and slowly ran my fingers through my hair. I took several deep breaths and wondered when I would stop having the dream.

I opened my eyes, and as the room began to focus, I rubbed my eyes. Where am I? It all came flooding back. I remembered the fire and escaping from the ship. There was a knock on the door, and when it opened, I saw Amanda. She smiled at me, "You are finally awake. It's almost noon, and I thought you would sleep the day away. Get dressed and come downstairs. I will prepare a meal for you."

My stomach rumbled as I dressed quickly and went downstairs. Amanda laid out a small feast on the kitchen table. She looked at me and said, "I wasn't sure what you like to eat, so I put a little of everything out."

I was speechless. I sat down and began to gorge myself. Amanda sat beside me and watched with pleasure as I enjoyed my meal. After my fill, I sat back in his chair and looked around the room. "Mum, where is your husband?"

Amanda beamed at me and replied, "John is at his business. He wanted to talk to you this morning but needed to go to work."

I nodded. "Thank you for 'he meal."

She reached over and patted my shoulder. "When was the last time that you were home?"

"No' sure, been a long 'ime since I saw my mum."

She slowly shook her head and sighed. "Tell me about your family."

I sat there with my elbows on the table. "My dad is dead. Mum was 'akin care of me and my bro'hers an' sisters. We were destitute."

I could see the look of pity on her face.

"What do you do on the ship?"

I didn't make eye contact, "I help 'he cook prepare meals and serve 'he cap'ain."

Out of the corner of my eye, I noticed a boy standing by the stairs. Amanda noticed where I was looking.

"Oh, darling, come here and meet our guest."

The boy dutifully came to the table.

"Robert, this is Peter. He was on one of the British ships and came here when the fire started." She then turned to me. "Peter, this is our son Robert."

I nodded at Robert. He looked to be about my age but was frail and sickly. He didn't say anything but stared at me with a troubling glare.

Amanda seemed not to notice. "Now, where were we? Oh yes, the ship."

I fidgeted in my seat and started to sweat. I didn't want to talk about the ship. After a few minutes of awkward silence, Amanda reached across the table and hugged me.

"Peter, it will be alright. You are in a safe place. If you are uncomfortable talking about the ship, that's okay."

The whole time I was being hugged, I watched Robert. He continued to glare at me.

"Mother, how long will this boy stay with us?"

She released me and looked at her son. "Robert, Peter is our guest, and you will treat him as such."

I was shocked when Robert let out a loud huff and walked away. When I looked at Amanda, she just shook her head.

Amanda stood up and said, "We need to get you some proper clothes."

I looked up at her and just stared. *What if they are looking for me? I can't go out there.*

"Come on, we are going shopping."

Chapter 19

Captain Auger

Find the Boy

I had to see it for myself. There were reports all night about the disastrous fire. When I reached the top of the ladder, I was overwhelmed by the stench of the smoke which had drifted over from Boston. It was dawn's first light, but I clearly saw small fires continue to burn. The air was heavy with ash that rose from the burning embers. Many people were actively fighting to prevent the spread of the flames. It must have seemed so hopeless for them. I felt pity for the citizens of Boston. They weren't true Englishmen but were still a part of the empire. I knew it was pure luck that the ship escaped with no damage. I gave the order last night to have the crew assist in firefighting duties. I knew that would promote goodwill among the townspeople.

"Captain, sir."

I turned to see Harris standing behind me. He had a troubled look on his face. "Yes, Mr. Harris, what is it?"

His face glowed with light from the fire. He fidgeted with his hat in his hands. "Captain, sir, I am here to report that we are missing seven crew members."

I approached him and asked, "Who are these missing men?"

"All seven were from the last batch we collected back in Portsmouth."

"Go on."

"The seven include the cabin boy, Beale."

I was incensed, and my body shook with anger. I wanted to scream at Harris. "How did this happen?"

Harris kept control of his emotions. "They must have snuck off during the fire. I took a roll this morning when the crew who fought the fire returned."

I held out hope that some of the crew stayed back to assist. "Are you sure some missing men aren't in Boston fighting the fires?"

"Captain, I was there. I made sure everyone came back."

"Very well. What have you done to find the missing crew?"

"I have ordered a search party to go into town and look for the men."

I loudly blew out a breath of air but nodded my head. "You will lead the search, Mr. Harris. I will hold you accountable for finding all the men. Especially the boy!"

"Yes, sir."

My mind raced. This is how the crew repays me for my leniency. There will be no pardons for any of those men.

Well, for the cabin boy.

Chapter 20

John Smith

Spared

My mind was still troubled when I thought about the boy. What should we do with him? Amanda will want to make him her "project" and take him in. That might be a good thing. But what if the British come looking for him. Do we protect him? I can't afford to anger them. That would be bad for business.

I heard the voices of men shouting echo across the water. I looked up from the small boat I was sitting in and started to get a good look at the damage. I might have more problems than worrying about the boy. I started getting anxious as I was rowed from Charlestown to Boston. What would be left of my office and warehouse?

Shaking my head, I could still see burning embers, and the air was still thick with the stench of burnt bodies and smoke. I was stunned by the sight of survivors wandering around the devastated streets, still in shock from the experience they underwent. I blinked my eyes from the acrid smoke. I was born in this town. My parents came here from England to build a better life. They instilled a work ethic into me at an early age. I tried hard to live up to their ideals. Still, I felt that I needed to be better. They died before they could see the business that I built on my own.

The ferry had to be diverted to another landing spot due to the damage done to the pier. I followed the other passengers up a small hill. When I got to the top, I stopped to catch my breath. It was hard to breathe with all the smoke in the air. I had a coughing fit to try and clear my lungs. I stood tall to get a better view of the extent of the damage. There was also an exorbitant amount of destruction to buildings and even some of the ships tied up to the pier. My God! How many died?

I forced myself to continue walking toward my office. Part of me wanted to turn around and go back home. What if everything is gone? Looking at all the devastation, I didn't feel confident that my property had been spared. I wandered through the debris until I came to Lynn Street on the North Battery. Almost there. Rounding the corner, I held my breath and shut my eyes. Taking a minute to delay the inevitable, I slowly opened them. I let out a small laugh and clutched my chest. The building only had minor exterior damage, and the warehouse looked intact. I couldn't believe my good fortune.

I stepped into the warehouse, still not believing I had been spared. I opened some of the crates of books, clothing, and dishes. I noted minor smoke damage. I would still be able to sell them. I turned and walked to the rear of the building. The large pieces of furniture and artwork were still in pristine shape. I said a quick prayer of thanks.

Grateful I had been spared, I went to see if I could help my neighbors.

Chapter 21

Peter Beale

Close Call

A manda had me by the arm and dragged me through the streets. I tried to plead my case for not going near the drydock. "Mum, I don' want' 'o ge' caugh' 'his close 'o 'he ship."

Her stern look told me she wouldn't be deterred. My head swayed as we walked to the shop, which was too close to the waterfront. I trembled at the sight of the Progress's masts in the drydock. My first instinct was to run away, but I didn't want to disappoint Amanda. She paid no attention to my objections; she was determined to purchase clothes that would benefit a young man from a middle-class family.

We stood in front of the haberdashery. "This is it." She grabbed my hand and led me into the shop. When we entered the small business, I looked around at the narrow space overflowing with clothing. We were the only customers. I couldn't let my guard down, so I kept an eye on the front door while Amanda picked through the clothes. She held up each piece, trying to determine what was appropriate. She smiled while rummaging through the piles of clothing. She looked like she was enjoying herself.

I walked over to the picture window at the front of the store. I timidly peered out at the street, searching for any familiar faces.

"Peter, come here. I want you to try on these clothes." She was motioning with her arm to a room in the back.

I took one more glance out the window. Nothing. As I went to Amanda, she handed me an armful of clothing. My eyes pleaded with her to stop this and go back home. She shooed me toward the dressing room. I had a bad feeling that something was wrong. Still, I stepped to the rear of the shop.

She made me show her each item of clothing I tried on. I was embarrassed as the owner stared at me over the fuss she was making. Amanda pushed her lips together while she appraised each item. Nodding her head, she was satisfied. She turned to the merchant. "Edward, I think we have everything we need."

"Very well, Mrs. Smith. Let me tally what you owe." He led her up to the front.

While she went to pay for the goods, I went back to the window. Suddenly, I jerked my head, and before I could shout out, I felt the hot flow of urine running down my leg. My amazed eyes saw a small group of men who looked familiar. They were striding down both sides of the street, looking at every shop they passed. How did they find me so quickly? I was in shock and didn't realize I had wet myself. As the men approached, I yelled, "I won' go back!"

Amanda turned at the sound of my voice. She noticed me staring out the window. Amanda dropped everything and ran over to me. Grabbing a hold of me, she tried to follow my stare. I could only point at the group of men. She instantly realized what that meant and pulled me away from the window. She quickly gathered the clothing and led me to the rear of the shop. She exited the back door, grasped my hand, and led me back to the house.

She said, out of breath, "My sister lives in Chelsea, and I will take you there so that they can't get you again."

I snapped out of my shock. I smelled the unmistakable odor of urine. I felt ashamed for wetting myself. I had tears in my eyes as I looked up at Amanda. "I'm so sorry, mum." Grateful for her help, I still feared having to go back to the ship and face more abuse.

She stooped over and looked me directly in the eyes. "You have nothing to be sorry about. We need to get you to safety. Go upstairs and change into your new clothes." As I went up the stairs, I watched her run to the carriage house from the back of the home.

I was still shaking as I changed clothes. I heard Amanda bound up the stairs. She opened the door, gathered me up, and stuffed more clothes in a satchel. She turned to me when we got to the bottom of the stairs. "Go out the front door. The carriage should be there. I need to write a note to Mr. Smith to let him know what happened."

I did as I was told and ran out the front door. About that time, the hired hand, a man named Chester, pulled a carriage around to the front of the house. I looked back and saw Amanda following me. She turned and yelled back to the house where the servant girl was standing, "Sarah, keep an eye on Robert. I'll be back later!"

We climbed up on the carriage.

"Let's leave, Chester. On to Chelsea."

We both turned around to see if the sailors were following us. The street was empty. I could breathe again.

The carriage ride through the countryside was peaceful. We passed several small farms and villages. Everything was neat and orderly. The air was crisp and clean. No open sewers. I leaned out of the buggy, watching the scene go by. I had never seen such a beautiful place. This was my first carriage ride, and I forgot there were men looking for me for a while. We traveled northwest along the Mystic River until we came to the bridge that crossed over to the Chelsea side. My senses were overloaded, and I couldn't believe people lived like this. It was a world away from the slums where I grew up.

As we neared Amanda's sister's house, she explained. "My sister's name is Jane, and her husband, Joseph Adams, is a clergyman at the local Puritan Church. They do not know about you, so I must talk to her first. I'm sure they will be willing to let you stay with them until it's safe for you to come back home with me.

Pulling to the front of the Adams's home, Amanda told me to stay in the carriage. I silently watched as she took long strides to the front door and knocked. She turned my way to make sure I was okay. The front door opened, and I watched as Jane Adams put her hands on Amanda's face and squealed. Amanda reached out, grasped her sister, and gave an enveloping hug.

"What do I owe for the pleasure of your company, dear sister?"

Amanda smiled. "I have come to ask you a favor."

Jane was a pretty young woman with green eyes and flowing blond hair. She dressed plainly due to her Puritan beliefs. Standing back at arm's length from her sister, she cocked her head while looking at her.

Amanda pointed in my direction, "I would like you to meet someone I have in my carriage. He is a young boy who has come into our life and needs to stay with you and Joseph for a while."

Jane furrowed her brow. "What has he done?"

Amanda continued to smile at her sister. "He is just a boy and was taken from his home back in England and forced to work on a ship. He escaped, but they are looking for him. I feel I must protect him."

Jane stared at Amanda momentarily, "Well then, I should meet this young man."

Jane and Amanda stood at the doorway and motioned for me to enter.
I cautiously stepped down from the carriage and timidly approached the
house.

"Peter, this is my sister, Jane. Jane, this is Peter."

Jane smiled at me. "It's a pleasure to meet you, Peter. Please come into
my home."

I entered the small cottage, which was nice and tidy but not as big as the
Smiths' house. Jane led us to a small sitting room to get some tea. I was
still confused by all of this. I asked Amanda, "How long will I have 'o s'ay
here?"

Amanda bit her lower lip and stared into my eyes. "Hopefully, not long.
We need to ensure the sailors stop looking for you first."

Jane returned from the kitchen, carrying a tray, and poured us some tea.
Amanda filled her in on all that had happened to me. Jane agreed to let me
stay and told us Joseph wouldn't be home from the Meeting House until
later that afternoon. She assured us Joseph wouldn't have any objections
to me staying with them. Once Amanda was sure I was safe, she returned
to the carriage to go home.

I was conflicted. My mother was the only woman who ever cared about
me, and she seldom showed any affection. Now, two women were show-
ered with affection. It all happened so quickly. Should I trust them or run
and try to make it on my own? I was exhausted by all the activity. For now,
I will stay here. That doesn't mean that I shouldn't look for other options.

Chapter 22

John Smith

The Jealous Son

After a long day of sorting through my possessions at the warehouse, I returned home to check on our new addition. The familiar scent of home greeted me as I walked in the front door. I found Amanda standing near Robert, her face etched with worry. I could see that our son was terrified, his eyes wide with fear. Then I turned to see our servant girl, Sarah. She was a sixteen-year-old, mousy girl we paid to help with the cooking and cleaning. She was trembling all over, her hands shaking as she clutched her apron.

"What is the problem, Amanda?"

She turned and noticed that I was home. "Your son told the British about Peter."

I asked Robert, "Why would you do that, son?"

He looked up at me, his eyes darting back and forth between his mother and me. "I don't want that boy living with us," he blurted out, his voice trembling with a mix of fear and defiance.

I panicked and scanned the room for any sign of Peter. "Did they take him back to the ship?"

Amanda glared one more time at Robert and turned to face me. "I took him to Chelsea to stay with my sister. He should be safe there."

I sighed and walked to my son. I sat down next to him. "Robert, what made you think telling the British about Peter would be a good idea?" I asked, my voice filled with a mix of concern and confusion.

He stared at his feet and, barely above a whisper, stated, "I don't want you to love him more than you do me."

I took him in my arms. "That would never happen. We must welcome him into our home and give him a chance at a normal life." He started to sob and held onto me tightly. I glanced back at Sarah. "Tell me what happened?"

"Oh, Mr. Smith, some men came to the door looking for the boy. I didn't know what to tell them. When Robert told them he was here, I tried to get them to leave." Her eyes shifted to the boy and then back to me.

"Did they leave?"

"Not at first. The men pushed past me and searched the house. When they couldn't find him, they screamed at me, wanting to know where he was."

"Did you tell them anything?"

Sarah began to cry. "I told them he left, but I don't know if they believed me."

"Robert, did you tell the men where Peter went?" I could feel him shake his head from side to side.

"Sarah, when did they leave?"

"They left a few hours ago."

I let out a long breath, my shoulders relaxing slightly. "You did the right thing. No one is to mention Peter while the sailors are looking for him. We'll keep him safe, I promise."

I then held Robert at arm's length. "You must promise me you won't do something as foolish as that again."

He just nodded at me.

"Go get ready for dinner."

As he ran off, I turned back to Amanda. "Why would he do that?"

She came over and sat next to me. "Robert has been the only child and must have felt threatened by a new child in the house."

I dropped my head. "Should we be concerned? With his issues, do you think he understands what he did was wrong?"

She clutched my arm, her voice filled with conviction. "There's nothing wrong with Robert! They just need to get to know each other. It will take time, but I believe they can build a bond."

"I pray you're right." I whispered, my voice filled with a mix of hope and fear, as I held Amanda's gaze, searching for reassurance in her eyes.

Amanda then lifted my head so she could look into my eyes. "What was damaged in the fire?"

I was relieved to be talking about something else. "We were very fortunate to only have some minor smoke damage. There was so much destruction everywhere. I don't know how it will all be rebuilt."

Chapter 23

Peter Beale

The Boy Shall Stay

We sat in a suffocating silence that seemed to stretch on forever. The walls of this unfamiliar place closed in on me, amplifying my unease. The last day had turned my life upside down, and now, even though I was further away from the ship, I felt no safer. Jane, perceptive as ever, seemed to sense my discomfort.

"Please, forgive my oversight. Allow me to show you around and guide you to your room," Jane said with a warm smile, her kindness a balm to my unsettled heart.

She stood up, and I followed her, my footsteps echoing in the small cottage. We walked through the narrow hallway, the walls adorned with faded family portraits, and I was in a fog as she talked about each room. At the end of the tour, she showed me to the bedroom where I would be sleeping, a small, cozy space with a window overlooking the garden.

"Take some time to unpack your belongings, and then come eat some lunch."

As Jane closed the door, leaving me to my thoughts, I felt a sudden wave of vulnerability. I unpacked my meager belongings, hanging them in the bureau against the wall. The small bed in the corner was the only other piece of furniture. Overwhelmed by exhaustion, I slumped onto the bed. I must have dozed off, for I was startled awake by a gentle knock on the door. The door creaked open, and there was Jane, her concern evident in her eyes.

"Peter, are you alright? It's time for lunch."

I rubbed my eyes and stood up, the fatigue of the journey still lingering in my bones. Jane came in, her presence a comforting warmth in the room. She gently grabbed my hand, her touch soft and reassuring, and led me to the kitchen. I didn't realize how hungry I was until I smelled the yeasty aroma of freshly baked bread, the scent filling the room and making my stomach growl. I sat down and started to shovel bread and cheese into my mouth, the taste of the simple meal a welcome comfort. Jane reached out and touched my hand, her touch a gentle reminder of the kindness I had found in this strange place.

"We need to thank God for our meal before we eat."

I didn't know what to do. I had never prayed before, never believed in a higher power. The piece of bread slipped from my fingers, my hand pulling back instinctively. I felt a mix of fear and guilt, unsure of how to navigate this unfamiliar territory.

She smiled. "Bless us, O Lord, and these Thy gifts, which we are about to receive from Thy bounty, through Christ our Lord. Amen."

She dipped her head, and I started to eat again.

"You are very quiet, Peter. Can you tell me about your life in England and on the ship?"

I froze, my mind racing with the things I could never tell Jane. The truth about my past, about the ship, about the men who were still looking for me. Would she make me leave if I didn't talk? She sat there, her eyes filled with a mix of curiosity and concern, waiting for me to respond. Gathering the courage to speak, I took a deep breath. "I was born to a poor family in

England. My father died when I was young, and I had to help my mother make ends meet." She leaned in, waiting for more.

"One day, some soldiers made me go on a ship and sail here 'o figh' 'he French." I hoped she wouldn't make me say anything else and returned to my meal.

I sensed she had more questions but remained quiet while I ate. I felt like I was disappointing her with my silence. I took my last bite and said, "Wha' can you 'ell me abou' your life?"

She perked up at that. Smiling broadly, she started to babble. "I was born in Boston and have lived in this area my whole life. I have always wanted to travel but have not been able to. My parents urged me to marry a clergyman and be a dutiful wife. My life has been tied to attending church and performing chores around my parents' home. My sister and I were taught to read and write. This is not normal for women, and I am grateful." She had to take a breath after saying all that. She narrowed her brow and asked, "Do you know how to read?"

My cheeks turned red. "No, mum."

"We shall do something about that. We need to also work on your accent."

When her husband's return approached, Jane warned me, "You must not be afraid of my husband. He is earnest, but I know he will want to help you as much as I do." We sat there silently while waiting for Joseph Adams to come home.

The front door opened, and in stepped Pastor Joseph Adams. A tall, thin man with dark eyes and chestnut hair. His face was long and dominated with a dour look. Joseph wore a dark frock coat and short pants. He very much looked the part of a serious man of God. He saw Jane and me sitting at the table and asked, "Wife, what is the meaning of this?"

"Husband, this is Peter. He is a boy that Amanda brought to our home. She asked that we take care of him for a few days."

Joseph remained silent. He looked at his wife for more information, but she stared at him.

He turned his attention back to me. "Why should we have the honor of caring for this young boy?"

She sighed and told him the whole story about me being taken from my home in England to serve on a British Naval ship and how I had escaped my captivity and was currently hunted by members of the ship's crew. She explained that her sister will take care of me once it's safe to return to her home.

Joseph rubbed his chin while considering all that he had been told. "It would be our Christian duty to care for the boy, but I am concerned about angering the British Navy."

After a few more minutes of thought, he announced, "The boy shall stay, but he is not to leave this house until he returns to Charlestown."

Jane stood up and hugged her husband. I sat there quietly while others decided my fate.

Chapter 24

Captain Auger

Hang the Deserters

The tension was eating away at me while I waited. The daily business of running the ship seemed unimportant. I had to know what the men I sent ashore had found of the deserters. These men, who had abandoned their posts and fled, were not just any crew members. They were traitors to the ship, to their duties, and to me. I, who had provided them a future as part of the greatest military power the earth has ever known, was now determined to make it my life's mission that they paid once they were returned to the ship.

I stood up on the quarterdeck until the sun's last rays dipped below the horizon. It had been a long, stressful day. I turned to the officer of the deck. "Mr. Williams, I am going to my cabin. You shall direct Mr. Harris to report to me upon his return."

"Aye, sir."

I picked at the meal that the old cook brought me. I couldn't take my mind off the fire and the escapees. I considered trying to get some sleep when I heard a gentle rap at my door.

"Come in."

I watched the ragged face of the master-at-arms appear. "Is this a bad time, Captain?"

I tried to maintain my composure. "No, Mr. Harris. Make your report."

Harris didn't make eye contact with me. "Sir, I am proud to report that we have found four of the deserters, and they are locked below, awaiting your orders."

I rose abruptly, my voice thundering, "What do you mean only four? What of the other three, and what about the boy?" My disappointment was palpable, a heavy cloud that hung in the air.

I watched Harris melt from my fury. He recovered and pushed out his chest. "Captain, we searched every business, home, stable, barn. Everywhere." He was close to being insolent. "At one of the nicer homes, a young lad told us that the boy fitting the cabin boy's description was there earlier."

Suddenly hopeful, I took a step toward him, my voice filled with anticipation. "Go on. Tell me more about this boy." The possibility of finding the boy, my young cabin boy who had shown such promise, filled me with a renewed sense of purpose.

Harris stood his ground, "Sir, the house servant declared that the boy wasn't there. We still searched and could not find him."

I sank into my chair. "What of the others?"

"We found the four men drunk in pubs and had no problem bringing them back. We can send more men out tomorrow if you would like."

I stared at him with cold eyes, my mind racing. The news of the repairs and new orders was unexpected, but I was a captain who could adapt. "No, Mr. Harris. I have been informed that our repairs will be completed soon. We have new orders to sail to the Caribbean to assist in an operation against the French installations in that area. We must be ready for this new mission."

Harris looked to absorb what I said, "What are your orders for the four men who were captured?"

"Mr. Harris, they will swing from the yardarm once we return to sea. That should set an ample example to the rest of the crew."

Harris kept his composure, "Yes, sir."

"You are dismissed, Mr. Harris."

Chapter 25

Peter Beale

Adoption

O ver the next few days, I settled into life with the Adams. I didn't let my guard down and continued to fight my demons. In my mind, every sound on the street was sailors from the Progress coming to take me back. The recurring dream of the captain became less frequent but was still as potent. I missed Charles and thought about him frequently. Was he still on the ship? Did he think about me? How could I ever be close to anyone if I couldn't move on from my past? I needed closure. I swore that I would never share my secrets with anyone else.

Jane was persistent in teaching me how to read. She set aside time every morning after breakfast and prayers. Her lessons were taken from the Bible. The words were difficult to understand, and I would get frustrated. Through it all, she would remain patient with me. I was still a child, and she had to be stern to keep me on track. She seemed to be fixated on saving me. This included making me lose my accent. "A proper young man doesn't speak as if he came from a gutter," she would tell me. I had never been concerned about the way I spoke. It was how I was taught.

Joseph took time in the evenings to guide me through the books of the Bible. Growing up in England, I had a rudimentary understanding of

Christianity, but my family did not attend church services. Between Joseph and Jane's constant lecturing, I understood that education would open up more doors for me in the future. I was still full of doubts and constantly felt the shame of being violated by that horrible man. I wasn'terved all the attention they gave me.

One morning, while we were in the middle of a reading lesson, there was a knock on the front door. I instantly became rigid and started to quake. Jane turned to me and hissed, "Go and hide!"

I ran out of the parlor and hid in the pantry, closing the door. I strained to listen as Jane opened the door. I could hear a conversation going on. Jane sounded pleased. Then I heard her call for me. "Peter, come and see who is here."

My curiosity peaked, and I opened the door to see Amanda. My tension instantly melted away, and I let her take me in her arms.

"Peter, it is so good to see you." She released her hug and took a good look at me. "You are looking well and have grown."

I shyly looked at her, "Thanks, mum."

Amanda barely contained her excitement. "Peter, I have great news for you!" With her arms flailing all over the place, she looked back and forth between Jane and me, "Peter, the ship has left Boston! It's safe for you to come home."

I stood stiffly, stunned by the news. I thought the captain would have me hunted until they finally found me. "Are you sure?"

"I'm sure. I even went down to the wharf and asked about the ship. One of the men who worked at the drydock told me the ship set sail to the Caribbean. Isn't that wonderful news?"

I glanced at Jane. She returned the look and said, "That's great news, Peter. You can now have a normal life."

Amanda shook her head in agreement. "Go get your belongings, and we shall return to Charlestown."

I was overcome with emotion and just stood there. I could see that Jane had started to tear up.

Amanda said to her sister. "You can visit as often as you would like, dear sister."

Jane sighed, "I have become very fond of Peter. Even Joseph has taken a liking to the boy."

I felt like I was intruding on their conversation and started to leave to get my possessions. When I was out of sight, I stopped to listen.

Amanda looked at her sister compassionately, "You know we can provide so much more for him. John has even talked about teaching him the family business."

"What will you tell people when they ask where Peter came from?"

"John and I have decided that we shall tell anyone who asks Peter was orphaned, and we have adopted him to raise as our own child. There is a legal process that John has spoken to a magistrate about so that we can make it official."

"Have you told Peter about it?"

"Not yet. John and I will sit down with him tonight and tell him."

I was stunned by Amanda's revelation. Then Amanda called out, "Peter, we need to leave."

I quickly went to my room and packed my clothes in the satchel. When I returned, the sisters were in an embrace. Jane was still crying. I wasn't sure what to do. No one had ever cried about me before. Jane saw me standing there and stepped back from Amanda. She wiped her eyes with the hem of her dress and walked to me.

"I shall miss you, Peter. I have enjoyed having you in my home." She then gave me a stiff hug.

I wasn't sure what to say. "Thank you for having me mum. I won" forge' you."

"You won't 'forget' me." She corrected me.

"Sorry, mum."

That night at dinner, John looked directly at me. "Peter, we have something we would like to tell you." He fidgeted with his fork and was sweating. I didn't want to let on that I already knew what it was about. I nodded my head.

"Mrs. Smith and I have adopted you into our family." He paused for my response. I looked at Amanda, who was beaming. Then I turned toward Robert, who glared at me with nothing short of hate. I was surprised by his reaction.

"Wha' does 'ha' mean, sir."

"That means you will officially be a member of our family. Your name will be Peter Smith."

I thought about my mother, and I was troubled. "I will no longer be a Beale?"

John frowned. "Is that a problem?"

"No, sir. I was jus' 'hinkin abou' my mum."

"I'm sure that she would be happy for you."

I gave him a timid smile and noticed that Robert was ready to scream. Amanda squealed with pleasure.

John glanced at me sideways but looked appeased. He then added, "There is more. I would like you to learn the business, and after your schooling is done, I want you to come to work with me."

I was startled by the loud crash of a chair tipping over. I saw Robert jumping up from the table and leaving the room. Amanda looked embarrassed. "I'll go talk to him."

Chapter 26

Captain Auger

Back to Work

Since sailing from Boston, my mind has been troubled. We have not accomplished anything of value during the war. The desertion remained an issue. I have second-guessed my decision not to send additional search parties to find the other traitors. I still think about the boy. I must put it behind me. There are more important matters to consider.

There is a loud knock on my cabin door. "What is it?"

"Captain, the crew is assembled. It's time."

"Very well." I grabbed my hat and straightened my uniform. I feel the warmth of the midday sun. The sound of the wind beating the sails tells me we are progressing well. I walk to the railing and look at the crew standing at attention. The look on their faces is pure hatred. I have little respect for these men. My gaze turned toward the four men. Their feet and hands are shackled, so they can't resist. A noose had been placed over their heads and tightened around their necks. The rope's end has been fed up through a pulley over the yardarm. I see the master-at-arms staring up at me.

"Mr. Harris, carry out the sentence."

He has a grim look of determination on his face and nods.

"You men have been charged with the crime of desertion and have been sentenced to hang. Do you have any final words?"

Two men have defiant looks while the other two struggle with their chains. One of them calls out, "Captain, please have mercy. I will not try to escape again."

Mr. Harris looks over his shoulder at me. I shake my head no. Harris then points to a team of sailors holding the ends of the ropes. Each man pulls the rope taunt until the sentenced men are hanging just below the yardarm. The crew watches in horror as the men flail about, struggling to fight their death sentence. After a few minutes, the men end their fight. I continue to watch as they are lowered to the deck. Then, one by one, they are unceremoniously thrown overboard.

Mr. Harris calls out, "You are dismissed. Get back to work!"

I linger to see how the men react. Some of them maintain their look of hatred. Others reflect fear. This is what I desire. I do not intend to be popular. My only motivation centers around my prospects for promotion. These dreams are fleeting now as we are delegated to escorting supply ships to protect them against a French threat that is nowhere to be seen. I shall be relegated to command this aged ship for the rest of my career.

Before heading back to my cabin, I turn toward my executive officer. "Mr. Crittenden, maintain our course toward the Bahamas. Wake me when we are within sight."

"Aye, sir."

Chapter 27

Peter Smith

The Tutor

O ver the next three years, I worked hard to fit in. No matter how much I tried, I could never repay everything the Smiths did for me. My adoptive parents hired a private tutor. I struggled to learn, and my accent reminded me of my meager beginnings. There was also the tension between Robert and me. I couldn't understand what I had done to offend him. Each time I tried to talk to him about it, he would abruptly leave. There was something not quite right about him. I began to notice a strain between him and our father. John showed impatience with Robert and never nurtured the boy. When I could no longer ignore the issue, I spoke with Amanda.

I finished my studies for the day and went into the kitchen to find her sitting at the table, drinking tea. I must have startled her because she jumped when she noticed me.

"Mum, can I speak wi'h you?"

Her face softened. "Of course, Peter. What would you like to talk about?"

I pulled a chair out and sat down. Amanda noticed how nervous I was. "What's wrong?"

I folded my hands in my lap and turned my eyes away from her. "I was wondering why Rober' ha'es me?"

She put her teacup down, reached out, and patted my arm. "Oh, Peter, Robert doesn't hate you." She paused. "He is –slow– and doesn't understand why we adopted you."

I needed clarification on what she meant. "He won" talk 'o me, and I notice 'ha' Mr. Smi'h is some'imes mean 'o him."

She sat back in her chair and looked like she was carefully weighing her words. "You must be patient with Robert. He will come to care about you as his brother. Mr. Smith is disappointed with how Robert turned out. He loves him, but Robert can never take over the family business. That's why he is so happy that you came into our lives. He has big plans for you."

"Wha' if I'm no' able 'o be wha' 'e wan's me 'o be?"

She leaned toward me and frowned. "You must not let your father down. Continue to work hard on your studies, and lose that ungainly accent."

She got up and left me sitting there.

I felt the pressure of the lofty goals that were set for me. I also continued to have nightmares involving my time on board HMS Progress. I would wake up screaming, and when my parents came to comfort me, I would beg ignorance about the cause. It added to my low self-esteem. I could never open up to them about my actual past. Do I give up or exercise my demons? How do I go about doing that?

As hard as I tried, I struggled to grasp my lessons. My tutor was a young man named Carlton Stevens. Carlton was a recent graduate of Harvard College. He was using the tutoring job to gain connections with businessmen in Boston to further his opportunities. The tutor was severe and stern when dealing with me. I didn't want to disappoint my parents, but I dreaded when he would show up at our home every morning. A typical morning would be spent listening to him flatter Amanda while leering at me. Amanda would walk away, blushing, leaving us alone in the study.

"Young Master Smith, have you worked on your reading lesson from yesterday?"

I sighed. "Yes, Mr. S'evens."

I felt the sudden flash of pain on my knuckles from the wooden rod that he carried.

"That is Mr. S-t-e-v-e-n-s!"

Rubbing my hand, I said, "Sorry, sir."

"Fine. Take out your Primer and start reading where we left off yesterday. After that, we shall work on your mathematical tables."

Chapter 28

John Smith

The Family Business

My business, which had miraculously grown since the devastating fire, was thriving despite the ongoing war with the French. The conflict had not impacted the volume of goods I could import and export, a testament to the resilience of my operations. However, there was a growing concern among the businessmen in Boston about our ability to trade freely with countries other than England. This was not just idle talk, but a potential threat to our business. As I searched through a pile of invoices, I realized the need for assistance with the increasing paperwork. I looked up at the clock on the wall. "Noon already. Where has the morning gone?"

I grabbed my jacket and hat and headed out the door. This is my favorite part of the day. I strolled down to the waterfront to catch a launch, go home for lunch, and fetch Peter for his afternoon to work with me. I stared back and admired the work that has gone on to rebuild the city. Then, my thoughts returned to Peter. He is still a boy. *Am I putting too much pressure on him?* That unpleasant tutor tells me the boy is progressing with his studies. Still, I wonder if he will be ready for everything I ask. The boy needs a proper education befitting a gentleman to move up the social ladder.

I knew that Joseph Adams was distantly related to the esteemed businessman Samuel Adams. This connection, if properly utilized, could be the key to Peter's future success. With this in mind, I resolved to devise a plan to have introductions made for Peter's advancement, ensuring that he would have the best possible opportunities to succeed in his future endeavors.

I climbed out of the ferry and made the short walk home. With all the excitement about Peter, I had forgotten about Robert. It was a sore subject between Amanda and me. I still hadn't recovered from the shock of learning that my son would never be "normal." His future options were bleak. I hoped to give him a comfortable life, but I stupidly blamed him for his condition. I will never forget the doctor's unkind words, "simple-minded."

We quickly ate a simple meal of stew and bread. I was in a hurry to get back to the office. "Peter, eat your meal. We need to catch the one o'clock ferry back to Boston." He looked at me with sadness in his eyes. He had hardly touched his lunch.

"What is troubling you, son?"

"I had a difficul' day of schooling."

I sensed trouble. "Should I be concerned?"

He shook his head, but I knew better.

"You understand how important your education is. I want you to be successful, and that takes hard work. You must redouble your efforts. Do you understand?"

He pushed himself away from the table. "I'm done ea'ing."

The ride back to Boston was spent in silence. The boy usually enjoyed going to the office and learning the business. Not today. He was distracted by something.

"Peter, last week I had you complete an inventory of all the stock in the warehouse." He dutifully waited for more.

"Today, I want you to learn how to keep the accounting books in order. This is where your mathematical skills will come into play."

I was still concerned about his lack of excitement. There may be a problem with the tutor. I made a mental note to check into it. "I want you to sit with Mr. Henderson. He will teach you how to enter income and expenditures into the ledger. Pay close attention. This is an important part of our business." I watched him for some kind of response. He finally nodded and went to find the accountant for his training.

There was too much going on to be distracted by Peter right now. I made a mental note to talk to him again on the way home.

Chapter 29

Captain Auger

Going Home

I grew restless while we languished in the Caribbean, protecting British supply ships. I thirsted for glory, which would only come from defeating the French Navy. What should have been the pinnacle of my career was spent babysitting unarmed transports in "paradise." The tedious duty also took its toll on the crew. There was still an issue with desertions, which forced me to limit granting liberty. It was too tempting for the men to take permanent leave. I understood the impact of my decision on the morale of the crew. What else could I do?

It seemed like a daily occurrence for me to receive reports of fighting, theft, and even death among the crew. I blamed all this on our present duty. I could not bring myself to take responsibility for the actions of the rabble. Still, it was concerning that the crew's numbers diminished, and the possibility of mutiny grew. I was more concerned about the effects this had on me. My mind was dulled, and the ailments of old age were catching up. The worst part was being deprived of an outlet for my "urges." I wondered what my cabin boy was doing.

I spent another stifling hot day locked in my quarters. My staff had addressed their concerns about the crew's welfare, but they had the audacity to demand I do something about it. I sent them away and am now considering my options. The all-too-common knock on my door pulled me back to reality.

"What is it?"

"Captain, we received orders addressed to you."

I stood. "Enter."

Mr. Crittenden entered with a hopeful look on his face. Could we be ordered back to action?

"Captain, we just received these sealed orders from the supply boat." He reached out and handed them to me. I watched him take a step back and lick his lips. His anxiousness was intoxicating.

I broke the seal and unfolded the parchment. My eyes widened.

"What are the orders, sir?"

I let the orders drop to the floor. "The war is over. We have been ordered to return to England."

"That is great news. Permission to share the news with the crew."

I waved at him, and he fled from the room. The orders were two months old. We have wasted away here for no reason.

As we approached the English coastline, I assembled my staff in my cabin. I scanned the room and stared at each man with my face embroiled in a scowl.

"Gentlemen, we will dock in Portsmouth. We look to repair the ship and bring the crew up to full numbers. Before sailing from the Bahamas, I knew of the growing unrest in the American colonies. We are to await further orders but must be prepared to sail as soon as possible."

Ambrose Crittenden looked sideways at the other officers and spoke for the group. "Sir, how soon do you expect until we get underway?"

I scowled at the man, "That is not up to me, Mr. Crittenden."

"Would this not be a good time for the crew to spend time with their families after being away so long?"

I sighed loudly, "Mr. Crittenden, my duty is to the King, and we shall do as we are ordered."

Crittenden nodded, but I knew he had more to say.

After silence, I bellowed, "Any other questions?" Without waiting for a reply, "Good, you are dismissed to prepare us for our landing in Portsmouth."

Chapter 30

Peter Smith

Harvard

I reached my sixteenth year. My circumstances couldn't have been any better, considering where I came from. My adoptive parents were supportive, if not obsessed with my success. It was a burden to constantly please them while maintaining my sanity. Through it all, I worked hard to master my lessons and the intricacies of my father's business. There had been little time for me to deal with my demons. This was probably a good thing. I just wish the dreams would cease.

Today is the day that my father had scheduled an interview with Samuel Adams. Getting accepted to Harvard was all John talked about. It was undoubtedly more important for him than for me. I just couldn't let him down. I wasn't sure how it would get me past my need to avenge my innocence.

"Peter, it's time to go."

I sighed and felt the pain in my stomach that wouldn't go away. "Coming, Father."

As we walked through the streets of Boston, I noticed an energy from the citizens since the end of the war. The city bustled and prospered. There were no remaining signs of damage from the fire.

"Today is an important day for you, Peter. Your uncle introduced me to Mr. Adams. You must make a strong impression on him. He is a mighty and influential man."

"I understand, Father."

We reached Purchase Street and stopped in front of a two-story red brick dwelling. John placed a hand on my shoulder and gently squeezed.

"This may be the most important interview of your life. Just be confident and answer his questions."

"I will do my best, Father." My voice cracked, and I felt like vomiting.

We were escorted to an office on the first floor and invited to sit. I looked around the room at the ornate furniture. A large world globe caught my attention. If my mum, back in England, could see me now. The door swung open, and we turned to see the figure of Samuel Adams. He was a large man, over six feet tall. He was dressed in a fine suit made of silk. His face was pleasant and welcoming.

"Gentlemen, I'm sorry to make you wait. Peter, your father tells me that you are interested in attending Harvard. Is that true?"

I could feel my father's eyes burning a hole in the side of my face. "Yes, sir. I' has been my dream to attend college there." I stiffened. "Excuse me, 'it'."

I saw a slight smile on Mr. Adams's face. I didn't dare look at my father.

"Tell me, young Master Smith, why should I recommend you for entrance?"

I had prepared for this question. "As I'm sure you have been told, I come from humble beginnings in England. I have been blessed to have been adopted by the Smith family and have worked hard to study while learning the family business. By furthering my education at Harvard, I can hopefully take over the family trade someday. This would allow me to pay back my debt."

He leaned forward with his elbows on his desk. He put his hands together, interlocking his fingers. I could tell he was studying me. The silence was punishing.

"You are an impressive young man. I will see what I can do."

"Peter, are you paying attention?"

I glared at Carlton Stevens. "I was dozing off."

"You need to take this seriously. These examinations are difficult. I'm not sure if you are ready."

The next step in the process was to take the entrance examinations, which were geared to test overall knowledge. I spent the last few weeks preparing with my old tutor, Carlton Stevens. He had completed his apprenticeship and was employed as an attorney. My father was persuasive, and he couldn't say no.

I blew out a breath through my parted lips. "I'm as ready as I can be."

"Your father will be disappointed if you don't pass."

"I will."

Harvard College was only located three miles from our home in Charlestown, but the ride there seemed to take forever. I sat rigidly on the family horse during the ride to Cambridge. My head ached as I continued to think about all the knowledge crammed into my brain. Carlton had been an excellent source for the types of questions that were typically asked. I didn't want to fail and let my parents down after all they had done. There was so much pressure on me.

I rode up to the entrance of the college and gasped at the beauty of the campus and imposing stone structures. The campus was laid out along tree-filled streets. There was a large green area surrounded by large ornate buildings. My pulse raced at the thought of what obstacle I would face. The closer I got, I saw a group of young men lining up. I'm private by nature—and experience—and as I congregated with the other aspiring students, I was intimidated. These young men were richly dressed and carried themselves confidently. I was told that they were sons of some of the wealthiest families in the colony.

The testing lasted all day and was a grueling affair. It included both written and oral examinations. I felt prepared, but self-doubt crept into my mind as I tackled each subject. My weakest course was Latin. As things worked out for me, this was the last subject of the day. I grasped both sides of my head and pulled at my hair while struggling through the Latin section. I had grave misgivings about how it would affect the overall outcome. I was warned that class sizes and the margin for error were relatively small.

As I rode home at the end of the day, I stooped in the saddle, drained and full of doubts. What would I tell the Smiths? I could only stare down at my boots with the thought of letting the Smiths down and endangering my future plans. How could someone like me, who came from such a disadvantaged position, ever amount to anything. It would be another challenge I had to face at such an early age, waiting to see if I would be admitted to the school.

I deflected most of my parent's questions. Surprisingly, they sensed my anguish and didn't press for answers. To distract myself, I threw all my energy into the family business. We were busier than ever and had to hire additional help to keep up with deliveries of our goods. At this time, I also heard rumblings about the challenges the American colonies faced from controlling British authorities. Even though the war had ended, the British government still decreed that the colonies only trade English goods and not expand to other countries. This action incensed my father and other business leaders around town.

After a few weeks, I was in my room getting dressed for the day. I heard the front door open, and Amanda cried out, "Peter, you have received a letter from Harvard."

I had honestly put it out of my mind. The familiar burning sensation returned to my stomach. Time to face the truth. I walked downstairs like I was walking off to the gallows. My parents stood at the base of the stairs. They had cautiously optimistic grins. My mother handed me the unopened letter. I tried to compose myself as I ripped it open. I could feel both of them staring at me as I read the letter.

"Tell us, Peter, what does it say?"

I slowly looked up at them. "I passed! I have been accepted into Harvard College."

They screamed with joy. They grabbed me, and we danced around the room. Out of the corner of my eye, I saw Robert standing with his arms crossed, showing no emotion.

"The letter stated that my scores, while not outstanding, were adequate. There was an indication that the decision had more to do with the recommendations the school received on my behalf."

"All that doesn't matter, son. You have been accepted, and I couldn't be more proud of you."

"Thank you, Father."

I knew this would start the next phase of my life. It wasn't what I wanted. Still, I couldn't make a mess of it.

Chapter 31

Peter Smith

Making Friends

I moved onto the campus of Harvard and began my studies. It was one of the most lonely times of my life. I was cut off from my family and left to sink or swim. My days at Harvard were highly regimented. I took a full course load, and the students were required to attend regular church services and dine together. I was socially awkward. Most of the students ignored me.

The day that changed my life was the day I met Moses Fairchild and Henry Stiles. Both young men came from wealthy, well-connected families. They took notice of me sitting by myself at dinner and approached me.

Moses sat next to me. He was tall and thin, and his dark hair stood in stark contrast to his blue eyes. "My name is Moses, and this is Henry," he said, pointing at his friend. Henry was the polar opposite. He was short and chubby, with short cropped auburn hair. "What is your name, and why are you sitting alone?"

I cleared my throat. "My name is Peter. I don't know anyone here."

"Then Henry and I will have to do something about that, won't we, Henry?"

My new "friends" introduced me to a world that I would have never known back in Portsmouth, or Boston, for that matter. Moses and Henry came from respected families in the colony. They were carefree and taught me to enjoy life and not be so serious all the time. This included taking me to social gatherings where I was introduced to young ladies. I had no experience with the fairer sex and was ultimately out of my element. These women both thrilled and frightened me. I was charmed by their beauty and threatened by their intelligence. It gave me a glimmer of hope that there was more to life than school and business.

I started to blossom during this time and became more confident in myself and my abilities. At times, I had to pinch myself that life had turned around like it had. I still had my nightmares, but I stuffed my demons down deep in my soul. The question was, "How do I close and lock the door?"

My deepest fear remained that someone would discover the truth about my past, and I prayed that would never happen. Even with my prospects looking up, I needed someone to confide in. I trusted Moses and Henry, but I doubted they would understand what I went through and the abuse I suffered from Auger. No one else knew what I went through other than Charles Tildon. It wasn't likely that I would ever cross paths with him again.

Chapter 32

John Smith

Anarchy

With Peter away at school, my entire focus was growing my business. The Stamp Act, which was enacted and approved by the King, became a divisive issue in the colony. The law was vast and overreaching in the number of items requiring a tax to be paid on all legal documents and printed materials. It was to be the first time that individuals would be directly taxed. It could have a lingering effect on me and other business owners in the colony.

I was recruited along with several other "like-minded" members of the merchant class of Boston to meet at a secret location. Each of us was a respected businessman in the community and well-connected. We are not politicians but have friends who serve in the Massachusetts House of Representatives. We are motivated and determined to do anything necessary to protect our interests.

The room was crowded, dark, and filled with smoke from the gathered group's pipes. The air was thick with anticipation, and each man looked resolutely as if aware of the magnitude of what we were about to discuss. After pleasantries were completed and a hush fell over the chamber, I stood and adjusted my top coat to address my peers.

"Gentlemen, we are gathered to discuss the grave issues that our businesses are facing due to the latest acts ordered by the Crown." I gazed at the assembled men, confident I had their attention, and continued, "We must come together as a united front to respond to these travesties."

There was a general murmur from the crowd. One of the merchants, Arthur Jacoby, stood red-faced and stated, "It is a mockery what they are doing to every one of us. How can we profit by paying these levies, especially for soldiers living among us and keeping us under their control? Don't they know the war is over?"

The crowd reacted in unison with loud shouts and pounding fists on tables. Mr. Jacoby cocked a quick look at me and took his seat.

Then, the oldest man in the room stood. His name was Silas Grainger. He was slightly stooped over with flowing white hair and a long, wrinkle-lined face. Grainger owned several businesses in town and had the most at stake to lose. "Gentlemen, I agree that we are faced with serious challenges, but let me caution all of you on acting too rashly." He glared at each man around the room, "I have lived a long life and have seen many things. I have not agreed with every edict from the Crown, but it makes no sense for the King to interfere with our commerce, which also enriched the merchants of England. They are trying to raise revenue to replenish all the funds spent to protect us from any threats from foreign powers. Surely, the King's motives are pure."

There was some agreement from the crowd with Mr. Grainger's sentiment, but most of the men in the room remained silent.

I stood again when the room was silenced. "I would like to thank Silas for his valued experience and thoughts. However, we must come to an agreement as to what course of action we should take in response to these acts."

Several men stood and voiced agreement, "What shall we do then?"

I waited stoically for the crowd to quiet, nodded my head, and grinned. "I'm glad you asked. I agree that the Crown wants us to succeed, but they also want us to trade exclusively with them and not with the other European nations. This action puts us at a disadvantage. It would be in our best interest to continue our unauthorized trade and consider boycotting all English goods until there is change."

Someone shouted, "That would be very dangerous for us to take that action."

A few others shouted in agreement to take a less provocative stance, but I noted that the majority continued to stare at me for guidance.

I let the shouts die down and sensed the overall mood of the room. "We cannot continue to let the British dictate how we run our businesses. We must take a stand for our survival. It starts with taxes on certain items and housing troops, then leads to them taking over all aspects of our lives. I don't know about you, but I chose not to be guided by a king who lives thousands of miles away."

Most of the crowd rose to their feet and pledged their agreement to take action. I pursed my lips and frowned at the few gentlemen in the room who remained seated, their faces shocked.

I understood that unity was necessary if we were to survive this threat. "Gentlemen, I know the risk of what I speak. Let us think on the matter and agree to meet again this time next week. Gather your thoughts and come ready to discuss the course of action we shall agree on."

The crowd nodded, and everyone stood, preparing to leave the meeting. Hands were shaken, and goodbyes were bid as they filtered out of the small room over a local tavern.

When everyone else had left, a remaining member of the group walked up to me. His name is Albert Shelby, and he is a close friend of mine, but more importantly, he is a member of the Sons of Liberty.

"That went well, John."

"I agree, but I was surprised by the number of men who aren't as committed to the cause."

"They will come around. What will you tell Samuel?"

I smiled at the mention of the name, "I will tell Mr. Samuel Adams that we have a group of merchants who are prepared to do what must be done."

I struggled with whether to tell Peter about my decisions, which could significantly impact his future. After discussing it with Amanda, I decided to visit him in Cambridge. When I got to Cambridge, I picked up Peter and took him to a local tavern so we could speak in private. Peter looked at me, and I could see the concern on his face. The stress of making a stand against England was taking its toll on me.

We picked out a corner table and ordered tea. When I was sure it was safe to talk, I leaned in, "I have come to talk to you about some developments with the business."

Peter leaned closer and clasped his fingers tightly together in anticipation.

I continued, "I have decided to be an active member of the Sons of Liberty. As you know, there is a growing rebellion against the Stamp Act."

Peter nodded and waited for me to continue.

"I feel it is important for you to understand the dangers involved in that decision. There could be possible repercussions, not only to me but also to our business. The British aren't likely to let us protest without reacting." I let that sink into Peter for a minute. "It's only fair that I make you aware of how my decisions could cost you and your future."

Peter sat back in his seat, considering what I had told him. "This is something that we have discussed in my classes, and I have come to believe that it is important that we stand up to any British tyranny. I have no great love for the English, even though that is where I come from." Then, lifting his shoulders and placing his palms flatly on the table, he looked into my eyes. "I have some things that I need to tell you."

I cocked my head while continuing to look at my son.

"You know I came from humble beginnings, but you don't know that I had to resort to thievery just to survive. I was arrested and put in jail at a very young age. It was there where I was taken away to serve on the ship." Then he paused.

I was distressed about anything else he would divulge. I could see the pain on his face. "Go ahead and tell me what you want to say."

He hung his head and then raised it slowly, "That's all I wanted to say."

I knew there was more. I didn't push the issue.

Peter sat up and puffed out his chest. "Then you should allow me to also join the Sons of Liberty so that I too can make a difference."

I smiled at his enthusiasm, "I appreciate your willingness to serve, but I think it is more important for you to focus on your schooling right now."

Peter deflated and shrugged his shoulders.

"Let us drink our tea and discuss other issues."

Chapter 33

Peter Smith

Meeting Anne

I worked hard to focus on my studies at Harvard while putting my past behind me. I felt selfish for being away from home with all my father was facing. I was troubled by our last conversation and the way he had aged in a short period. With the help of my friends Moses and Henry, I blossomed socially. They introduced me to the "right" people. I felt like a fraud at times, but it buoyed my confidence. I had to think about my future and trust my friends to look out for me.

Part of their plan was to drag me to social events where women would be present. As I had never been around women my age, I struggled. My heart raced, and my cheeks would glow from the excess blood flow as I turned the heads of the women I met. I was tongue-tied and would sometimes slip into my cockney accent. In the back of my mind, I would never be able to be intimate with a woman due to the abuse I endured. It was troubling, but my thoughts would return to Charles during these encounters.

At one of these parties, I was introduced to Anne Proctor. Anne was a beautiful, tawny-haired, brown-eyed, somewhat frail young woman. Two years younger than me, Anne was the daughter of a pastor from a local church in Cambridge. Moses must have seen me take notice of the young maiden. He smiled and grabbed my arm.

"Come with me."

"Anne Proctor, this is Peter Smith."

She slightly bowed. "It's a pleasure to meet you, Mr. Smith."

I wasn't able to say a word. Moses elbowed me in the ribs. "Sorry. The pleasure is mine, Miss Proctor."

I succumbed to what could only be an infatuation with the stunning young woman. This feeling was foreign to me. I don't recall the rest of our conversation. It was a dizzying experience.

I successfully maneuvered through my last year at Harvard. Four years had been a whirlwind filled with classes, sermons, and social events. I continued to see Anne socially, but part of me kept my distance from her. I sensed she thought I was a fraud and was holding back something. I could never share with her what happened to me. Still, she pursued the relationship, and I was resigned that we would wed at some point. Despite my doubts, I longed for the precious moments I spent with the vivacious pastor's daughter.

Along with my self-doubts, I never got to the point of being comfortable around her father. Every time that I would accompany Anne to one of Pastor Proctor's church services, the sermon always seemed to be directed at me, like the occasions that he preached on the subject of the lust of human flesh and would stare down from his pulpit at me. My intentions with Anne were always honorable.

I knew I was destined to take over the family import business, but I became interested in the law. My favorite classes involved debate, which I excelled at. Both my friends, Moses and Henry, prepared to become lawyers and often tried to convince me that's where my future should lie. I couldn't disappoint my adoptive parents, especially after all they had done for me. However, it was intriguing to consider a life spent in the law, with the impending disruptions with England, who knew what would happen. It was debate where I cut my teeth on extolling both sides of an issue to attempt to come to a conclusion. While there were times when passions ran high, there was always a free and open discussion, and dissension was welcomed and encouraged. I learned important lessons of life I would use all my days. These debates were vital to my development, and I knew I belonged there. In the past, I belonged to the street gangs back in Portsmouth. Then, I was part of the ship's crew during the war. Now, I indeed found where I was supposed to be. My college experience turned me from a shy, abused, lost boy to someone who was treated like an equal and whose opinion was valued.

The day's current events in Boston were intriguing to the students and faculty at Harvard. A solid majority's loyalty remained with the Crown, and they arrogantly viewed the treasonous acts being committed against the King's representatives in Boston by the mobs of miscreants with great disdain. Not all of the staff and students were as supportive of the King, and some were outspoken about their concerns about overreach by the government. My mindset strongly agreed with the minority. I loved to openly debate anyone who disagreed with me. My views had been shaped by my father's opinions and my experience as a boy serving in the British Navy.

My favorite professor, James Edwards, taught rhetoric based on classical philosophers like Aristotle, Cicero, Erasmus, and Francis Bacon. I thoroughly enjoyed the class and the discussions that went on among my fellow students. When word reached the college that more British troops were being sent to enforce the Townshend Act, class deliberations were inflamed by the passions of the opposing sides.

Professor Edwards broached the subject during one class and opened the discussion to the students, "Men, we are faced with the prospect of King George sending additional troops to our area to instill order. Let us discuss the merit of such action." Edwards' eyes averted directly toward me, but another student stood before I could take the floor.

"Professor Edwards, fellow students. We are facing difficult times where the rabble of Boston has taken it upon itself to defy the King, who clearly has the best interests of his subjects at heart. We are an integral part of the empire and need the protection of these troops if we are to survive. It will be the duty of gentlemen like us to uphold all English laws and actively support our King in expanding our way of life. By supporting the King, we shall also have the best interest of all the subjects in the American colonies and prosper."

A few of the students clapped their hands in support of the speech.

His name was Carlton Hughes, and he came from one of the wealthiest families in the Massachusetts colony. His father supported the King and held large tracts of land in the southern part of the colony. Carlton was uptight and smug. I detested him.

Professor Edwards stoically looked around the classroom. "Thank you, Mr. Hughes, for that spirited argument. Would anyone like to share an opposing view?"

I leaped out of my seat and stood ramrod straight. "Professor Edwards, fellow students. I agree with my learned classmate, Mr. Hughes, in that we should uphold the law so that society would not spiral out of control."

I noted the smug smile on Hughes' face.

"However, that is the only point that I agree with. What is at stake here are our basic freedoms. As British subjects, should we not have a voice in our governance? Are we to be treated like dogs if we attempt to have our opinions heard, even if they go against those of the ruling class? These are the true questions that need to be answered."

There were murmurs of agreement in the classroom, and I saw Hughes wearing a frown.

"We should have the right to govern ourselves and determine our best path. That can still be done equitably with an agreeable relationship with England, and we can all live in harmony. However, when the King sends troops to control our every action, can we truly be an equal member of the empire?"

Several classmates stood and applauded loudly when I sat down in a heap. Some went to me and patted my back.

Professor Edwards beamed at me but stood to calm the room, "Gentlemen, please return to your seats."

As the room quieted and the students returned to their seats, Carlton Hughes stood shaking his fist in the air and shouted at me, "Smith, what you state is pure treason and will be the destruction of all of us. We can't live in a society where all classes of people would have a say over how they are governed. It would be ruinous."

Deflated, Hughes took his seat and continued to glare at me.

I had crossed a line but regained my feet, and with my arms clasped behind my back, I faced the class again.

"Gentlemen, I realize my words may have come across as harsh and unrelenting. I have no desire for a war with England. I only state that we should have some control over how we are governed, especially how we are treated as equals and not as unruly children needing to be punished by our elders."

Professor Edwards dismissed the class and, as the students left the room, called out to me, "Smith, a moment, please."

I turned around, facing the teacher, prepared for a lecture.

Edwards smiled and shook his head, saying, "Well done, Smith. You made a strong argument, but you should not have apologized for anything that you said. Make sure that you remain strong in your convictions. They will carry you through your life."

I smiled, "Thank you, sir."

Chapter 34

John Smith

Sons of Liberty

M y disgust with the English authority continued to boil. The local group of merchants continued to meet in secret. We tried to devise plans for the best course of action to respond to the Townshend Act. It took some arm twisting and cajoling to get unanimous backing from the group. Initially, we agreed to have handbills printed and distributed around the city, pointing out the unfairness of the taxes and the resulting impact on the local economy. The group of businessmen planned to get the support of the local citizens in Boston to strengthen our cause. We reluctantly agreed on a partial embargo of British goods, which would directly impact the merchants in England. There was much debate about this action because it could place us in the most danger and hurt our businesses. We continued our illicit trade with French and Dutch merchants in opposition to the English.

I found myself in a constant battle, torn between my personal interests and the greater cause. Samuel Adams and the Sons of Liberty exerted immense pressure on me to take more radical steps. Caught in this tug of war, I did my best to appease both sides. Samuel, sensing my internal conflict, pulled me aside after one particularly heated meeting.

"John, you know how important our cause is. The British will never leave us alone if we don't take action. While I appreciate the steps the merchants have taken, it won't have the impact that we need to change how we are treated."

"Samuel, I understand what you are asking of us. You must understand that these businessmen only understand what impacts their bottom lines. It has been difficult for me to convince them to do anything that would harm them financially."

"I also am a businessman, John. They must understand that all of what we have worked so hard to build could be taken away anytime by a King who doesn't care about us."

This was an old argument from Samuel. I crossed my arms on my chest and slowly shook my head from side to side. Indeed, the King wasn't utterly callous toward all his subjects.

Adams' face flushed with anger. "We cannot afford to wait any longer, John. We must act now, before we find ourselves forced to submit to more than just a few disagreeable taxes!"

"Samuel, I will continue to work on the group, but they will need to see that the risks they are taking are worth the danger they could face."

"John, there is a growing movement among all the colonies. England will be made to understand how united this cause is in America."

I raised my eyebrows, a flicker of surprise crossing my face. I had been focused on the local movement, unaware of the protests and actions brewing across the colonies. The realization of this growing unity among the colonies was a revelation.

"Let me know what you would like us to do."

"That's exactly what I want to hear."

Chapter 35

Captain Auger

New Orders

"Captain Auger, the admiral will see you now."

I stood and straightened my uniform. I entered the lavish office and spied Admiral Ingram sitting at his desk. "Captain Auger reporting for orders."

The balding man looked up from his paperwork. "Auger, what shape is the Progress in?"

I remained standing at attention. "Admiral, we have gone through our refit period and are ready to set sail."

Ingram's face looked like he had swallowed something bitter. I knew he didn't think very highly of me.

"Fine. Here are your orders." He handed the papers to me. "You are to sail back to the American colony of Massachusetts, escorting troop ships. We are sending 4,000 soldiers to quell the unrest in Boston."

My shoulders drooped. It felt like I was punched in the stomach. Not escort duty again.

He must have read my mind. "You shall take this duty very seriously, Captain. We are trying to prevent open rebellion in the colony. We need you to intimidate these Americans who think they can disrespect their King."

—·—

I watched as the crew took on supplies from my perch on the quarterdeck. I looked up and saw a gray slate sky. A crossing during this time of year will be difficult. I see Crittenden coming toward me out of the corner of my eye. He went behind my back to get the crew some time off the ship while we were in port. I will make sure that he pays for that action.

"Captain, we are taking on the last of the supplies. We should be ready to get underway soon."

"Very well, Mr. Crittenden."

The ship's crew has been supplemented with "conscripts" replenishing the depleted ranks. The excellent work of Lieutenant Pressley. This included a new cabin boy for me to amuse myself with. I still can't get that Beale boy out of my head.

I call out to the master-at-arms. "Mr. Harris, a moment."

There is reluctance on his face as he climbs the ladder to the quarterdeck.

"Yes, sir, how can I be of assistance?"

"How is the training progressing for the new crew members?"

He snorts, "It's going as well as expected."

"Tell me we will not have the same issues as the last group."

"Me and the other able seamen will do all we can, sir."

"See that you do."

We both heard the order, "Cast the lines to make way!"

Harris turned to me and touched the brow of his hat. "Permission to see to the crew."

"You are dismissed."

I stayed on the quarterdeck to watch the evolution that always fascinated me. A man of war getting underway from a congested port full of ships. I'm always surprised how smoothly the crew can pull off the feat without damaging the boat. As we put the coastline out of sight, I notice the chill in the air. I wrapped my frock coat tightly around me. Will this be a harbinger of things to come? Sailors are very superstitious.

Our last journey to the new world took a tremendous toll on me. I wondered if it was due to our failure to accomplish anything significant or if my age was finally catching up with me. I have lost much of the fire I had. My reading of the new orders to the crew was uninspiring. I couldn't let the crew see any weakness from me. What will it take for me to regain my rage?

The transit across the Atlantic was uneventful. After a three-month passage, I was notified that land had been spotted, so I went topside to see the welcome sight of the coast of Massachusetts.

The small armada of ships sailed into Boston harbor, where the troops disembarked and set up camp on the Boston Commons. We stayed anchored in the harbor to ensure the Americans didn't attempt any shenanigans.

Chapter 36

John Smith

Resistance

I stared out at the mass of British soldiers assembling on the common. A cold chill ran down my spine. It all seemed so hopeless. I knew that the incursion of British troops would immediately impact the merchants of Boston. Our foreign partners would be hesitant to trade with the colony for fear of reprisals from England. We would also be pressured to pay taxes and only deal with British merchants. I put out the word for an emergency meeting with fellow businessmen.

"Gentlemen, we face the gravest threat to our livelihood ever known." I paused for effect. There was an air of near panic in the room.

"What shall be done to combat the harassment from the British against our businesses? Do we fold and acquiesce to the government's will and, pay our taxes and only trade with the English like good little children? Or do we continue on our path of deciding who we do business with and take control over our own fates?"

The spattering of discussions simultaneously resulted in mixed opinions on what should be done. I needed to gain unanimity from the group to create a united front. I watched the wave of discussions taking place around the room. I scanned the back wall, attempting to make eye contact with my son. I summoned Peter to attend this meeting as it might impact the family business. I wanted Peter to know the risks involved in rebelling against the British. Peter leaned against the wall with his arms folded across his chest. He met my stare and smiled brightly. I returned the smile and redirected my attention to the babbling group of merchants.

Unable to read the room, I looked at my friend Arthur Jacoby. "Arthur, what is your opinion on the matter?"

Arthur looked every part of his sixty-two years old, with graying hair and tired green eyes. His business centered around the tea trade. He slowly stood up and looked around the room. "Like John, I am concerned about the latest developments that we are facing. I also believe that we need to make a stand and not bow down to the demands of the British. We can't live in fear of the troops sent against us."

The group showed a smattering of approval, but I could still see disagreement on the faces of many of my peers. I understood their concerns. I turned my attention to Benjamin Little's reaction, who owned one of the largest bookstores in the colony. A nervous, short, bookish man, Little relied heavily on England for his books.

Benjamin noticed me staring at him and stood to face the crowd. "You all know me, and you also know the impact the tax has on my books. I do not support the government's actions, but we are at a crossroads. If we continue down the path that we are on, we could face more than just a loss of business. We could be placing our lives in danger."

I nodded to Benjamin as the old man took his seat. I had anticipated some doubt from a few of the gathered men, but I was unprepared for the pushback I received. I would need to be resolute in supporting our cause without alienating anyone in the room.

"Clearly, there is danger in our resistance to the Crown and its policies, but I submit that there is more danger in not doing anything. What is to stop them from taking away our businesses or taxing us into oblivion even if we go along with their every whim? We continue to fight the injustices that have been placed upon us. We need to hit the English where it hurts them most: not buying their goods. Due to the British fleet in the harbor, we face additional challenges in obtaining goods from other countries. We need to explore other options."

I let out a breath, and I could see most of the men in the room nod their heads in agreement. "I have invited Mr. Noah Mast to speak with us concerning some alternatives for boycotting English goods. Mr. Mast is from Providence and would like to present us with that other option."

Noah Mast was a handsome man standing more than six feet tall with a full head of blond hair and sparkling blue eyes. He exuded confidence and stood to face the men with a massive smile. "Thank you for allowing me to speak to you gentlemen today. Mr. Smith has kindly invited me to share an alternative to your trade difficulties."

Every eye in the room was riveted on him. They sat on the edge of their seats, waiting to hear what Mr. Mast had to say next.

"It is clear that your businesses will be impacted by the closing of the port of Boston. Please allow me to assist in opening up other accesses for your trading partners. I also trade with other countries and would like your goods to be shipped through the same ports that I use and have those goods transported to Boston over land. This would be more expensive, but the cost would be small compared to the English tariffs and the exclusiveness of only buying and selling their goods. This would allow you to continue to show resistance to the King."

The rest of the meeting involved answering questions and detailing the logistics of setting up this new distribution system. I sat quietly, observing my fellow businessmen for any signs of opposition or doubt. The reaction in the room lifted my spirits, and a weight was lifted off my chest.

Preliminary discussion continued about fees that Mast would charge to make these arrangements. Mast owned several small sailing boats that could easily smuggle goods from various locations along the North Atlantic coast without detection by the British Navy. He also had access to a dedicated system of men, wagons, and horses to move the goods over land to any location.

I watched intently as the plans were ironed out with most of the men in the meeting. I dropped my head, closed my eyes, and remained silent because I couldn't convince everyone about the plan's advantages. I would have to be content that most came around to my way of thinking. What I didn't know at the time was a British mole in the room, noting what was said and by whom.

When the meeting ended, and the men left the upper room of the tavern, I motioned for Peter to join me so that I could introduce him to Mr. Mast.

"Noah, this is my son Peter."

Mast shook hands with the young man. "Pleased to meet you, Peter. Your father told me that you are attending Harvard College."

"Yes, sir. I will finish in the spring and look forward to helping run the family business."

"I've also been informed that you have some experience working on a sailing ship."

Peter cocked his head slightly at me in disbelief that I would tell anyone about that part of his life.

I noticed the anger on my son's face, "Peter, I only mentioned that you worked on a British frigate during the war until I adopted you."

Noah seemed to notice the anger and added, "Your father did not share any information that I shouldn't know. There may come a time very soon when we will need men who are experienced sailors to combat the British."

Peter's eyes became round as saucers, "Do you think it will come to that, an actual war with the British?"

"Yes, I do. If we are ever to be free from the tyranny that we face, there will need to be blood shed for us to gain our freedom."

I feared for my son. He was quiet, and I couldn't tell what he was thinking.

Chapter 37

Captain Auger

Back in Boston

I stood on my usual perch on the quarterdeck and gazed out at the tightly packed city. It was different from the last time we were here. The colonists had admirably rebuilt much of the damage caused by the fire, a fact that both impressed and unsettled me. I couldn't help but wonder, what did they expect? How dare they resist the edicts of their King. We should hang the whole treasonous lot.

Life aboard the HMS Progress continued to be monotonous for the crew and me, day in and day out of the same meaningless duty only a few yards away from Boston and its temptations. I wrestled with the need for more activity or orders to be of more use. I maintained the facade of running a tight ship and being unbending about the draconian rules the crew lived by. I couldn't forget what it was like to face discipline for minor offenses in my youth. So I wasn't without sympathy. Boredom breeds strife, especially with sailors locked on a ship for long periods. It was inevitable there would be incidents of fights breaking out. While I couldn't condone wholesale liberty for the men to go ashore, I decided to permit limited leave. "Mr. Condone, have Mr. Crittenden meet me in my cabin."

My executive officer, Crittenden, was a man of knowledge and experience, but his soft spot for the crew's feelings was a constant source of internal conflict for me. As the door opened and he stepped in, my face twisted in a slight breach of protocol. But for now, I let it slide.

"You asked to see me, sir?"

"Mr. Crittenden, I have given the matter some thought and will grant liberty for the crew."

He smiled broadly. "That is great news. It should go a long way to improving morale."

I felt like wiping that smile off his smug face. "There are conditions." I watched for his response. To his credit, he stood waiting for more without comment.

"The men will likely get drunk and visit the houses of ill repute. This could lead to issues with the local officials. I will not have the low-life men on this ship ruin the ship's reputation." I paced the room, my hands clasped behind my back. I stopped and turned to him. "Therefore, I will hold you accountable for their behavior."

Crittenden tried to remain stoic, but I could tell it affected him. He recovered and stood ramrod straight. "Yes, sir. Then, I propose a senior crew member escort each group of men. These trusted crewmen will look out for the men to keep them in line."

I thought to myself, *Very wise. Deflect the responsibility to others.*

"What is your plan to prevent the men from deserting like the last time we were here?"

For an instant, he actually glared at me. He was treading on perilous waters.

"I shall take responsibility for that and will personally direct the escorting officer to be watchful to prevent that from happening."

"Very well. Understand this, Mr. Crittenden, punishment will be severe for any transgressions. Any issues could also affect your chances at promotion and command of your own."

"I understand, Captain. Can I be excused?"

I nodded my head. I was feeling better about the whole ordeal. I even dropped the man a couple of notches down the chain.

The memory of the desertions was still painful, especially the loss of the cabin boy, Peter Beale. What is that boy doing right now?

Chapter 38

Peter Smith

Reunion

I left the meeting with my father and the other business leaders in utter disbelief. My head felt like it would explode, and I needed to walk to clear my mind. I couldn't believe he exposed part of my past to a stranger. How could I ever trust him with my darkest secrets? I just wanted to be alone. I stuffed my hands in my pockets and walked, trying to come to grips with events I had hoped were finally behind me. Added to my frustration, I struggled to get over the fact that the academic exercise I went through at school now played out in the reality of severe acts against the King and his government. I turned down near the pier with my head down. I wondered how I would fit into all that was happening around me. The conflict with the British could directly impact my future.

I ignored the others walking along the pier and accidentally bumped into another man. When I looked up, I saw a group of three men facing me. The one that I bumped into leered at me and said, "Watch where you're going, mate."

I tilted my head and squinted while looking at the man. "I'm sorry, sir, I did not see you."

The other two men prodded the third man, "Are you going to let this boy get away with assaulting you like that?"

I saw the telltale signs that all three men were drunk and didn't want to escalate the situation. "Gentlemen, I meant no harm. If you please, I need to be somewhere else."

"Did you hear that, Cook; he thinks we are gentlemen."

I noted the thick English accents and looked again at the men. Instantly, I knew that they were sailors. It then registered with me that one of the men had been called "cook." My heart skipped a beat. I stared at the man. I nearly cried out when I recognized him. It was the cook from the Progress standing right in front of me. Several thoughts were running through my mind. Should I remain calm and take my leave, or should I run as fast as possible?

As I stood there wondering what to do, I watched in horror as the cook tried to steady himself and take a good look at me. I could see that there was a hint of recognition in his eyes.

"Do I know you, lad?"

Taking every ounce of self-control I could muster, I replied, "I don" believe so." Damn, my accent!

"I never forget a face, and I know you. I just can't remember where."

I just stood there and didn't say anything. Cook continued to stare at me. It was good that he was drunk, and I no longer looked like the boy held captive on that ship.

The other two sailors stood there watching the conversation. One grabbed the cook and said, "Leave the poor boy alone. We need to get some more ale before we return to the ship."

Cook stopped staring at me, looked at his fellow sailors, and said, "Right, the night is still young. Off we go."

I didn't wait for the man to change his mind and continue to reminisce. As I turned and started walking away, the cook called over his shoulder, "I know I have seen you before. I have a good memory, and it will return to me."

I didn't turn back but said, "Goodnight, gentlemen." I then picked up my pace and tried to get as far away as possible before the old cook remembered me. I clinched a fist and hit the side of my leg, chiding myself for being so ignorant about the possibility that the Progress could be in Boston. I would be safe in Cambridge, but I would be graduating soon and needed to help my father run the business in Boston. I couldn't make that mistake again about carelessly wandering around town.

As I melted into the night, I started to feel safer. I turned around one last time to ensure no one was following me. Suddenly, I heard a shout.

"I know that is you, boy. I told you I have a good memory. We will come looking for you. The captain misses you!"

I stood there frozen, and a shiver overcame my body. The memories of the ship flooded back. I remembered all the times that I was trapped in the captain's cabin and assaulted by the man I had grown to hate. It was unfair. My innocence and childhood were taken away from me. I wanted to take vengeance against the man and the crew that did nothing to stop him. I calmed down and made a promise that I would get my revenge.

For now, I would stay away from Boston.

Chapter 39

John Smith

Informer

I wasn't comfortable sneaking around to meet with colleagues. The chill in the air fit my mood. These times called for caution, and I was careful with whom I trusted. We agreed to meet in secret at the home of a mutual friend. We went separately and entered the dwelling from the rear. I disguised myself and glanced constantly around to ensure I had yet to be followed.

We were informed about the true nature of Gerald Aston and his position as an informant for Governor Hutchison. We had taken the news roughly as we all knew Aston and trusted him to be loyal to our cause. The meeting was between Arthur Jacoby, Benjamin Little, and myself. We were tasked with deciding what was to be done with Aston. We had to be cautious if we chose to have him killed. This action could raise the alarm with Hutchison, who would, in turn, have the British soldiers come after all of us. Still, we had to do something. We couldn't just capitulate to the authority of the British government.

The hostess served tea in the home's parlor. The outcome of the meeting could decide the fate of our businesses. I started the conversation.

"Gentlemen, we must decide what to do about the governor's informant in our midst." I leaned forward with my hands folded under my chin, staring at the other two men.

Both men turned their gaze from me to stare at each other. Eventually, Arthur spoke up, "I would just as well have the bastard murdered, but I suppose that would be too risky. How do we know there aren't more Hutchison spies in our meetings?"

"Good point."

I turned toward Arthur. "I wondered the same thing. I arranged for everyone who attends our meetings to be followed, including the two of you."

Benjamin sat back in his chair as if slapped on the face. "Who was following you?"

"That's a fair point, Ben. We have much to lose if we can't trust each other. I just had to be sure that Aston is the only spy."

"So, what do we do?"

"I only see two options. Either we eliminate Aston, or we surrender to the edicts of the British authority and pay their taxes and only trade their goods."

"You know that we can't give in to them. But how do we eliminate Aston?" Arthur mumbled.

"I agree that's the only option," added Ben.

"We have to make it look like an accident. There can be no incriminating evidence to tie it back to us."

"How can that be accomplished?" Arthur wondered out loud.

"Wouldn't Hutchison be suspicious if Aston were to die or disappear?"

"That's why we must make it look accidental or even from natural causes. Aston is not a young man. Gentlemen, I have come into possession of some belladonna berries that should work quite nicely."

Arthur frowned, showing deep burrows in his aged face, "Are we sure that it would work? How do we get him to eat the berries?"

Ben looked doubtful. "Wouldn't he show obvious signs of being poisoned?"

My face displayed an evil grin. "All good questions. It should only take a couple of the berries to do the job. Aston regularly takes his lunch at the pub across from his shop. I have already convinced the barmaid to place the berries in his meal. He should not be suspicious because I am told that the berries taste sweet. As far as the signs, I was also told that it would appear that he was having a heart ailment or a stroke."

"It sounds like you have figured everything out already, John," Arthur said.

"If we all agree, I will set it in motion." I looked at my co-conspirators, waiting for their response.

Both men nodded in agreement. "It has to work for all our sakes."

There was too much at stake, so I accompanied Noah Mast to retrieve the first shipment of goods from France through the French West Indies. I stood stoically on the stern of the small craft while the supplies were unloaded. Many finished goods were included, like furniture, clothing, books, weapons, and tools. The operation took place off the coast of Rhode Island. The supplies were taken from a single French ship and loaded onto four smaller vessels owned by Noah Mast. These smaller vessels then transported the goods onto land, eventually sending them to the merchants in Boston. It was a dark, moonless night, which added to the danger of the enterprise.

I turned to Noah. "Do you always complete your operations under these conditions?"

He looked like a man who didn't want to be interrupted with trivial questions. "This is to ensure there is less chance of discovery by the British. The small vessels easily avoid discovery at night. They are piloted by skilled sailors who know the area well."

"I'm sorry to doubt you. You can appreciate my concerns." I stood and looked at the light from lanterns bouncing off the calm sea.

Mast's tone softened. "This area is perfectly suited for this type of operation. A series of small islands lead into Providence Bay, providing multiple landing spots. The downside is that there are too many opportunities to run aground while sailing up the Sakonnet River. I ordered each ship to navigate the area slowly to avoid collisions with the land or other vessels."

I was impressed by his professionalism. I knew we had made the right choice to trust him with our livelihood.

Mast barked orders out to his crew. "Be cautious, men. We are coming up to the landing."

He then turned to me. "It is fortunate that you caught the spy. Otherwise, we could be in a perilous position."

I knew how close it could have been had we not discovered Aston's treachery. Landings were made at a remote spot in the Little Compton area, where the goods were transferred to waiting wagons under the watchful eye of Noah Mast.

We exited the ship and stood on dry ground. "The next phase is just as dangerous. The wagons are directed by firelight onto back roads to keep them from prying eyes. The roads are little more than paths carved out in the thick woods in unpopulated areas. They are manned by associates of mine who are strategically placed to ensure no one gets lost along the way."

I stood quietly as he continued.

"Due to the change in plans, the route is less direct and will take longer."

This was directed at me. "It is far better that it takes longer than the British confiscating our goods. Don't you agree?"

"Of course, but remember, you merchants are responsible for smuggling the goods into Boston."

"We already have a plan in place. The loads will be taken into Boston piecemeal over several days to evade unwanted attention. British troops are stationed at the only road leading into the city. These soldiers have been alerted to check for the smuggled goods. To avoid the troops, the supplies will be loaded onto small water skiffs and moved onto the peninsula, avoiding the troops altogether. This will be done at night to reduce the risk of being caught."

He patted me on my shoulder. "Let's hope for all our sake that we don't get caught."

Two days later, I met with the barmaid, Ruth. She is a single mother in her late thirties with few prospects. I almost hated myself for taking advantage of her situation to accomplish my goals. I convinced myself that it was for the greater good. I took a seat at an empty table in the Lazy Goat Tavern. I waited patiently for her to notice me. She was smiling and flirted with her customers until she saw me. Her expression changed suddenly, and I saw sadness in her dull gray eyes. She was beefy, and her unruly red hair was tied up in a green sash. She hesitated but slowly crossed the room in my direction.

"Ruth, so good to see you. Can you sit and talk to me?"

She glanced back to the bar where the tavern owner was washing mugs. She nodded and sat down.

"Can you tell me what happened?"

I saw that her eyes had started to swell up with tears. She absently wiped them away. "I did like you told me and mixed the berries you gave me in Mr. Aston's mashed taters." She hesitated.

"Go on."

She looked over her shoulder again. "It was terrible. After a few minutes, Mr. Aston started to act strangely. He had a confused look, and his right arm trembled. He suddenly grabbed his chest with his left hand and then fell off his seat and hit the floor with a loud bang." She started to sob again and drew attention from the other patrons.

I reached out and grabbed her hands. "It's okay, Ruth. You did the right thing."

She tried to compose herself, and her cheeks turned a bright red, matching her hair. "I'm so sorry, sir."

I released her hands and reached into my jacket. Everyone turned their attention away from us, so I slid the small purse to her. She opened it, and her eyes got wide.

"That will help you take care of your children."

She picked at the money and said, "Please don't ask me to do that again."

Chapter 40

Peter Smith

Graduation

O ne of the proudest days of my life finally came. I completed my education at Harvard, and it was graduation day. A culmination of all the hard work I put in to overcome my meager beginnings. My proud adoptive parents and Anne attended the ceremony. The commencement was an all-day affair with morning, mid-day, and evening activities. I sensed an overriding gloom that settled over the festivities due to the ongoing conflict between the colonies and the British. Still, it was a time for celebration by the graduates and their families. The pent-up stresses of the last four years were temporarily forgotten, and copious amounts of food and strong spirits were consumed.

I wasn't much of a drinker, and the strong glasses of rum took away some of my inhibitions. Moses, Henry, and I started drinking early that morning, and I opened up to them.

"Gentlemen, a toast to your health and success."

Moses laughed. "Peter, I have never seen you like this."

Henry joined in, "Moses, I think our young friend is drunk."

"I need to talk to you as my best friends in the world."

"What is it, Peter?"

A fog had overtaken my brain. "I have serious doubts about what I should do. Both of you have tried convincing me to follow you in practicing the law. My father wants me to work in the family business. I also feel pressure from Anne to commit to marriage."

Both of my friends paid closer attention to my words.

"I should be grateful for everything that has been done for me. I didn't want to go to college. I only did it to make my father happy. I'm not ready to settle down. There are things that I need to do first." Before the following words escaped from my lips, I took a deep breath and realized what I was doing.

Moses must have noticed. "Is there something else you wanted to say?"

My head spun, and I felt like I would be sick. "It's nothing. What should I do?"

Henry looked troubled. "Peter, you need to decide what is best for you and not try to please anyone else."

"I wish it were that simple. You have been such good friends. I don't deserve either one of you."

Moses slapped me on the back. "Nonsense. It has been a pleasure knowing you."

We realized we were late and ran off to the great hall for the ceremony.

After the morning ceremony, I sought out my parents and Anne. I had sobered up some and regretted my outburst with my friends. The look on my mother's face was alarming. She still grieved for my brother Robert. He had run away and had not been heard from in days. Word of my graduation must have been the final straw. It bothered me that my father was not concerned about his eldest son.

"Mother, Father, I'm so glad you could make it."

My father radiated his joy. "Nonsense, son. We wouldn't have missed it for the world. This is a big day for you."

I turned my attention to my mother. She was still distracted but offered a curt smile. Anne stepped forward. "Congratulations, Peter, on your accomplishments."

How she said was unusual, almost like what an acquaintance would say. Even though our relationship was strained, I couldn't get over how beautiful she was. "How are you, Anne?"

She looked serious. "I'm fine. Can I talk to you?" She turned and walked away.

I shrugged my shoulders at my parents and followed Anne. She stopped under a magnificent oak tree and turned toward me. "I'm very happy for you, Peter, and I'm sorry to do this now." She looked for a reaction.

"What is it, Anne?"

"I have been very patient with you. You are hiding something, and you won't confide in me. You also have been distracted lately. I won't wait for you forever. I need to know what you are thinking."

I was overwhelmed by what she had just told me. This was a moment of truth for me. Should I tell her everything about myself, or should I continue to string her along? I wasn't ready to share. "Everything is fine. I have been busy with school. Things should be better between us."

She furrowed her brow and looked directly into my eyes as if making a judgment. "Well, I guess I just got my answer. I can no longer see you. I hope you find what you're looking for." She then turned and walked away, leaving me standing there speechless.

I was shaken by Anne's actions. With one less distraction, it may have been easier for me. I decided to put all my energy into the family business. After my earlier encounter with the crew from the Progress, I was cautious about staying away from the piers of Boston to avoid any other incidents. Now that I lived in Boston, I had to remain vigilant in avoiding the sailors. I wasn't even sure that the ship was still in the harbor. I couldn't live my life in fear.

I immersed myself in my work. My initial responsibility centered around keeping the books for the business. My father put intense pressure on me to take over more of the day-to-day operations. He was busy attending to other issues, and I was well aware that meant Sons of Liberty duties.

While I was hovering over the books, he called out to me one day.

"Peter, come here. I want you to see this."

I rubbed my eyes and went outside to the sound of his voice. He was standing at the entrance to the office, watching a man hang a sign.

"It's about time that I did this." He said, pointing to the sign.

Emblazoned in bold letters was "Smith & Son Importers."

"It's official. You are now an equal partner in the business." He reached out and shook my hand. "What do you think?"

The first thing that came to my mind was 'Trapped.' "It's wonderful, Father."

Due to the continued embargo of British goods and the tightening of the noose around the city to prevent the smuggling of outside merchandise by the British army, the business was losing money. We faced mounting pressure to pay the taxes imposed by the Townshend Act. Governor Hutchison had appointed agents in the city to enforce the taxes, which only inflamed the passions of our opposition.

I was included in every meeting that the local merchants continued to have concerning schemes to avoid trading British goods and paying the imposed taxes. I noticed that security for these meetings had tightened after the Gerald Aston affair. Still, there was mistrust among the attendees, and reaching a consensus became more difficult. All of us were losing money, and it was harder to stay the course. There wasn't any indication that our actions were making any difference to the merchants in England or the politicians in parliament. We considered ourselves abandoned bastards as we were isolated from the rest of the colonies and fought the battle ourselves.

My hatred for the British grew.

Chapter 41

John Smith

Massacre

I was given advance notice that something big was about to happen. It was a bitterly cold March night. I walked through the snow-covered streets to one of the local print shops we used to spread our messages. I stepped into the shop and removed my topcoat to shake off the snow and ice. I searched out the pot-belly stove to warm myself when the owner saw me. His name was Charles Bradford, and he was a serious young man who was an ardent supporter of the cause.

"Mr. Smith, I'm so glad you came. We are still waiting for the boy to return with the news. Please help yourself to some coffee and make yourself comfortable."

"Thank you, Mr. Bradford. Do you know what this is all about?"

He smiled. "We all shall know very soon."

I looked around the crowded room at the large, motionless printing press. There were several men standing around, but no one seemed to be doing any work. Still, there was excitement in the smoke-filled air. I grabbed a cup of coffee and settled in to wait. I stared out the frosted windows at the activity on the street. A commotion was going on, and the sounds of people yelling could be heard.

It wasn't long until the door flew open, and a young boy stepped in. He was shaking and looked like he was in shock. His name was Jonas Welch. A ten-year-old lad with a slight build for someone his age. Jonas wore shabby clothing, barely protecting him from the harsh winter elements. I watched someone go to the boy and direct him to the stove. I could see that he was intimidated by all the men who watched his every step. The boy stood by the stove and held his shaking hands up to the radiating heat that emanated. He looked unharmed, but I sensed there was something wrong.

Mr. Bradford pushed through the crowd and grabbed the boy by his shoulders. I moved closer and spotted tears running down the boy's face. Bradford took a step back while the boy stared up at him with lifeless eyes. Bradford looked around the room and motioned for the boy to sit in an empty chair. He sat beside the boy and put an arm around him. As the other men in the room crowded around, Bradford, in a soft and gentle voice, asked the lad, "Jonas, tell me what you saw."

Jonas looked around the room at all the men who stared at him and wiped his eyes with the back of his hand, "It was horrible, sir, all those bodies lying on the street."

Bradford looked at the boy and said, "Start at the beginning and tell us everything."

"I stayed like you asked after delivering the prints to Mr. Archer in the tavern. I found a good spot near the front of the Custom House where I could see the guard. I then noticed a group of men and boys who started to yell hateful things at the guard. Then, after church bells rang, more people came to yell at the guard. It was when more soldiers came that it got bad."

I was mesmerized and crowded closer to the boy to hear every word.

Jonas looked like he wanted to escape but continued, "It was then that I saw the crowd throw things at the soldiers, and someone fired a gun. Then, the other soldiers fired their guns. People were screaming, and when the crowd started to run away, I could see the bodies in the snow."

One of the men asked, "Wasn't it the soldiers who fired into the crowd first?"

Jonas looked up at the man and shook his head no. "Sir, it was the crowd that started it."

Mr. Bradford stood up and addressed the room, "Gentlemen, we shall report to the world the atrocities committed by the British on peaceful protestors. It shall be called the Boston Massacre."

I tried to understand what I had just heard. The radicals in the movement had plans to force the British's hand, but why this? I grew concerned that things would only get worse.

Chapter 42

Peter Smith

The Dinner Party

There was a noise at the front door. I turned and saw my father. He looked like he had seen a ghost.

My mother gasped. "John, what happened?"

I was stunned as I watched him collapse into a chair. He was in shock and half frozen from being out in the elements. "Father, are you alright?"

He blinked and tilted his head in my direction. "I have horrible news. There has been an incident with the British troops."

Amanda went to him and stroked his wet hair.

I knew there had to be more, so I said, "Go on, father."

He appeared to be reliving the event in his head. "There was a group of citizens who were rallying against the soldiers being stationed in Boston. Things got out of control, and the soldiers opened fire on the crowd. There were a number killed."

I was appalled by the murder of "innocent" citizens by the British troops. It was another reason to be ashamed that I was born an Englishman. "How could that have happened? Were you there?"

He gazed my way but seemed to be looking past me. "No. I heard it from a young boy who witnessed the event. After hearing the tale, I had to see it for myself. Bodies were lying in the snow, and blood was everywhere."

"What would provoke the soldiers to kill innocent people?"

He didn't say anything, but there was fire in his eyes. I could tell he held something back, but I didn't force the issue.

I took on more responsibility for continuing the smuggling operation with Noah Mast. I made the perilous journey to Providence and back multiple times to ensure everything went smoothly. I even sailed on the transport ships and met with the French. The experience was both exhilarating and nightmarish. Boarding the small sailing vessel brought back a flood of memories I tried hard to bury. Even with the bad memories, it was actually enjoyable being back on the ocean. It was always dark, and I couldn't see the open water that calmed my nerves in the past, but it felt right. I used some of the sailing skills I had picked up serving on the Progress. Mr. Mast and the crew acted impressed with my bearing and knowledge. I found a confidence that I usually needed to improve. I took charge of navigating the small vessel, to the surprise of Mr. Mast. Noah offered me a job captaining one of his vessels. It was flattering, but I had more important priorities back in Boston.

I was at a crossroads and made some very adult decisions. I realized I would surrender to my father's wishes to work in the family business. I owed him that much. My other change was to move out of my parents' home and get my own place in Boston. There was a risk of being detected by the Progress crew, but I couldn't live in fear for the rest of my life. For the first time, I lived independently, which was refreshing.

As I threw myself into my work, I became more active in the dissent going on in Boston. I attended meetings and participated in protests against the British authority. As with everyone in Boston, I closely followed the trial of the soldiers involved in the massacre. When the verdicts were reached, I sought my father's reaction. I found him at the Lazy Goat tavern. He was sitting in the back, drinking a pint of ale. It was unusual for him to be drinking this early in the day. He saw me walking across the nearly empty room and smiled weakly.

"Father, have you heard the news?"

He raised his stein and shrugged. I sat next to him. "How could any jury in Boston find those criminals not guilty?" He didn't say anything. I was incensed. "I still don't understand why John Adams defended them. Isn't he loyal to our cause?"

He waited for me to calm down. "Son, there is a reason for everything. There had to be the appearance of equity under the law. We needed the British people to see that we could handle our affairs in America fairly. We desperately need them to be on our side."

I sat back and considered what he told me. "You mean that it was all for show?"

"No, it was a real trial. You never know what a jury will do. Mr. Adams was very compelling."

"So what happens now?"

"We continue the struggle."

I had been waiting to hear from Anne since my graduation day. I was so caught up with my responsibilities and the day's issues that I had not considered her. So I was surprised to receive an invitation to attend a dinner party at her father's home. I was intrigued and decided I couldn't refuse. Was this Anne's doing or her parents? I barely knew Pastor Proctor or his wife, Hester. As I rode to Cambridge, I still needed clarification on the invitation. Anne made it clear that she no longer wanted to be with me. What happened to change her mind? I also considered how much of my business activities I would share with them. I could never read the Pastor concerning his allegiances and was unsure where the man stood on colonial independence as he never discussed politics with me.

The small stone house was located near the campus of Harvard, right next to the church Anne's father presided over. I had only been here a few times but marveled at the quaintness of the cottage and the immaculate garden, which was Pastor's pride and joy. I stood at the front door, took a deep breath, and knocked. When the door opened, I was face to face with Anne's mother, Hester. Hester was an elegant woman with graying hair pulled back neatly. She dressed conservatively, as one would expect. I always thought she had a mischievous look.

"Hello, Peter."

"Missus Proctor."

"It's been a while since we've seen you. How have you been?"

I wondered if Anne had told her about our breakup. "I know. I'm sorry, but I've been swamped."

Hester led me into the parlor where the other guests were gathered. I looked around the room and saw some familiar faces. There were also ones that I didn't know. As introductions were made, I saw Anne. She was as lovely as ever. She still increased my heart rate and took my breath away. She came to me and grabbed my arm. I was bewildered by her response at seeing me. I tried to question her with my eyes. She whispered, "We will talk later."

That's when I noticed her father. Abraham Proctor was an imposing figure. Tall with piercing eyes that would look through a person, Abraham always seemed to have a scowl. This was the exact facial expression that I was looking at now.

"Pastor Proctor," I said, bowing my head.

"Mr. Smith. How good of you to come."

The other guests stared at me because of the tone of the statement, and I sheepishly looked around for somewhere to escape. Anne detected my discomfort and squeezed my arm. She led me into the dining room, where dinner was ready.

Four other couples attended the dinner. I recognized two of them as Harvard faculty members and became acquainted with them and their wives. The other two couples were introduced as members of the church. After dinner was served and the Pastor said grace, the real discussions commenced.

One of the men introduced as Abel Chase looked at me and said, " What do you do, Mr. Smith?"

I finished chewing on a piece of roast, wiped my mouth with a cloth, and replied, "I help my father run our import business."

"Is that so? Has your business been impacted by all the rebellious actions in Boston?"

I forced myself to remain calm, sensing the danger in the question. All eyes were on me. "Mr. Chase, as you may be aware, there are many factors that impact business. We have been fortunate to continue to prosper through all the upheaval that has taken place."

Anne gave me a subtle smile, but I was more concerned about her father's continued scowl. Is this a test?

Another guest I was unfamiliar with, William Tate, added, "I don't know how anyone can feel safe going to Boston these days with all the rabble about."

I noted that everyone at the table except Anne nodded in agreement to the statement. I knew what I was up against now. In college, I had been an excellent debater, but it was all academic back then. For the sake of Anne, I would tread lightly.

"Mr. Tate, I have not encountered any unsafe conditions while living in Boston."

Pastor Proctor had remained quiet until now, added, "Would you have my daughter live in a city that is in open opposition to the King, Mr. Smith?"

Again, all eyes turned on me, and I clenched my fists under the table to maintain my composure. "Sir, if I were ever to be blessed enough to have Anne as my wife, I would feel confident that she would be safe in Boston from the local citizens." At the end of my statement, I placed too much emphasis, indicating to the group that the danger was from the British, not the "rabble."

The Pastor's stare softened a little, and he changed the subject to church matters. After another two uncomfortable hours, I got up and made an excuse to leave due to an early meeting in the morning. I bid my goodbyes and thanked Mrs. Proctor for the dinner. Anne walked me out to my horse.

"What was that all about Anne? I thought you didn't want to see me anymore?"

She grabbed my hands in hers and stared into my eyes. "My parents don't know about our situation. They are pressuring me to marry. They wanted to see you to gauge your intentions."

Shaking my head, I said, "You made it very clear to me that you ended our relationship."

"I told you that I can't be with someone who won't be honest with me. That doesn't mean that I don't care for you. You will come to your senses and let me know your secrets."

I got up on my horse and headed back toward Boston, as confused as ever.

Chapter 43

Captain Auger
Cabin Boy Sighting

As much as I enjoyed keeping my staff in the dark, I called for a meeting to discuss the recent events in Boston. I sat behind my desk, watching each man enter my cabin. I needed to dispel the rumors and clarify our orders. The officers were usually chatty but were subdued as they filtered in. I tried to count heads as the room filled.

"Is everyone here?"

Ambrose Crittenden stepped forward. "Yes, sir. All accounted for."

"Good. Let's begin." All eyes were riveted on me. "As I'm sure you have all heard, the troops billeted in Boston have been moved to Fort William. The King has deemed it prudent not to prevent any more events from happening between the soldiers and the citizens. We should maintain a strong presence, but it's not up to me to challenge His Majesty's orders." I noted there were a few shocked faces. So be it. "Our role is to protect the fort against any threats. This means the limited liberty available to the crew has effectively ended."

I could see that Crittenden was nearly jumping out of his skin. "What is it, Mr. Crittenden?"

"Sir, with respect, the crew will take it as another blow to the already precarious morale on board the ship."

"What would you have me do? We should not provoke more conflict with the "good" citizens."

Crittenden was dejected as he slunk back into the crowd of officers.

"You must maintain discipline on the ship. I will hold each of you accountable. Questions?"

A voice from the back of the room asked, "Captain, do you know how long we will protect the fort? Do we expect more problems from the locals?"

"Who was that?" No response. "We will be here as long as we are ordered to be. As to your other question, there better be no uprising from the peasants for their sake. That would be a regrettable choice for them."

I glared at each man. "You are dismissed!"

Over the next few days, I roamed through the spaces of the ship to get an idea of how the crew was reacting. In my presence, there was little discussion, but when they thought I was outside of earshot, they spoke openly about the incident in which the civilians were killed. Most were surprised as they were unaware of the tension between the colonists and the government. As rumors grew, the crew debated openly if this would lead to another war. Most of these men still had fresh memories of the war with France.

I was pleased at the grumbling about me and my orders keeping them on board. My staff had done an excellent job maintaining discipline, and there were only a few incidents. The crew seemed resigned to their present fate, at least for now.

Part of my daily tour of the ship took me to the galley. I noticed Cook preparing the evening meal. His back was turned away from me.

"Ahem. Cook, what are you preparing?"

He jumped and turned to see that I was standing behind him. "I'm sorry, Captain, you startled me." He put down the knife he was holding and wiped his hands on his apron. "I am preparing a stew for the crew. Is there something I can get for you?"

"No. I am just taking a tour of the ship. How are you doing?"

I could see from his expression that he was surprised by my show of empathy. I rarely showed any interest in the crew.

"I'm doing well. I keep busy to pass the time.

"What are your thoughts about liberty being canceled?"

There was doubt on his face about sharing his opinion. Cautiously, he replied, "That is your decision, and I'm sure you have your reasons."

"How do you spend your time in town?"

I could see the alarm on his face. I was rather enjoying this.

He put his hands on his waist. "Well, sir, I usually spend my time in a tavern drinking ale. I'm not one to take in the sights."

I smiled at his honesty. I then saw a look on his face that showed he remembered something.

"Sir, the last time I was in Boston, I saw something I should have told you about."

My grin turned into a scowl. "What is it?"

"Well, as I said, I had a lot to drink. Walking along the pier, I ran into a young man." He paused and started to fidget with his apron string.

"Go on!"

"I think it was Peter Beale."

I exploded. "Why didn't you tell me about this sooner?"

He shied away from my wrath. "I was not completely sure at the time it was him."

"Why are you so sure now?"

"I've had some time to think about it."

I couldn't respond and wanted to reach out and strangle the man. I took a few deep breaths and left him standing there.

Chapter 44

John Smith

Out of Control

I was called to an emergency meeting of the local merchants. Since the massacre, things had seemed to go back to normal, and most of the ridiculous taxes had been repealed by parliament. As a group, we boycotted English goods and continued to smuggle merchandise through Noah Mast. This could have had the desired effect. I grabbed Peter and rushed out the door. There was chaos when we got to the upper floor of the tavern. Peter and I stood in awe at the shouting and unruly behavior of men we respected.

I spotted Arthur Jacoby sitting at a table, watching the melee.

"Arthur, what is this all about?"

He had a troubled look on his face, and barely above the noise in the room, he stated, "The parliament, in their wisdom, has passed a new set of taxes called the Tea Act, apparently for the sole purpose of saving the East India Company from insolvency."

He must have seen the confusion on my face. "John, the act makes buying or selling any other tea brand in the colonies criminal. There will be a duty paid to representatives of the British government after the tea is sold here in the colonies. It would effectively give a monopoly to the East India Company."

Looking around the room. "I'm not sure why there is such an uproar over tea."

Arthur patiently explained the bigger picture as the order was slowly brought to the room. "It's true that parliament repealed all the taxes imposed on the American colonies after the backlash from the Boston Massacre, except those on imported tea. The British want to maintain their control over the colonies without us having any say in the matter."

What he was saying suddenly dawned on me. The Crown wants complete and utter control over us, and we would never have any representation. As each man took his seat, Samuel Adams stood before the group.

"Gentlemen, I know that the news is troubling to all of us. We have also received word from our contacts in London that seven English ships loaded with tea have already set sail for America. Four ships will land in Boston, and one ship each will go to New York, Philadelphia, and Charleston."

There were more rumblings from the group. Adams raised his hands. "It's not just that we are faced with another senseless tax; our greater concern continues to be Parliament's overreach to legislate us without our having any say."

I smiled, knowing that Adams was in his element.

"We must fight this tax like we have fought the others until England finally takes us seriously."

The room erupted in cheers.

"Once we have a better idea of when those ships are to land, we will meet again to decide our response.

Peter looked at me. "Father, everything seems to be spiraling out of control."

"We can only hope that it doesn't come to that."

Chapter 45

Peter Smith

Tea Party

The first ship entered Boston Harbor in late November. Samuel Adams called a meeting of the local citizens to determine the best course of action. By this time, I was fully immersed in the movement and knew ahead of time what would be discussed. I attended the meeting without my father. All the stress had been too much for him, and he wasn't as involved. As the crowd settled in, Samuel Adams addressed them.

"Good citizens of Boston. I have met with Governor Hutchison to convince him that sending the ship away is in our best interest. He politely refused to do so."

There was a spattering of cat calls from the crowd. Adams smiled. "We have no choice but to pressure the ship's captain to sail back to England with his cargo without paying the duty. The Governor has already ordered that the ship would not be allowed to leave without paying the tax. This has caused a stalemate. By British law, the ship has twenty days to unload its cargo and pay the duty of the local customs officials. If the duty isn't paid, the officials could confiscate the goods. We don't plan on letting that happen."

The crowd cheered wildly and marched down to the pier to keep watch. I focused on Adams' face as he soaked in the crowd's reaction. As Adams came down from the podium, he looked at the other members of the Sons of Liberty. "Make sure that the tea does not get unloaded. We shall prepare for the next stage of the plan." I followed the group of men to the pier.

Nearly three weeks later, I met with a few dozen other members. Samuel Adams told us he would have one more meeting to resolve the Governor's disagreement. He told us to get prepared. As we commenced to apply soot to our faces and change into our costumes, we could hear the roars from the public meeting at the Old South Meeting House. We were kept from talking while we went about our business. I saw the same determined look on the faces of the other men while we dressed as Mohawk Indians. I'm still determining whose idea it was, but we would at least be disguised.

It was a crisp night. A layer of fog covered the pier, and no breeze could carry it away. We were given the sign to start our short walk down to the pier where the ship was located. To a man, we knew there was danger in what we were about to do. We also knew the significance of our actions. We were under strict orders not to harm anyone or destroy any property other than the tea.

I took my place and followed the group that I had been assigned to. The freezing cold air beat against my exposed skin. I pulled the blanket I was wrapped in tightly around me. I clutched tightly to the hatchet I would use to perform the task.

The group made our way to the ship Eleanor. As we neared the ship, one of the crew called out, "Halt, what is your business here?"

I could see the fright on the man's face, and one of the Mohawks replied, "Move aside. We have no dispute with you or any of the crew."

The sailor tried to stand his ground, and I could see other crew members come forward to see what was happening. By this time, thousands of people lined the pier, watching eagerly. It appeared that half of the town came to witness the historical event. The ship's captain came forward and surveyed the situation. Standing at the railing, he stared at the crowd massed around his boat and then turned his attention to the men in the strange costumes. The captain must have instantly realized the danger of resistance. It would be better to lose his load than have the mob confiscate his ship or, even worse, have his crew be injured or killed.

"Stand down, men. Let them pass."

The crew stood stunned but complied and retreated, letting us climb onto the ship. We then fanned out in search of the crates of tea. Someone shouted, "It's down here in the hold!" We formed a chain and began passing the crates up on deck. We commenced to destroy the boxes and throw them into the harbor. One of the sailors held up his hands and walked toward me. "Why are you dumping the tea in the harbor?"

I paused from my work and glared intensely at the man, replying, "We are protesting against the King and his policies of taxing us without our say in the matter."

The sailor didn't seem to understand what I meant by the puzzled look on his face. The conversation with the sailor broke my focus on the task, and I suddenly became aware of the large crowd of witnesses on the pier. I stood up, still tightly gripping my hatchet, and shook my head at seeing many people scooping up the tea that had fallen from the destroyed crates. I didn't see that anyone, including any city officials, had tried to stop them. Surely, Governor Hutchison had spies watching all this take place.

We continued to quickly do our assigned responsibilities. Then, when all the crates were destroyed, we exited the ship and melted into the crowd.

Chapter 46

Peter Smith

Escape

I peeked out the window to the empty street below. I jumped at every noise and expected to be taken into custody. The city of Boston was a military encampment. The British military has control of every aspect of life in the city. They monitored the comings and goings of the citizens and prevented any unauthorized meetings or gatherings. More importantly, they closed the harbor to trade until the destroyed tea was paid for. The Intolerable Acts were passed as nothing more than retribution against everyone in Boston. I don't regret playing my part in destroying the tea, but I never expected this to happen.

My father and I struggled to keep the business going during this time. With the military presence, smuggling goods in and out of the city was nearly impossible. I'm concerned for the safety of my parents. My mother is not strong, and she is visibly showing signs that her health is failing. My father seemed to be in denial. Still, a majority of the citizens remain steadfast against paying the reparations. Even as Boston is being held hostage, word reaches the city that the other colonies have rallied in support of us.

Even with all the hardships we were facing, my most significant concern centers around the question as to why the British soldiers weren't actively hunting the members who had taken part in the supposedly treasonous act of destroying the tea. I would sit in my room at night anxiously facing the door, convinced that any minute, there would be a knock at my door, and I would be arrested. I remained vigilant not to be out in public too much, but as I hid safely away, I considered myself a coward.

I knew that I reached the point where I had to take action. It's something I've been thinking about for some time. There is no hope of me making a difference by staying in the city, and we must leave. I have brought up the subject a few times, but only to be met with objections from my parents. Today will be different.

I leave my room and walk downstairs with resolve. "Father, Mother, I need to talk to you."

My father is standing by the fireplace, staring into the flames. He doesn't seem to hear me. I turn and watch my mother come into the room. The sadness on her face is too much for me to bear.

"Listen. We are no longer safe here. We must leave – now."

My father turns and takes notice of me. "Son, we can't leave. Who will take care of the business?"

"There is no business to take care of. The British have seen to that."

His face is gaunt and emotionless. He turns to my mother, "Your mother is ill, and it wouldn't be prudent for her to take a journey right now."

I was beginning to get angry. "Then I shall have to go by myself!"

"Peter, where will you go?" My mother said weakly.

The look in her eyes made me take a step back. I softened my gaze. "I have heard that militias are forming in the colony. I need to do something about this British invasion."

I saw my father's eyebrows rise. "Are you sure that is a good idea?"

"I have to do something. I can't just sit here and wait for the army to arrest me."

——ℓℓℓ——

I picked a dark, moonless night to make my escape. I arranged for a small rowboat to be made available for me to cross to the mainland, avoiding any British patrols. I packed lightly. A part of me felt I was deserting the people I owed the most. On the other hand, there was a strong pull for me to do something that would make a difference.

My parents are standing by the back door. I go to my mother and hold her tightly. "I promise I will write and tell you how I am."

She cries silent tears and doesn't say anything. I put my hand out toward my father. He looks at it and gradually shakes it.

"Father, you must remove mother from this terrible place before it's too late."

He doesn't meet my watchful eyes. "Be careful, son."

I slowly opened the door and carefully looked for any signs of danger. I crept around the building, hugging the wall. I don't look back. It was a short distance from our business down to the pier. My heart is beating outside my chest. I jump at every sound and stop often to calm myself. I reached the dock without being detected. I didn't consider how dark it would be, and I struggled to find the rowboat. Relying on my memory of where the boat should be tied up, I go hand in hand to see it. I lost my footing and stumbled down the bank, crashing into the water.

"Damn it!" How could I be so careless? I sit in the water and listen for any signs of being discovered. The only sound I hear is my thumping heartbeat. After an agonizing few minutes, I determined that it was safe. Soaking wet, I dragged myself out of the water and felt around for the boat. As I reached to untie the line holding the small craft, I heard footsteps on the pier above me. I catch muffled voices that are close. I need help to make out what they're saying. I calmed my breathing and waited. There isn't a call of alarm.

Finally, after a few unbearable minutes, I heard footsteps going away from me. I gave it a few more minutes to ensure it was safe, and then slowly, I pushed the boat out from the bank and started to row away from the pier. I still had to be careful not to bring attention to myself and try to stay as close to the land as possible. There were faint lights from the city, and I made out the outline of other boats in the harbor, including a British man-of-war.

I plan to go north around Boston and cross west to the Cambridge River to land near Cambridge. A shorter route to Charlestown would have been easier, but I would have had to walk a long distance to get to Cambridge. I even considered going to my parents' house and taking a horse, but that might be dangerous if the British were looking for me.

After two hours of rowing, I reached the mouth of the Cambridge River. Due to the darkness, I ran aground several times and had to push off with my oar to get back underway. This made for slow going up the murky river. I planned to get as close to Cambridge as possible without being seen. I struggle to judge distances in the dark, and when I get as far as I dare, I pull the boat out of the water and tie it up in some trees where it will be hidden. I immediately lay down beside the river, breathing heavily from my exertions. Exhausted and still wet from falling in the harbor, I curl in a ball to fall asleep. My last thoughts are to wait until dawn to get my bearings and go to Cambridge to see Anne. I then drifted off into a deep sleep.

Early the following day, I abruptly sat up, startled awake by the sound of a wagon passing by. It took me a couple of minutes to remember where I was. I stretched the sore muscles in my arms and back. Slowly, I stood up to see that I was next to a small dirt road leading from the river toward Cambridge. I remembered the bag I packed and looked frantically for it. I must have lost it during the night. I catch sight of the back of a wagon pulled by a team of horses. I wasn't sure if it was safe to catch up with the wagon to get a ride, so I walked. Fortunately, my clothes were dry, and I felt rested. It was a glorious, warm morning, and I looked forward to the walk. It would give me time to think about what I would tell Anne.

The walk took longer than anticipated, and I reached Cambridge in midday. I didn't see any soldiers during my walk, and the few people I passed kept to themselves. As I neared Anne's home, I realized I must look like a mess. I tried to smooth out my clothes as much as possible and combed my hair with my fingers. I hesitated while standing at the front door. I may not be welcome. I looked around me to make sure no one was watching and knocked. When the door opened, I stood face to face with Reverend Proctor.

The reverend looks up and down at me and slowly shakes his head. "Mr. Smith, what brings you to our door this day?"

I stood tall and answered, "Sir, I hoped to see Anne. Is she available?"

Reverend Proctor eyed me suspiciously and opened the door to let me in. "You look ruffled; what have you been doing?"

"It was a long journey from Boston."

"How is Boston these days? We have heard that it is hard to live there with all the soldiers."

"Yes, sir, they are making life very hard."

"Please have a seat, and I will go find Anne."

When Anne entered the room, she gasped at the sight of me. I stood and strode over to her.

"What's wrong, Peter? You look terrible. Why haven't you come to see me sooner?"

I stared into her eyes; it was so good to see her. "I escaped from Boston overnight and feared that I would be caught by the British."

"How bad is it? We have heard several rumors."

"Ever since the tea incident, the British have been bent on punishing us. The harbor is blocked, and we can't trade; there is no business. I stay hidden each day, afraid that I will be arrested. That's why I'm here. My parents agreed I should leave Boston until all this is cleared up."

"What will you do?"

I have Anne take a seat and sit next to her. "I came here to talk to you about that. I am considering joining the militia to defend us from the English."

Anne's face contorted into a scowl, "Do you think that's wise to do?"

"I can't sit idly by and watch while there is so much suffering and unfairness in the world."

"But you are not a soldier, Peter."

"I can learn to be one. This is something that I must do."

"What about us then? Have you thought about that?"

I take her hands in mine and see that she is tearing up. "What would you think of me if I ran from this fight instead of standing up to the British?"

"I would think that you are wise beyond your years." She says sarcastically.

"I will do this with or without your blessing. I hope you will support my decision.

"How can I support the man I love going off to die in a hopeless cause."

Her statement surprises me. "I thought you told me you couldn't be with me." I instantly regretted saying that.

She would not look at me as I stood up to leave. I glance back one last time and walk away.

Chapter 47

Peter Smith

Joining the Militia

I walked in a daze, replaying the conversation with Anne in my mind. Why didn't she see the merit in what I wanted to do? Despite her lack of support, I remained steadfast in my decision. The streets of Cambridge, though familiar, seemed to hold new challenges. *Where does one go to find out where to join the local militia?* I hadn't thought that part out when I made my plans. I stuffed my hands in my pockets with my head tilted down, realizing I should have planned better for my new adventure. I needed to devise a solution with only the clothes on my back and some spending money. Where is the best central location to go when trying to meet with people who have connections? I knew exactly where to go.

It had been some time since I last entered the Tattered Hat tavern. It was an establishment frequented by some of my fellow classmates at Harvard. We would go to drink and talk freely, away from the prying eyes of school administrators. I turned down a side street littered with filth and arrived at my destination. The pub looked the same as the last time I had been there, with the familiar sign representing the tavern. An old, worn hat hanging above the door. I entered the pub, and my eyes tried to adjust to the dark and dingy room. I smiled, gazing around, and saw the usual population of some of the more unsavory people in town. I didn't know any patrons and walked to the bar to get some information.

"Excuse me, sir. I was wondering if you could help answer a question for me?"

The bartender was a rough-looking man with a growth of whiskers and a painted-on scowl that covered his face. He eyed me suspiciously. "What do you need, boy?"

With a cautious glance around, I leaned in closer to the bartender and asked, "I was hoping you could point me in the right direction. I'm looking to join the local militia."

The man firmly placed his hands on the bar top and leaned toward me, "What makes you think I would know anything about what you're asking? This is a loyal establishment to the King."

I stood closer and laughed, "I have been to this establishment many times, and it is anything but loyal to the King's policies."

The man laughed loudly and said, "You can never be too sure who you are talking to these days. Well, young man, your best bet is to go up the road to Lexington and look for a John Parker or William Tidd. You look to me as someone too young and inexperienced for such work."

The comment slightly deflated me. But I was determined to prove myself. In a confident voice, I said, "I came from Boston, where there is much suffering, and I need to do something about it."

"I meant no disrespect, young sir. You should be careful, or you might get what you are asking for."

I felt considerably better than I did that morning. I'm off to Lexington. The bartender gave directions and told me it was about ten miles from Cambridge to Lexington. I didn't want to spend any money to hire a horse or carriage, so I decided to walk there.

The early afternoon sun shone brightly through the trees lining the dirt road where I walked. I whistled as I rhythmically put one foot before the other, almost like I was marching to war. I pursed my lips together as I thought about the reality of my situation. I have no idea where I will live or how I will support myself if I stay in Lexington. I have no military training other than when I was on the HMS Progress as a young boy. I never fired a weapon or had a physical altercation with anyone. These are skills that I need to learn. Despite all my doubts, I was confident I was making the right decision.

It takes me about three hours to reach Lexington. The town isn't more than a small sleepy village. There is a scattering of small businesses and homes. *How could this be the center of militia activity in the area?* I hadn't eaten anything all day and was debilitated from all the walking. The bartender in Cambridge didn't indicate where I should meet Mr. Parker or Mr. Tidd, but it worked going to a pub to get information, and I would try that again. I asked a man I passed on the street where I could find lodging and was directed to the Munroe Tavern. The man pointed over his shoulder toward the business.

The building was a two-story structure with redwood slates and adorned with double-hung windows. The inside of the tavern was spacious, clean, and neat. After washing my face, I rented a room and went back downstairs for dinner. While I ate my meal of boiled meat and potatoes with a pint of ale, I listened to the other diners' conversations. Most of the discussions centered around the events going on in Boston. The mood is strictly anti-British, and I am determined to be in the right place. After eating, I approached two gentlemen in an intense chat, demeaning the King for his actions.

"Excuse me, gentlemen. Could one of you direct me to where I could find a Mr. John Parker or William Tidd?

Both men stopped talking and looked suspiciously at me. One of the men, who appeared to be in his fifties and, by his dress, was wealthy, replied, "What is it that you want with John Parker, young man?"

I motioned toward an empty chair, "May I sit down?"

Both men nodded. I sat down and leaned toward the men, and in a shaky voice, I stated, "I'm from Boston, and I am looking to join the militia. I was told to find these two gentlemen."

"How do we know that you are not a spy for the British trying to gain information to take back to the army?"

I sat back in my chair and rubbed my sweaty palms on my pants. Then I took a deep breath in through my nostrils. "Sir, I assure you that I am not loyal to the King or his policies. My family business in Boston is in ruins due to those policies. I know Samuel Adams, who was directly involved in the tea incident in Boston Harbor." I was out of breath and sat back, awaiting their response.

Both men laughed. "One can never be too sure these days. We shall check about you knowing Mr. Adams, but let me introduce you to John Parker." The older gentleman pointed to the other man sitting at the table.

John Parker was in his mid-forties and was more plainly dressed than the other gentleman. He told me he was a local farmer and mechanic. I learned that Parker had served as a colonial soldier for the British during the French and Indian War. I watched the man's eyes roll over me as if trying to assess me, "What's your name?"

I hold my hand to Parker and say, "Sir, my name is Peter Smith."

Parker shook my hand. "Why do you want to join the militia, Mr. Smith?"

"As I said, I'm from Boston, and I couldn't stay there and do nothing while the British disrupt our lives and take away our freedoms."

"How is it that you know Samuel Adams?"

"He is a friend of my father's, and he helped me to gain entrance to Harvard College."

"Is that so? You are then an educated man."

"Yes, sir. I planned to take over my father's trading company."

"Do you have any military experience, young man?"

I paused and thought about how much I should share with these two men. "Mr. Parker, I served in the British Navy as a young boy during the war with the French. The ship I was on was involved in the battles in Canada."

John's jaw dropped as he continued to stare at me. "I was also involved in the fighting up there. That means that we were both there at the same time. How is it that you live in Boston?"

"I escaped from the ship during the great fire and was taken in by my adoptive parents, the Smiths."

"It seems you have lived an interesting life in your short years. Well, you have come to the right place to join our militia. Do you have a place to live or any means to support yourself?"

"I had not thought that through yet. Please assist me.

Parker looked at the other man and said, "We need a teacher here for our children. Do you think you would be up to the task?"

"Certainly. That would be a suitable position for me."

"Great. Then it's settled. Do you have lodgings here for the night?"

"I do."

"Someone will collect you in the morning to familiarize you with the town and the school. We will also find a place for you to live. One last question, did you bring a rifle?"

"No sir, I do not own a gun."

"We shall have to do something about that."

ele

The next morning, I met a man named Silas Mercer at the tavern. Mercer told me that he was the self-proclaimed town elder. A smallish, wiry man, Mercer seemed very nervous and looked around the room continuously with his head on a swivel.

"Good morning, Mr. Smith. I was directed by John Parker to meet with you to discuss filling the position of town instructor. Do you have any experience teaching children?"

"Good morning, Mr. Mercer. I do not presently have any experience teaching."

"What would qualify you to tutor our children?"

"I have a college degree from Harvard and am well versed in all study subjects."

His head bobbed up and down. "That should work just fine. When can you start?"

"I can start today if needed. Why do you have an immediate need for a teacher?"

Mercer fidgeted even more. "The last instructor left when his political leanings became known around town. He also attended Harvard."

"I see. You will find that my leanings are more in line with the rest of the town, Mr. Mercer."

"Let me show you to the schoolhouse. I will also direct you to where your lodgings will be while you are here with us."

Mercer gave me a tour of the village, including the one-room school-house. The building was a one-story rectangle, deep but not very wide. Inside, my desk was located at the front of the room, and there were four rows of tables and chairs facing toward the desk. There was little room for anything other than a small pot-belly stove to heat the room. I keep my opinions to myself, but internally, I'm surprised by the size of the small classroom.

Mercer sees the look on my face. "The school is adequate for our needs. You are responsible for teaching fourteen children, ages six to sixteen."

Mr. Mercer decided that I would start teaching on Monday. This gave me the weekend to acclimate to the town and get my bearings. The grand tour ends at a boarding house operated by Mr. and Mrs. Townsend, where I would have my own room.

On Saturday afternoon, I hear a knock on my door, and when I open it, I am face to face with William Tidd. Tidd introduces himself as a lieutenant in the local militia under Captain John Parker.

"Mr. Smith, I was told you want to join our local militia."

"Yes, sir, I would like to do that."

"Excellent, we are always in need of good men. I understand that you do not have any experience with a gun. Is that true?"

"I do not have any experience, that is true. Were you told I served in the Royal Navy during the war with the French?"

"I was so informed. However, you must still be trained to drill and fire a weapon. I was also told that you do not have a rifle."

"No, sir."

"We are in short supply of weapons now, and you must make do for now. We meet on Monday in the commons area at four o'clock. That should give you time to finish the day's lessons and meet with us."

Monday morning, bright and early, I went to the school house. I had no training for teaching and would have to fall back on my experience in the classes I took at Harvard for a guide. I was both curious and apprehensive about how it would go. Mr. Mercer told me to stick with the basics, such as reading, writing, and arithmetic, and to ensure discipline was consistently enforced. I wondered about that and knew that I would not be able to dole out any form of corporal punishment.

I stood at the entrance of the schoolhouse while the children began to filter in. I made sure to wear a bright smile and noted that the children had curious looks on their faces, wondering about their new teacher. I politely bade each student a good morning. I was surprised that four girls were in attendance because education for women then was limited. There weren't any women allowed to take classes at Harvard. When all the students had taken their seats, I stood in front and addressed them, "Good morning, children. I am your new instructor, Mr. Smith."

The children responded in unison, "Good morning, Mr. Smith."

I smiled and continued, "I was told that you are learning to read, write, and solve mathematical problems. Can anyone tell me what progress you have made?"

A tall boy, who looked to be the oldest student in the room, stood up. "Sir, we were being instructed to read the bible and to study English law. Our last teacher didn't try to help the younger children, and he was strict."

"What is your name, young man?"

"Sir, my name is James Walters."

"What happened to your last teacher?"

James looked around the room at the other children. "He was dismissed."

"Do you know why?"

"My father said it was because he was a Tory."

The other children chuckled at the statement.

"Very well. Thank you, James. Please take your seat. I would like to speak with you individually to see how much you have progressed in your learning. Then I will determine what the next steps will be for your education."

Each student came to my desk individually, and I assessed their ability to read, write, and do basic math. I then separated the students into three groups; advanced, intermediate, and beginners. Four boys were in the advanced group, as it was apparent they had mastered the basic requirements. The intermediate group consisted of six children and included two of the girls. The last group of four children was young; clearly, they needed individual attention for their education. I would keep the groups separated and place my attention on the needs of each. The day went quickly, and I was pleased with my progress. I had been so busy that I almost forgot I needed to go to the common area for my first drill. I dismissed the children and headed off to start my new career as a soldier.

It was a short walk from the school to the town's common area. I could see that several men had already gathered. I increased my pace to join the group. I spotted John Parker, who motioned me over. He got the attention of the group. "Men, this is Peter Smith. He is a new member of our militia all the way from Boston."

The other men came over and introduced themselves. I instantly noticed that each man carried a rifle, and I felt naked without one. William Tidd handed me a broom handle and told me to use it instead of a gun until they could get me one. I watched closely as the men were organized into two lines and were given commands.

William turned to me. "The drills were copied from the British Army order of drill and manual exercise handbook. This was the same document that John Parker used when fighting the French and Indian War. The manual addressed close-order drills for the loading and firing muskets, going from a line into columns and back. It also addressed advancing and falling back."

I desperately tried to keep up but needed help. Part of my learning process was to pay close attention to what the other militia members were doing. To the amusement of the others, I tripped over my feet multiple times. I quickly learned to respect the work the other men in the company had put in. They followed the orders given by Parker and Tidd without hesitation. After nearly two hours of running through the drills, we were dismissed. Captain Parker pulled me aside as the other men went in separate directions.

"You looked like you were grasping the drills. How do you feel?"

I shook my head, "It will take me some time to learn all that is required, but I am confident that I will master them."

Parker slapped me on the back. "Hopefully, we have time for you to learn before the British do something foolish."

I looked at Parker, "When will I be taught how to fire a weapon?"

"In due time, young man, in due time."

Chapter 48

Peter Smith

Anne's Visit

O ver the next few weeks, I taught myself how to become a soldier. I was having the time of my life and learned that I had an aptitude for both vocations. Drilling with the broom handle had been hard, but I eventually received a rifle. The day William brought me the musket, he said, "Let's go out in the woods and practice."

I grasped the weapon and looked at the ornate designs on the long rifle. It was heavier than I thought. I grinned at him and said, "Do you think I'm ready?"

"One way to find out."

I followed him to the edge of town. He stopped and pointed at some wooden targets that had been set up. "We are about twenty paces away from those targets. First, I need to teach you the basics of loading." He handed me a powder horn and a small bag filled with musket balls and patches. "Observe as I go through the steps of loading and firing."

I watched as he deliberately went through each step.

"First, you set the butt of the rifle on the ground and pour in a small amount of powder." He turned to see if I was paying attention. "Then you take a musket ball wrapped in a patch and set it in the muzzle." He pulled out the ramrod and pushed the lead ball down the rifle. "Make sure it is seated, but don't jam it in." He replaced the ramrod and picked up the gun. "Next, fill the flash pan with powder like so. Then you half cock the hammer, and the powder will fill the touch hole." He stood up and pulled back the hammer. "Take careful aim at your target through the sight on the rifle's top. Hold the rifle tight against your shoulder and fire."

I jumped from the explosion and turned to see if he hit the mark. There was an apparent hole in the middle of the circular wooden target. He smiled and handed me the musket.

"Your turn."

I was nervous and a little overwhelmed. I went through the steps in my head and did as I was instructed. The whole time, he stood watching me without any comments. The musket ball came tumbling out when I got to the part where I was filling the flash pan. I cringed.

He calmly said, "What did you do wrong?"

Embarrassed, I muttered, "I didn't firmly set the ball."

"Do it again."

I went through the steps again and was ready to fire my weapon. I looked at William for approval. He only slightly raised his eyebrow. I took a deep breath and pulled the trigger. The kickback from the rifle nearly broke my shoulder. After the smoke cleared, I searched for the results of my effort.

"Where did I hit the target!"

Tidd maintained his patience. "You missed. You also didn't hold the rifle firmly against your shoulder."

He patted me on the back. "You have a lot of practicing to do."

I diligently maintained a steady correspondence with my parents and with Anne. I was incensed by the news from Boston of the ongoing deprivations laid upon the citizens by the British army. It made me more committed to the cause. I received word that there continued to be a stranglehold on the comings and goings of the locals and an exodus of many of the families from the city. My mother's letters were too optimistic, and I genuinely feared for their safety. I urged them to come to Lexington and stay with me. My father would have none of that and wanted to keep the business alive.

Anne's letters were filled with more trivial matters, and she seemed unaware of the danger lurking from the British. She showed curiosity about my teaching role and longed to see me as soon as possible. I realized that I missed her more than I would admit to myself and relented, sending an invitation for her to come.

Anne arrived, escorted by her mother, on April 1. It would have been improper for Anne to come calling unescorted, and her father could not make the trip. It was a glorious spring day, and the sugar maple, northern red oak trees, and wild rose bushes had started to bloom. I arranged for lodging at the Munroe Tavern, where I met them. Upon seeing Anne, my heart leaped with joy, and I could hardly contain myself. I could see by the glowing expression on her face that Anne felt the same way.

As I helped both women down from their carriage, I stated, "Mrs. Proctor, it is so good to see you. Welcome to Lexington."

I then held Anne's hand as I assisted her out of the carriage. I didn't show any other sign of affection, as it would have been inappropriate.

"Anne, I have missed you. Thank you for coming."

"It is lovely here, Peter. When do we get to see your school and meet your students?"

"School is out for the day, but you can meet them in the morning. I have talked often about you and your parents. They will be thrilled to greet you."

As I led them to the tavern, Anne took my arm and asked quietly, "How are your other endeavors going?"

I looked to ensure Mrs. Proctor couldn't hear, "They are progressing well. I am told that I have an aptitude for it. We have been drilling constantly to be prepared for any contingency."

She squeezed my arm harder and looked serious. "I only pray that you will not have to use your new-found skills," she said.

I assisted them in checking in and carried their bags to their room. We had dinner at the tavern after they were given time to freshen up from their travels. After we ate, I escorted them around the small town, giving them a guided tour. I realized how much I truly had missed being with Anne. Still, I knew I would have to remain steadfast to focus on defeating the British. If it came to that. There could be a future with her. However, I would never share my secrets with her even though it might mean never marrying her. For now, I would just bask in the joy of spending time with her.

Over the next few days, we were inseparable. We were still escorted by Anne's mother, but Hester remembered what it was like to be young and in love and allowed us some time discreetly to ourselves. Anne and Mrs. Proctor told me how impressed they were by the school and my handling of the children. They were pleased that girls were allowed in the class and that they took an active role in their education. Hester told me that she would bring the subject up with her husband to include the females in classes back in Cambridge. Anne also indicated that she would pressure her father to give the girls a formal education.

The ladies attended the drilling of the militia, a popular attraction for the town folks. There were about one hundred fifty men in the militia company in Lexington. Weeks of practice had made us a cohesive unit under the tutelage of John Parker. Anne and her mother expressed how impressed they were as the company went through our drills following the officers' orders. The company was ordered through all the movements addressed in the manual. We were also allowed to practice loading and firing our weapons. Anne squealed as she watched me. She told me that it looked like I belonged with these men. Anne shared with me that her mother avoided politics. She didn't know what Hester's thoughts were about the British. On the other hand, her father tended to lean more toward the Tory side, although he would never preach about which side he supported. Even though Anne was enthralled by all she saw, she couldn't hide her concern for my safety.

The few days passed quickly, and it was time for Anne and her mother to return to Cambridge. I dreaded having to say goodbye; it didn't help that Anne was in tears as I helped her climb onto the carriage. I tried to remain stoic, but it was tough for me to keep my decorum.

Before they left, Anne leaned over and whispered in my ear. "Please be safe, but you must still be honest with me, or we can't have a future together."

I stood there stunned as the carriage pulled away.

Chapter 49

Peter Smith

The First Shots

I was startled from a deep sleep. There was yelling, and when I ran to the window, I saw a single rider speeding through the town. It was still dark out, and it was hard to make out the shapes. What time is it? Then I heard someone yell, "Captain Parker ordered all the militia to assemble."

I grabbed my rifle and, along with more than seventy company members, quickly gathered in the town square. Parker stood erect in front of us. Someone held a lantern up, which cast an eerie glow. I noticed the severe expression chiseled on the Captain's face. Parker addressed the mustered men about the course of action to be taken.

"We have been advised that the British are coming here to collect Mr. Adams and Mr. Hancock. They also plan on going to Concord to confiscate our supply of powder and guns. We must decide if we should stand up and prevent the British from accomplishing their mission or let them pass unmolested."

He silently made eye contact with each man crowded around him. Murmurs generally supported taking a stand against the British, but a few expressed concerns about fighting. I leaned on my musket, trying to comprehend what was happening. I shook my head as I listened to each conversation without providing an opinion. When I served in the English Navy, there was never any question of the crew deciding the course of action. I watched Parker closely. He looked like he was gauging the mood of the men and ordered us to gather our rifles and report to the Lexington green to line up and await the British.

I tightly gripped my gun, wondering if this would be my last day on earth. I took my place as we filed out onto the green. We were ordered to fall into a line extending across the road the British would be traveling. I stood there, lost in my thoughts, and stared into the blanket of darkness, waiting for the British. The other men in the company were considering what was taking place. There was very little chatter going on.

At about 5:00 am, the outline of the British troops could faintly be seen entering Lexington. Their shapes were blurred by the darkness. Captain Parker repositioned us to face the road leading to Concord, but we didn't block the way. I held out hope that violence could be prevented. It was a chilly spring morning, and the ground was still damp from a rainstorm the previous night. I watched intently as the British troops spread out onto Lexington Green instead of continuing their march on the road to Concord. I couldn't help but be impressed as the British maintained their ranks and smartly closed the distance.

I turned my attention to Parker as he jerked his head left and right, trying to see if the militia line would hold. It was apparent that the British intended to engage the small company of militia assembled before them. I heard a British officer shout out an order for us to disperse. Some of the militia began to fall back and came into contact with a stone wall behind us. A shot rang out. With all the confusion, I wasn't sure who fired the shot. I turned to look for orders from the companies' officers when a volley exploded. The sounds of musket fire were deafening, and my view became obscured by the smoke from the rifles. There was a strong odor of sulfur in the air. Some of the men standing near me crumpled to the ground like sacks of potatoes. My first reaction was to go to help the wounded men. As I bent down to aid those injured men, I could see others flee. I saw the futility of staying as the British continued to come at us disorganizedly. I regained my feet and retreated with the other company members.

I never fired my weapon.

Most of the company made it into the trees at the edge of the town. I bent over to catch my breath. When I looked up, I saw the British officers were finally able to get control of their troops. As the sun's rays broke over the horizon, they lined up on the road again to continue their march to Concord. After the British soldiers were out of sight, I went back to tend to the wounded and dying men. We paid a heavy price for our actions that morning; eight men were killed, and another ten were injured in the volley. The wounds were atrocious, and I saw up close the damage a musket ball can do to human flesh.

I hung my head and slumped my shoulders after thinking about my actions, or lack thereof, during the heat of the battle. I heard Captain Parker walking among the men, giving them consoling words and trying to lift our spirits. I also noticed townspeople came out of their homes to assist the wounded.

After a short reprieve to rest, Parker rallied the men. He personally addressed every able-bodied militiaman. "Men, grab your muskets and get back into line. Our work is not done yet." He was incensed as he walked among us. "The British will pass back through Lexington upon their return from Concord. This will be our opportunity to take revenge for the mauling we have taken!"

This time, instead of lining us up to face them directly, Parker placed us behind barriers, like trees and stone fences, where we would be able to rain bullets on the advancing soldiers from protected positions. I witnessed

Parker's resolve as he shouted out his orders. "Find a place where you can fire effectively. There will be no retreat this time."

His words inspired me, and I found my place behind a stout oak tree.

We could hear the distant crash of rifle fire echo. I wondered if the militia in Concord fared any better. After a tense wait at our posts, movement could be seen. Parker pointed out to the road, "Here they come!"

The distinct red coats could clearly be seen. They came in a ragged line showing the heavy fighting that had taken place in Concord. When the British came into range, Parker yelled, "Fire!"

This time, I fired my rifle. I wasn't sure if I hit anything, but adrenaline shot through my body. I kept up a steady pace of fire from behind the tree where I stood. Those British soldiers hadn't directly abused me, but I screamed after each shot I fired. It was a partial cleansing for my being brutalized on the ship and for what they were doing to Boston. I wasn't sure if I struck down any British soldiers, but I knew that I added to their misery that day. We maintained our firing and continued to follow and harass the British until they were able to reach the safety of their lines around Boston.

It was a clear victory for the militia. We prevented the British from capturing John Hancock and Samuel Adams while thwarting the Redcoats from confiscating our supplies of guns and powder. We also showed the greatest army in the world that a ragtag group of citizens was not going away without a fight.

Chapter 50

Captain Auger
Catching Smugglers

I tilted my head as I broke the seal on our next orders. They came from the commanding general, Thomas Gage. I didn't know the man, but I understood he had descended from an aristocrat. Orders were orders, and having a purpose that didn't include being anchored in the Boston harbor would be good. General Gage specifically addressed the need to prevent smuggled goods from entering the colony. Gage dictated it was time to put a stop to this and enlisted the aid of the Navy. He ordered some of the frigates anchored in Boston harbor to patrol the waters along the Atlantic coast and seize any ships not carrying British goods. As an incentive, the ship's crew was entitled to a share of the spoils of everything they confiscated. This should be welcomed news by the men.

These orders were also a godsend for me. There continued to be discipline issues from staying tied up in Boston. I remained steadfast and unwilling to grant shore leave for the crew lest there be any embarrassing episodes. The whip had to be used liberally to quash the dissent. Now was time to get back to work. I had the officers gathered to share the orders. The spineless among them still followed my orders. There was a growing contingent that began to question my authority. This group was led by

Ambrose Crittenden. I didn't have proof of outright mutiny, but I knew to keep a watchful eye on these men. With everyone in attendance, I saw the familiar look of disgust on their pathetic faces. They had no idea why they were called, and I relished my power over them.

"Gentlemen, we have a new set of orders. This time from General Gage."

That grabbed their attention. I snorted and continued, "We have been ordered to set sail and patrol the coastline from Boston south to the Pennsylvania Colony, looking for smugglers."

They leaned in, listening for more. "We are to intercept and capture these pirates. Our discretion will be what to do with the crew, but we will destroy their craft. We have been granted a share of any captured goods, which will be distributed among the crew."

There was murmuring of chatter among my officers. Of course, Crittenden was the first to speak up.

"Captain, that news should go over well with the crew."

I rolled my eyes. "You have your orders. We set sail immediately. Dismissed!"

Once at sea, the men were called to assemble. I knew they heard the news of the army's defeat at Lexington and Concord. This would give them the opportunity for vengeance. I jerked my head around to get a last look at Boston. Good riddance. It felt refreshing to feel the sea air on my face. I grabbed the railing and squinted as we headed toward the setting sun.

"Men, we have been ordered to take the battle to the profiteers who bring supplies from our European enemies. I know that each of you is angry and ready to seek revenge against the colonists' actions. This is our chance."

There was a rumble of voices reacting to my words. Good.

"You don't need any additional incentive to do your job, but General Gage has seen fit to reward us with a share of any bounty we capture."

A loud cheer resonated off the sails. With my arms crossed over my chest, I soaked up the crew's reaction.

We had been at sea for more than a week. The only ship we spotted was a small, single-sleeved craft that hugged the coastline and had been able to avoid my much larger ship. I changed tactics and moved as close to shore as I dared to capture these smaller vessels and confiscate their cargo. It was a risk I was willing to take to trap my prey. When I shared the new strategy with my officers, they were skeptical. It would take due diligence to ensure we did not run aground and become a target for the Americans. The charts we possessed for the coastline in this area were rudimentary at best, so I ordered a constant watch to ensure that the ship would not be grounded. The downside of this strategy was that the Progress needed to be more maneuverable and slower. Since we could not rely on stealth and speed, we would have to depend on our numerous guns to stop the pirates.

This change in plans had its desired effect a few days later when we came across the silhouette of the smaller vessel flying Dutch colors. The Privateer hugged the coastline going northward toward Rhode Island. It was dawn. The last remnants of sunlight highlighted the outline of the smuggler. I took a quick glance at the sea. I smiled as I saw it was relatively calm. This would aid in the capture of the smaller vessel. The alarm sounded, and the crew was drummed to quarters to prepare for the chase. I personally directed the ship. We were off the coast from where the Dutch vessel was going northerly. Possibly due to the setting sun or even carelessness, they had not detected the Progress.

I stared intently with a steely eye at the smuggler through my telescope, following its heading. My blood was up, and I slapped the wooden railing.

They did not change course. I ordered the ship to come about to starboard to head off the smaller ship. As Progress closed the distance, I watched the crew efficiently go about their work to put the older vessel in position to capture its prey. Progress made a sweeping right turn and had come parallel to the Privateer. There was movement on the smaller ship. They spotted us. The Dutch tried desperately to maneuver closer to the coast to escape in one of the many coves where they could hide. I had already planned for this and had the cannons on the port side open fire. There was a risk in this action, as it could sink the smaller ship, and we would lose the cargo. Most of the shots went high, but a lucky cannonball struck the sole mast of the Dutch vessel, causing her to stall in the water. At this point, the tiny ship was only a few hundred yards off the coast of Rhode Island.

I grimaced as I watched the crew abandon the ship and swim toward shore. I yelled out, "Drop anchor!" I turned to my executive officer. "Mr. Crittenden, order a boarding party to take possession of the ship. Try to capture the crew."

There was an intensity on his face that I was not accustomed to. As he ran off, he shouted, "It shall be done, captain."

I took a couple of deep breaths and watched as the ship drifted to within a few hundred yards of our prize before the anchor stopped us in place. I rushed over to the starboard side in time to watch the jolly boats being lowered into the water. Good work, Mr. Crittenden. It was getting darker, but I made out the profile of Lieutenant Pressley leading the boarding party across the still sea.

I paced the quarterdeck, waiting for Pressley to return and make his report. It took two hours for the crew to complete. Darkness had fallen, and lanterns on board the jolly boats were the only indication that they were returning. I maintained my decorum and stayed on the quarterdeck. An out-of-breath Lieutenant Pressley reported to me.

"Sir, we have recovered twenty barrels of gunpowder and fifty crates of rifles from the pirate ship."

I shook my head in disbelief and waited for more.

He continued, "The crew had escaped by the time we arrived. It's a Dutch ship called the Bella." He gulped in a few breaths. "I ordered the crew to scuttle the ship, and she was sinking below the waterline as we rowed back."

I was troubled by the cargo we recovered. It was a good thing it was dark and no one saw the concern on my face. "Very well, lieutenant. Ensure that all the cargo is stowed aboard. It is time that we return to Boston to report our findings."

Chapter 51

Peter Smith

Standoff

I was among the thousands of militiamen who made their way to Boston after the battle in Lexington. We marched in jagged lines along the winding dirt roads, the same path where the British soldiers retreated. I was in a daze and moved like I was in a dream. I breathed in the dust raised by the feet of the weary army of men. I heard rumblings that we missed our opportunity to end the war.

"Why did we let the Redcoats escape when we had them whipped?"

"Did you see the way they skedaddled?"

Thomas Devaney, a common laborer in Lexington, asked me, "What do you think, Peter? Will the British up and leave?"

I glanced sideways at him. "I lived in Boston and don't think they are going anywhere."

"You think so? We beat, um, pretty bad. I think they had enough of us."

I shrugged my shoulders. I knew better.

I had seen the power of the British Empire. I got a small taste of what it was like to seek revenge against the hated British for what they did to me. I needed more to erase the bad memories from serving aboard the Progress. Especially what Auger did to me. That man had taken away my innocence, and I meant to take my vengeance on all the English I could. In my wildest dreams, I couldn't imagine that this ragtag army of shopkeepers and laborers had a chance to defeat the mightiest military in the world.

We camped around the area north of Boston across from Charlestown with little more than the clothes we wore. It soon became apparent that no one planned how to refit and feed our large army. I had grown to love my adopted country and hated to see what would happen when the British took this rebellion seriously. Still, I understood what it was like to stand up to them. I looked around at the sprawling camp, which resembled a squatter's settlement instead of an organized army outpost. I wondered if these men had the same motivation that I did.

Drilling continued. After our experience in Lexington, there was more of a focus to be prepared. I still felt the shame of leaving the field during the first encounter with the British. I didn't even fire my gun. It was a stain on my honor that I still carried. I could see the determination on the faces of my fellow militiamen. I knew we needed more leaders like John Parker. We heard that the army was reorganizing and the command structure was changing. No one was sure how the British would respond to the show of force, but it was unlikely that they would surrender and go home to England.

We had plenty of time to share gossip amongst ourselves. As lowly militiamen, we were not privy to the thoughts and schemes of the officers in charge. Thomas Devaney latched onto me, and we formed a friendship out of necessity. One night, as I sat by the fire, staring into the flames, he plopped beside me.

"What are you thinking about, Peter?"

He was a simple man, but I enjoyed his company. "Well, I was remembering our first contact with the British. I was impressed when they kept coming at us like they were in a parade." I turned toward him. "Then I ran away after the first shots were fired."

He grunted, "Me too."

I tossed a branch into the fire. "Made up for it when they came back. The thrill I felt from firing my rifle into the mass of retreating soldiers was more than I can explain. I want to do it again."

"Me too."

I continued to be concerned about the welfare of my parents and had the urge to go into Charlestown and check on their house. It was not safe because the Royal Navy was patrolling the harbor. That would have to wait for now. Some other men from Lexington were blessed with visits from their wives and children. I was jealous and felt an emptiness I had not felt since I was at Harvard. It had been weeks since I had last seen my parents or Anne. I tried to write letters when I could but had not heard from my parents, who were still trapped in Boston.

Thankfully, I did receive regular correspondence from Anne. She shared what it was like when the retreating British soldiers passed through Cambridge on their way back to Boston. They had not damaged the city but looked like a mob rather than the disciplined troops they were known to be. She shared her concern for my safety and only wanted what was best for me. I still couldn't bring myself to share with her the horrors of my childhood. I was more convinced than ever to see the war through to the end before I could have an everyday life with her.

Chapter 52

John Smith

Time to Leave

Amanda and I remained hunkered down in Boston, just trying to survive. We had gone through most of our food supply, and only a tiny trickle of relief could pass through the British troops guarding the city. Trade was suppressed entirely, so I could not keep the business open. We received little news and had been waiting to hear from Peter for weeks. There were rumors of a battle between the colonists and the British troops, but nothing that could be confirmed. Amanda's health continued to deteriorate from concern over our son and from lack of nutrition. I debated trying to get out of Boston, but I was a known supporter of the Sons of Liberty. It would be risky to try to pass through the British sentries. I did have money stashed away and could try to bribe my way out of the city.

When I felt we had reached the end of our wits, it was time to convince Amanda. I found her sitting alone, staring out the small window in our bedroom. I followed her gaze and saw her staring across the bay toward Charlestown. I pulled a chair next to her and grabbed her hands. She continued to look out the window.

"Darling, we need to talk."

She slowly turned her head with a blank expression on her face.

Maybe it was too late. "I think it's time that we left Boston. We're not safe here."

She cocked her head and squinted. "What do you mean, John? We have to wait for Peter to return to us."

I leaned closer. "We will go to Charlestown and wait for him there. Wouldn't it be nice to see our home again?"

She remained emotionless. "Whatever you think."

We packed a wagon with as many personal belongings as we could fit. I went to hitch up our horse to the wagon and saw the effect the siege had on him. He was gaunt and listless. The poor animal was another victim of the British. My mind raced with the possible outcomes of our attempted escape. Most of them were bad. I prayed we would be allowed to leave.

We set off late in the afternoon when there would be less traffic. We dressed as unassuming as possible by disguising ourselves as ordinary people. Amanda was very weak, and I was concerned that she wouldn't be able to complete the journey. The stress might be too much. I knew we had to try. We were as good as dead if we stayed in Boston. Slowly passing from the piers to Orange Street, we headed for the neck of the peninsula. Amanda clung tightly to me. As we seldom ventured out, I was appalled at the poverty and destruction we saw along the way. There was garbage everywhere and few people on the streets. The pockets of soldiers we encountered looked at us with contempt and loathing.

As we pulled up to a line of stragglers trying to exit the city, I noticed that only two British soldiers were guarding the road.

We waited our turn in line. When we got to the guards, one of the men looked sternly at me.

"What is your business?"

"Sir, we are trying to return to our Charlestown home."

Both sentries looked at us more closely. "What are you carrying in the wagon?"

"Personal belongings. You are welcome to see for yourselves."

One of the soldiers jumped into the wagon and began searching for the items in the back. When he was satisfied there were no dangers, he hopped back down next to the other sentry.

"Why should we let you pass; there are many criminals in Boston trying to flee."

"Sir, we are common people who want to escape the city's misery. We would gladly pay a toll to be allowed to pass."

"Is that so? How much would you be willing to pay?"

A shilling would be a fair amount.

The guard who seemed to be in charge stated, "Well, if you mean a shilling apiece, then I think that we can let you pass."

I handed the men their money and set off before they changed their minds. I could see Amanda's worried look, and I squeezed her hand.

"It will be fine. Let's go home."

Chapter 53

Peter Smith

Promotion

We spent weeks camped outside of Boston. Camp life was dull, and several men silently escaped into the night, never to be seen again. Those who decided to stay were tense because they did not know what would happen next. The remaining Lexington militia members were reassigned to Colonel William Prescott's command. I knew nothing about the man, but he seemed to have the same leadership presence as John Parker. He was a Massachusetts man, and that seemed important.

We continued to languish at the outskirts of Cambridge. Even though I was so close to Anne, I denied myself the opportunity to go and see her. I couldn't let my feelings for her distract me from my mission. Other than my real mum, Amanda and Anne were the only women who mattered to me. In my mind, a barrier was still preventing me from getting closer. I knew it stemmed from the abuse I endured and the shame I continued to feel. Even if I killed every British invader, would it ever be enough?

I spent my idle time gazing out at the vast number of Americans surrounding the British troops trapped in Boston. I felt the strength of that, but I also knew the truth: that it would take more than numbers to defeat the English. From my naval service, I learned firsthand how disciplined and trained the British were. I still replayed the image of those soldiers marching into Lexington. The reality of what we faced made me decide to be more assertive.

I needed to make recommendations to the officers we reported to. Captain Henry Skiles was a capable and respected man. He was an attorney from western Massachusetts with no military experience. After a long day of drills, I chased him down.

"Captain, can I talk to you?"

He stopped and turned around. "Peter. What can I do for you?"

I fidgeted with my hat in my hands. "Sir, I was wondering if you had some time to talk about my suggestions."

His green eyes flared, and he looked over his shoulder and back at me. "Very well. Let's take a walk."

"I know you are aware of all the men who are leaving. I think we need to focus on cleaning up the camp." I pointed at the shabby dwellings and filth. I continued, "We also need to provide better food for the men. That would go a long way to improving morale."

He stopped. "Where did you come up with these ideas, Smith?"

I turned to face him. "I served in the English Navy during the war with the French."

He took a step back. "You must have been a child?"

"Yes, sir, I was."

"I had no idea. What other suggestions do you have?"

"I'm concerned that we do not have enough ammunition and powder for the next battle. The British won't make the same mistakes again after the defeat they suffered at Lexington and Concord. We should be better prepared for that."

"Have you talked to anyone else about this?"

"No sir, I came to you first."

"Follow me. Colonel Prescott should hear about this."

Over the next few days, some of my ideas were implemented. The other company members came to respect me. Colonel Prescott told me it was evident that I was mature well beyond someone my age.

As was the custom of the time, the other members of the company elected me lieutenant. I was humbled by this and did the best I could to live up to their expectations. I wished I could share the news with my parents.

Chapter 54

John Smith

We Shall Rebuild

I looked back over my shoulder at the two British sentries. We did it. Amanda still held tightly to my arm and buried her head against my shoulder. As we slowly traveled down the dirt path away from Boston, I got a good look at the ring of rudimentary encampments. "My God!" What did it mean? "Amanda, you need to see this."

She lifted her head and gasped. "Are those our soldiers?"

"It appears so."

"Do you think Peter is out there among them?"

"Let's find out."

I felt a swelling of pride as I scanned the surrounding hills filled with American militia. I tried to push the horse past its limits. As we neared the city of Roxbury, we were challenged by American pickets. One of the men stepped in front of the wagon.

"Halt! State your business."

I pulled back on the reins. "We are trying to go back to our home in Charlestown." Amanda grabbed my arm again. I whispered. "It's fine, don't worry."

The sentry eyed me. "It's not safe here. You need to be on your way."

"Thank you. Do you know where the militia from Lexington is? Our son should be with them."

"The companies are all mixed up. They could be anywhere along the line." He turned and glanced at the mass of men behind him.

I looked up to where he pointed and saw thousands of men. I thought to myself. *Let's go home now and look for him later.* We continued on the twenty-mile trip to Charlestown. We got a good look at the army sent to defeat the British. While it was a welcome sight, I was appalled at the appearance of the men and the state of their lodgings. How could this gathering of citizen soldiers ever best the professional British army?

After being stopped several times, I finally steered the wagon onto the narrow peninsula that was home. The closer we got to Charlestown on the southern tip, the more damage we observed. I looked over at Amanda and saw concern on her face. There weren't any British soldiers in sight. It was different from Boston, but it wasn't normal either. There should be more people here.

We finally reached our street. I craned my neck to get a good look at our house. "My God!" My jaw dropped as I stopped the wagon. Amanda started to wail.

"John, what happened to our home?"

The front door was open, and all the windows were broken. Furniture was strewn all over the front yard. I climbed down from the wagon as Amanda continued to cry. My legs trembled as I climbed up the front stairs. I peeked in the front door and was suddenly frozen. The home had been ransacked, and many items were stolen. There were holes punched in the walls. Hay and fodder were scattered on the floor. It looked like British soldiers had been stationed here and were careless. Why would they put their horses in the house when suitable stables were in the rear? I walked the rest of the way through the empty dwelling. What do I tell Amanda?

Dreading it, I walked back outside and looked at Amanda. Her eyes pleaded with me. All I could do was shake my head and look down. I heard her start wailing again. I walked to the wagon and helped her down.

"At least the house is structurally intact, and we are away from Boston."

She wrapped her arms around me. "What shall we do?"

I looked at the surrounding houses and gritted my teeth. "We shall rebuild."

Chapter 55

Peter Smith

Here They Come

I received word that the officers were being assembled to meet with Colonel Prescott. I was out of breath when I reached his headquarters. The meeting had already started. Prescott noticed me. "Good of you to join us, Lieutenant."

There was a smattering of laughter at my expense.

"As I was saying, General Ward has received word from Boston that the British are planning to move on the Charlestown Peninsula." He pointed to a map that was spread in front of him. I inched my way closer.

He looked up. "Our orders are to dig into the high ground at the peninsula's center to prevent the British from capturing it. If we allow them to take those heights, it could threaten our position." The other officers started to talk among themselves.

"Gentlemen, go prepare your men. We leave immediately."

As the others drifted away, I walked up to the Colonel. "What is it, Smith?"

"Sir, how did we come by this news?"

He had a sheepish grin. "Appears we have a well-placed spy in Boston. Now go. We will need to be ready for anything they throw at us."

We reached the heights of Bunker Hill, which offered a commanding view of the area across to Boston. Orders rang out to start working on trenches. The men started putting their backs into the work when Captain Skiles told us to stop.

"Change of plans. We are to move down the hill and set up our defense on Breed's Hill." He pointed to another height closer to the possible British landing spot. I scanned the terrain. I wondered if this was a smart move, but orders were orders.

I turned to my company, "Let's move out." When we reached the spot, I ordered my men to work digging trenches and building abutments. They stood there looking at me. I took off my shirt and grabbed a shovel. I shouted, "Who will assist me?" As I bent down and buried the head of the shovel into the dirt, I saw the others grab their own shovel. "That's the spirit. We will make those redcoats sorry they picked on us?"

We labored the rest of the day, erecting a solid fortification. As I climbed out of the trench, I was beyond where my body could carry on. I stood leaning on my shovel and looked at the maze of trench work surrounding me. This would be different from standing in that open field facing the British like we did in Lexington. This strong position would give the men the courage to stand up to the British. I bent over to pick up my shirt and heard a familiar voice.

"Great work, Lieutenant! You and your men should be proud of your efforts."

I turned and smiled. "Thank you, Colonel. We shall be ready for any attack."

As he walked away, I looked into the tired faces of the men. "You heard the Colonel. Fine work men. Get some rest. Tomorrow will be a long day."

Early the following day, I was startled awake by the loud crashing sound of cannon fire. I jumped on top of the trench and stared out into the harbor. The British ships opened fire against the earthworks we erected. I watched with uncontained excitement as the cannon balls bounced off the earthworks with little effect. They aren't happy with us being here. I tried to see through the haze of smoke that covered the ships to see if I could recognize the Progress.

After the shelling stopped, I watched with fascination as hundreds of British troops were transported across the harbor on long boats. They looked like a swarm of red ants moving across the water. Transporting the initial load of soldiers to the eastern end of the Charlestown Peninsula took hours. Throughout this drama, Colonel Prescott kept a watchful eye out. He stood behind me, and I heard him speak to the assembled officers.

"Gentlemen, we must extend our defenses to prevent them from maneuvering around us and attacking from the rear. Get your men to work. I will see about getting some reinforcements."

I went back to my company. "Men, it is vital that we extend our lines to protect us against the British attack coming our way."

I knew the men were still exhausted from the previous evening's work, but they also saw what they were up against. Once again, we went to work strengthening the fortifications. I jumped right in to assist in digging the ground to extend the trenches. I could have easily avoided the hard work, but I wanted to be an example.

I looked to the rear for the promised reinforcements as the work progressed. No one was coming. I then jumped on top of the abutment, stared out down the hill, and watched the British line up for the pending assault. Beyond the mass of men, I saw that additional redcoats were being transported. This could be problematic. I walked across the trench. "Men, keep at your work. The British will be here soon."

The men dug with more gusto. It will make a difference.

I continued to watch the boatloads of soldiers being dumped on the shore. These men lined up smartly to join their fellow soldiers. There must be a few thousand men down there. Then, to my amazement, the British began their assault.

I yelled out, "Here they come! Men, drop your shovels and grab your rifles."

Other officers shouted similar things, and the men took their positions throughout the defenses. We all watched as the British marched in drill precision over the uneven ground in our front. The terrain was dotted with obstacles that prevented cohesive movement, but on they came. As the British passed Charlestown, I saw puffs of smoke coming from the city. We must have some militia there taking potshots.

Then, the familiar sound of cannon fire could be heard. I watched in horror as the shells rained down on the city. "Damn you!" I cried as I could see fires starting to burn among the wooden structures in town. This caused chaos among those who had remained there. I had a clear view of the smoke from those fires blowing across the peninsula. It was a prelude to the battle that was about to take place. I turned my attention back to the lines of attacking soldiers who were undeterred and continued their march toward our line.

I couldn't help but be impressed as our British counterparts moved toward us with such pageantry and precision. I looked at the men around me and saw fear in their eyes. It was time for me to step up and show leadership. I went from man to man and looked into their eyes. "Men, we shall prevail this day. Remember how these same troops ran from us at Lexington!"

The men let out a cheer, and I screamed along with them. It was then that I noticed Colonel Prescott pacing the lines behind me. He was shouting orders that were muffled. Then, with clarity, I heard him say, "Do not fire until you see the whites of their eyes!"

I jumped down into the trench and prepared my rifle. Onward, the British continued over the uneven ground. There were scattered shots fired from nervous militia, but most of the colonial line held their fire until the gap closed. At about fifty yards, the order was given, and we let go with a ferocious volley. I felt my musket jump when I pulled the trigger, and with the resulting smoke, I wasn't sure if I hit anything. It would have been hard to miss as the British were bunched together tightly. As I reloaded my musket, I could see that huge gaps were made in the enemy's ranks. There was also an overpowering smell of sulfur from the burnt gunpowder. The worst part was the cries from the wounded men that littered the field.

I took a few seconds to look around at my comrades and only noticed a few wounded. My blood was up. "Keep pouring into them, men!"

The men poured fire into the British lines. Slowly I could see that they were retreating. I heard the guttural cheers from the jubilant militia, but my eyes were fixed out to the front. As the smoke began to lift, I was shocked at the carnage. There were heaps of dead and dying men littering the ground.

I leaned my head against my outstretched arm. I said a quick prayer of thanks that I was still alive. I heard a commotion and looked up as reinforcements jumped into the trench. Then I heard someone yell out.

"Here they come again!"

I collected myself and jumped out of the trench. "Prepare yourself, men. Take good aim. Don't waste your ammunition."

The second wave had to step over and around their wounded comrades, but on they came. Our line opened fire again with the same results. My head swiveled around the trench while I loaded my rifle. *Why aren't there more casualties in our ranks?* I fired another round and felt my belt for more bullets. I was down to my last few and almost out of powder. This was my biggest fear, running out of ammunition. I knew it was only a matter of time before we would have to retreat and leave the field to the British. I continued to walk the line and encourage the men. I made eye contact with Colonel Prescott. He had an intense look on his face and nodded his head at me. How much more can we take?

In the third and final wave, the redcoats fixed bayonets and came straight to the center of our line. By this time, most of us were out of powder, and as the British closed in, many of the men scurried out of the entrenchments and hastily retreated from the line back to the relative safety of the rear.

I did what I could to keep the men calm to prevent a panicked mass exodus. My eyes burned from the smoke that covered the field, and my body was quickly passing the point where I could function. I tried to rally the men, but it was too much for many of them, who had little sleep the previous night and had been fighting most of the day. They saw those bayonets with the sunlight glistening off them and couldn't continue fighting.

We suffered most of our casualties during the retreat. Many of the militia who chose to stay and fight were bayoneted without mercy by the British troops, who had absorbed so many casualties. I retreated with my men and could only wonder how different it would have been had we not run out of powder to continue the fight. Many of the army leaders would continue to ask this question.

The British were ultimately left in control of the battlefield, but at a horrendous cost.

Chapter 56

John Smith

Refugees

W e finally cleaned up the mess and started repairs. I needed help finding someone with the proper skills, as they had either run off or joined the militia. My construction skills were put to a severe test, but I managed. Our problems followed us from Boston. I still had concerns about Amanda's health. She wasn't herself and retreated deeper into a shell. I could only assume it was over the possibility of losing her two sons. I needed to decide what we would do next. It was nearly impossible to resurrect my business with the British controlling everything. Our most recent concern was being located between the two armies. I watched last night as the American militia started to dig in on Breed's Hill.

The morning was like any other. I got up and made breakfast. Amanda wouldn't eat and was wasting away. As I set about doing the daily work of repairing our home, I heard shouting out in the street. I dropped everything and ran outside. People were fleeing from the waterfront. I yelled out, "What is happening?"

A gentleman, whom I didn't recognize, had a look of terror on his face, stopped and responded. "The British are coming across the harbor in boats." He then blended into the fleeing crowd. I had to go see what he was talking about for myself. When I got down to the piers, I could see dozens of boats loaded with soldiers heading in our direction. I thought to myself, *"What does it mean?"* Then I remembered our army digging trenches. It became apparent to me. I noticed a few other people standing and watching the sight. I shouted out, "We need to leave. It's not safe here."

One of the men turned to me and waved me off. Fool. I hurried back home to collect Amanda. When I got there, I heard the distinct sound of musket fire. I tried to see where it was coming from. I shrugged and went into the house. I found Amanda still in bed. I grabbed a dress and threw it on the bed.

"Amanda. You need to get up. The British are landing soldiers, and there will be a battle."

She stirred and sat up. The look on her face made me stop what I was doing. I went to her and held her in my arms. "We need to go now. Please help me pack a few things."

She reacted to my hug and, in a weak voice, replied, "If you think that's best."

While Amanda started packing, I returned to hitch the horse to our wagon. Suddenly, I heard the thunderous booms of cannons firing. I turned toward the sound and, to my astonishment, saw the projectiles arching through the sky in my direction. I was mesmerized by the sight and couldn't move. I followed the objects as they came down into the city. The percussion knocked me off my feet as they exploded a few hundred yards away. I was dazed and covered in debris. In my fog, I could see the horse panic. I slowly stood and went to calm him.

I pulled the wagon around the front with the shells still raining down. I went into the house to find Amanda on the floor screaming. I roughly snatched her and pulled her to her feet. I picked up all the belongings she packed and steered her out the door. We raced up the street as the cannonballs continued to fall around us. My eyes were wide with shock as I turned and saw the city engulfed in flames.

We turned onto Main Street, leading us off the peninsula, and fell in line with the mass of citizens trying to escape. Then, as the panic reached its peak, the cannon fire stopped. I sat up and continued to listen for any other signs of battle. Nothing. Amanda finally calmed down and laid her head on my shoulder, refusing to look at all the carnage. I looked off to my right at all the activity in the American lines as they prepared for the attack. I wondered if Peter was among those brave souls.

It took a couple of hours to reach the neck of the peninsula, and American militia were directing all the refugees toward Cambridge. Amanda stirred from her shell. "John, where are we?"

I put an arm around her. "My dear, we are on the road to Cambridge."

She sat up and looked around. "What happened to our home?"

"It was destroyed in the bombardment."

She deflated. "What will we do now?"

"I'm not sure."

We rode in silence the rest of the way. I wanted to utilize my network of friends to assist us until we could find a place to live. Cambridge was untouched by the battle, but there were hundreds of displaced citizens from Charlestown. Out of desperation, Anne's parents' home was the only place I could think to go. I had never been to their residence and had to get directions. As I turned the wagon onto their street, there was the muffled sound of gunfire. I gritted my teeth. It had started.

When we got to the residence, I helped Amanda from the wagon. We limped to the front door. Before we could knock, we were greeted by the sight of Anne.

She took one look at us and couldn't hide the shock she must have felt. We were filthy and must have looked like we had been through a biblical disaster.

"Mr. Smith, Mrs. Smith, what brings you here?"

Amanda recovered and stepped forward. She gave Anne a warm hug. "We have escaped Charlestown from the fires started by the British. They have destroyed our home. We hoped that you would have some news about Peter."

Anne ushered us into the house. "Please sit down. Is there something that I can get you?"

I looked at her sadly and said, "No, thank you. We were hoping that you heard from Peter."

"I have not heard from him in some time. The last I heard, he was part of the militia from Lexington. I don't know if he was engaged in the fighting there or in Charlestown."

Hester Proctor entered the room and saw us. Anne turned towards her, "Mother, this is Peter's parents, John and Amanda Smith."

"It is so nice to meet you. I have heard a lot about you from Anne."

Amanda looked at her, "We are so sorry to call on you unannounced, but we are looking for any news about our son."

Hester must have seen the hurt in Amanda's eyes, "Where are our manners? I will prepare you something to eat. Anne, please show our guests to the spare bedroom to clean up."

"We don't want to be a burden."

"Nonsense, we are very fond of Peter, and you shall be our guests."

"Mother, they had to leave Charlestown because the British burned the city down."

"I am so sorry to hear that. Now, I insist that you stay with us."

I looked down at my feet, feeling the shame of being homeless. "We are grateful for your offer."

Anne led us back to the bedroom while her mother prepared some food.

Chapter 57

Peter Smith

Decisions

We slowly retreated from the Charlestown Peninsula, the site of our most significant battle yet. It was an awful sight; our demoralized army escaped what could have been a glorious victory. I tried to comfort the men along the way, their spirits dampened by the sight of our retreat. I also looked at the destruction the British cannonade did to Charlestown. The flames were still burning, consuming the homes and lives of our fellow patriots. *Was my parents' house still standing?* There was an eerie mixed feeling of exaltation and utter despair. I knew we had severely damaged the British Army while retreating in defeat. Why were we not provided with enough ammunition to carry the day? We needed better leadership if we were ever to win this war. We needed to rest and care for the wounded from the battle.

I continued to grow into my role as Lieutenant, learning from the mistakes and successes of the battle. I had time to reflect on the battle and shivered as if chilled by the memory of what I did and saw. *How did I walk away from that day unscathed?* I learned important lessons from the mistakes that were made during the battle, lessons that would shape my leadership style in the future. Training would be paramount to our success, but the army needed to be adequately supplied. After the harrowing retreat from the British soldiers armed with bayonets, my men should get their hands on those also.

I spent as much time as possible with the senior officers, humbly seeking to learn as much as I could about the craft. I was especially in awe of William Prescott. He was a rock on that hill. How he kept his composure during the fight and rallied the men was inspiring.

I received an invitation to dine with Colonel Prescott. Both nervous and curious by the invitation, I had little direct contact with the Colonel since the battle. I had been busy rebuilding the ranks and training the men. There was little time for socializing on any level, and I couldn't help but wonder what this meeting could mean for my future.

At the appointed time, I reported to the house where Colonel Prescott had his headquarters. I followed an aide to the dining room, where Prescott and other officers had gathered. They were standing around talking and drinking. I was led directly to the Colonel.

"Lieutenant Smith, reporting as ordered," I said, trying to keep my voice steady.

Prescott smiled, "At ease, Lieutenant. This is a social occasion. Get yourself a drink and join in the conversation."

I started to mingle with the gathered men, my ears tuned to the conversations around me. I deliberately listened to the conversations centered on the new commanding general, George Washington. I heard rumors about the man and his heroism in the French and Indian War. There had also been some discussions about the fight on Breed's Hill. It was interesting to hear what the others thought about the fight, their perspectives and opinions. Most men I did not recognize knew they had not been on that hill.

The men who had fought there were mostly quiet, their silence speaking volumes about the horrors they had witnessed.

Dinner was magnificent and included many meat dishes, puddings, and an assortment of breads and desserts. There were also generous amounts of spirits available. After a toast was given to the new commanding officer, who was not present, we all pitched into the meal with gusto. It had been months since I had eaten this well. Conversations continued throughout the dinner, and I played the role of observer, taking in the sights and sounds of the room. As part of my schooling at Harvard, I was trained in proper etiquette in social settings. I knew I was very low on the rung of rank in the room, but I was content to listen and learn from those around me.

As the evening wound down, the other officers started to leave. I thought it was time to go back to check on my men. As I started for the door, I heard my name being called. I turned and saw Colonel Prescott coming toward me.

"Lieutenant, I hoped to speak with you before you leave."

"Of course, sir, I am at your disposal."

"Follow me into my office."

I dutifully followed the man into the office, where he shut the door behind us.

Pointing to a chair, "Please have a seat. I had hoped to be able to get to know you better tonight. The evening seemed to get away too quickly before I could talk to you."

I sat quietly, holding my hat in my lap, thinking that I had done something wrong and was to be chastised.

"Relax, Mr. Smith. I wanted you to know that I was very impressed by your actions during the battle, especially the way you looked after your men. I was not the only one who noticed, and if we are to win this war, we will need more leaders like you."

I didn't know how to respond to the compliment. "Thank you, sir," I managed to say, my voice barely above a whisper.

"You don't talk much, son."

"I was taught to listen and learn rather than babble to impress."

"That's a good lesson. I understand that you attended Harvard College."

"Yes, sir. I was able to complete my studies there and then apprenticed in my father's trade business in Boston."

"It is terrible how the British are treating Boston. How are your parents?"

"When I left Boston, they had stayed behind. I have not heard from them since."

"Were you born in Boston?"

"No sir, I was born in England," I said, my voice tinged with a hint of sadness. "I was very young when I was impressed by the Royal Navy to serve on one of their frigates during the war with the French. It was a difficult time, but it taught me the value of freedom and independence."

Prescott sat back and looked surprised. "I was not aware of that. How did you come to Boston?"

"After the war, the ship went to Boston to have work done in the dry dock. It was during the great fire that I could escape and was taken in by my parents."

"That's an incredible story, young man. It's true to say that you are not loyal to the King or his navy.

"That would be a true statement, sir."

"You will get more opportunities to serve on a ship again. I have heard that a Continental Navy will be built to combat the British fleet. They will need experienced men to man those ships. If you don't have any objections, I will provide your name to those in charge of that enterprise."

I perked up and could barely contain my reaction. This could be my chance. "As you see fit, Colonel."

"Is there anything that I can do for you, Lieutenant?"

"Yes, sir, would it be possible for me to take some time to visit the young woman whom I am courting? She lives in Cambridge."

"It would be my pleasure to approve that request. Take as much time as you need."

With that, I stood and bid the Colonel goodnight.

Chapter 58

Peter Smith

No Future

I packed lightly and was on my way to Cambridge. I had been through so much since the last time I saw Anne. How could I possibly share all the horror I had seen? There hadn't been time to let her know I was coming. I was given a horse to complete the twelve-mile trip from where my men were camped to the Proctor's home. As I pulled up to the front of the house and climbed off the horse, Anne came bounding out of the residence and gave me a lengthy embrace. I took in her aroma while I melted into her arms. As I was lost in the moment, I heard a familiar voice call out my name.

"Peter, is it really you?"

I looked up to see my adoptive mother and my father standing close behind her.

"Mother, Father, how can you be here?"

John came to me and shook my hand warmly. "We were able to escape from Boston, but during the battle in Charlestown, our home was destroyed by fire."

I stood there with my mouth hanging open and my hands raised at my sides. I was overjoyed to see my parents but was shocked by the loss of the family home.

"What will you do?"

John replied, "We have been blessed to stay with the Proctors for a few days. I have contacted friends from the Sons of Liberty, who provide us with lodgings. I hope to continue assisting the movement from there."

I noticed that my mother stood motionless and stared at me. Amanda's trance finally broke, and she came to me. She wrapped me in a hug and sobbed uncontrollably. I was choked up by her display of affection. After a few awkward minutes, Anne broke the silence.

"Let's all go in the house where we can talk more. I have prepared a meal."

I tied up the horse and followed Anne and my parents into the home. Inside, both of Anne's parents were waiting to greet me.

After some time spent chatting and catching up, lunch was served, and we all sat down to eat. The conversations continued during the meal, and I was surprised by Pastor Proctor turning to me and asking, "Peter, tell us about the part that you took in the battles with the British."

All eyes were now squarely on me. I wondered how to respond to the statement. I didn't want to go into too much detail about the bloodshed I witnessed, and I still wasn't sure what the Pastor's intentions were.

I looked around the room at each person sitting at the table. I put down my fork and folded my hands in front of me while I thought about how to respond. "Well, I was directly involved in the action in Lexington and Breed's Hill."

They continued to stare at me, willing me to provide more information. The look in their eyes was ghoulish with anticipation.

"There was much confusion during both battles. We tried not to confront the British at Lexington, but they came directly at us. On Breed's

Hill, we had strong defensive positions, and the British soldiers came foolishly at us until we ran out of ammunition." I stared off vacantly, reliving the memories.

Amanda came to my aid. "Son, we are relieved you are safely here with us."

John Smith wanted to know more. "Peter, do you believe that the British can be defeated?"

I cocked my head and looked at him. "Their army is very disciplined and well-supplied. The Colonial militias are still unorganized and not as well supplied. It could be a very long struggle."

I noticed that Abraham Proctor looked concerned. "Is it too late to reverse this action?"

I got a better impression of where his loyalties may be. "I fear, sir, that we are past that point. Many men have died on both sides, and I don't think the British are going to quit and go home."

Anne, who had looked back and forth as her father and I spoke, asked, "Peter, how long do you get to stay with us?"

I smiled at her, grateful that she changed the subject. "I have been granted a week to be away from my company."

After lunch was over, we took a walk to spend some time alone. Anne clutched tightly to my arm like she would never let it go. It was a magnificent, warm summer day, and it was good to get out of the house and away from all the questions. We walked silently for a few miles when Anne stopped and faced me.

"Do you have to go back and fight the British? Why can't you stay here with me?"

I looked directly into her eyes and weighed my response. "It is because of you and our future together that I must return when the time comes.

If we are truly free to live as we see fit, we must defeat the British. I cannot shirk from my duties and make others do the fighting for me."

I could see the hurt in her eyes as she looked away from me. "What shall happen to me if you are killed?"

I placed my hands on her shoulders and turned her to me. "I will have to make sure that doesn't happen."

Over the next few days, I enjoyed being with Anne and my parents. I concentrated on getting rest and recharging my energy for whatever lay ahead. Anne and I took a long walk every afternoon and seriously discussed our future. I remained adamant that we wait to marry after the war. On the other hand, Anne insisted that she would not marry until I was honest with her. I wasn't ready.

I learned that my parents had, in fact, found a place to live. John had also been appointed by the Continental Congress, through a recommendation from John Hancock, to serve on a board that was tasked with supplying the army. He would utilize his many contacts while smuggling goods into the colony to keep the Continental military supplied. Both parents were proud of me and supported my stance to actively serve in the army and fight the British. They were concerned for my safety, but they understood the bigger picture of the sacrifices that had to be made.

Anne and her parents were a different story. Anne clearly expressed her concerns about my service, but I was unsure what her parents thought. Abraham gave subtle indications of his loyalty to the Crown by what he said, while Hester would not offer an opinion during any discussion on the subject. I assumed that she played the role of a dutiful wife. I asked Anne about her parents' allegiances, but she was unsure. Through all this, Anne continued to push for me to open up to her before she would commit to a future with me.

The closer I got to report back to camp, the more I felt the pressure she applied. Finally, I took Anne aside the day before I had to leave. She looked into my eyes for any sign I would tell her my secrets. I took her hands in mine and hesitated.

"You know that I have strong feelings for you."

She had a troubled look on her face but remained silent.

"There are things in my past that I am not proud about. Those things I keep locked up, and I can't share them with you. At least not now."

She tore her hands away from mine, and I saw tears in her eyes. "Then there can be no future for us."

She walked away, leaving me speechless.

I mounted the horse early the following day and returned to the army.

Chapter 59

Peter Smith

On to Philadelphia

There have been many changes since I left camp for my week-long leave. General Washington officially took command of the entire Continental Army. In fact, the total command structure had been reorganized. I found out that I still reported to Colonel Prescott and led the same company of men. I quickly settled back into life in the army with its repetition and boredom. The men were also restless and impatient to return to their families and the life they left behind. It would be an ongoing problem as the war dragged on to keep the men engaged and willing to stay the course. I remained popular with the men and did not act as a marionette or a taskmaster. I was still haunted by the discipline expected on the HMS Progress and the punishment doled out for the most minor infractions. We still surrounded the British.

Good to his word, Colonel Prescott had conversations with his superiors about me concerning my naval experience. I was told that the Continental Congress voted to equip sailing ships to combat the British Navy and confiscate goods that could be used to prosecute war efforts. There was an urgent need for men to man these and other ships that would be built or captured. This was an effort to give General Washington his full support.

Therefore, it was no surprise that my name was mentioned in these discussions.

I received orders to report to Colonel Prescott. There had been talk in the company that I was a command favorite and destined for a promotion. I ignored the talk and was curious about what the Colonel wanted. I reported to headquarters as ordered and went directly to see the Colonel. I stood at attention in front of the Colonel.

"Lieutenant Smith, reporting as ordered," I said, trying to keep my voice steady.

"Relax, Smith. Take a seat."

I sat and waited for Colonel Prescott to explain why I was there.

"I have given your name to the senior staff of General Washington concerning your naval experience. You are to be interviewed by Congress in Philadelphia to see if you are a good fit for the new Continental Navy being formed.

I sat quietly and pondered the impact of what Prescott told me.

"Sir, I was a young boy when I served in the Royal Navy. However, I would be honored to serve in the Navy."

"Very well. You are to report to Philadelphia in one week."

"Yes, sir."

Prescott stood and held his hand, "Make us proud, Lieutenant."

My head was spinning as I left the office. This would be my chance to seek my revenge. The question would be overcoming the steep odds of confronting my old ship. It would take four or five days to complete the journey to Philadelphia, and I was given a horse, directions, and an allowance for food and lodging. I returned to the company and packed a bag to leave the following day.

I got an early start. This would be an adventure for me, as this was the first time I had been out of Massachusetts before I escaped from the

Progress. I always wondered what the other colonies were like; this would be my chance to see them. My thoughts turned to Anne. I hadn't been in contact with her since our argument. I decided that it would be prudent to stop and see her on my way to Philadelphia.

When I got to the Proctors' home, it was still early in the morning. Anne answered the door and was surprised to see me standing at the doorstep.

"Peter! What are you doing here?"

"Anne, I can't stay. I am on my way to Philadelphia to meet with the Congress."

I could see that Anne had a bewildered look on her face. "Why would you need to do that?"

"They want me to join the Continental Navy and are to interview me."

"Is that what you want?"

"It is."

"But why are you telling me? I thought I made it clear we have no future."

I desperately tried to explain my decision. "Can we sit down for a few minutes?"

She turned away from me.

I talked to the back of her head. "After we win this war, I will come back to you. I will tell you everything and make things right."

I left the house, remounted the horse, and rode toward Philadelphia. I didn't look back at Anne, who stood silently by the front door.

It was an overcast summer day with the threat of rain as I rode alone with my thoughts. I had only been given a week for travel and would need to make more than fifty miles daily to get there in time. I was instructed to stay on the main roads, the Post roads. I started on the Boston Post Road, which went toward Western Massachusetts. Even with the possibility of rain, I still enjoyed the scenery of the wooded, gently rolling hills. There wasn't a hint of the salt air I was accustomed to. I also couldn't see the ocean from where I was. There were other travelers on the road, but not many.

I wasn't in uniform, so as far as the others were concerned, I was just another citizen. I kept the horse on a steady gait so as not to wear him out prematurely. I passed through a dozen small towns along the way. These are places that I heard about from the men who served in the militia, like Sudbury, Marlboro, and Leicester. These towns were quaint and peaceful looking. Different from what was taking place in Boston. As a steady rainfall fell on me, I clutched my coat tightly and thought about how I got to this point. I wondered why the rest of the colony, and even the other colonies, would be caught up with the independence fever when they had not been directly impacted yet.

I hoped to make it to Springfield that first day, but due to the rain and not wanting to push the horse too much, I stopped at Leicester for the night. I found a small inn and took a room. After caring for the horse's needs, I had dinner at the inn. It was a small, crowded room lit by the glow of a roaring fire. I listened with great fascination to the conversations that were taking place around me. The room was clearly pro-rebellion, and I smiled as two gentlemen discussed how quickly the American army would whip the redcoats. If these good people only knew of the struggle that was going on. I slept well that night.

I got another early start the next day. This time, the weather cooperated, and it was a sunny, dry day. I was determined to make better today, but the muddy roads slowed me. It would make a better impression to be on time for my appointment with the Continental Navy board. Over the next three days, I passed through the same type of small towns in Western Massachusetts and into Connecticut. When I got to New Haven and turned onto the New York Post Road, my excitement grew over seeing

New York City. I heard tales about the city, which made it sound larger than life.

As I entered the outskirts of New York, I saw a city that was more expansive and grander than Boston. The streets were busy with people going about their business, and there was no sign of the trouble that was going on in Boston. The shops were full of customers and looked to be thriving. It made me think about our family business and all the struggles we were facing. I made good time up to this point, and even though I could have easily ridden another ten to fifteen miles, I decided to take a room for the night. I wanted to know the mood of the city for myself.

I had been on the road for five days and was tired and sore from all the time spent in the saddle. I had to walk gingerly to work out the kinks in my muscles from riding. When I went down from my room to eat dinner, I saw that the tavern was filled to capacity. I had to wait for a table, but it allowed me to watch the crowd and try to hear what they were talking about. I sensed that loyalties leaned more to the Crown than all the other places I had been. The patrons were openly in support of the King, and they seemed to be angry at the rift that was going on in Massachusetts. I heard rumors that New York was less supportive than the other colonies of the rebellion. Still, I was shocked at what I heard. I couldn't wait to leave this town and be on my way.

When I got on the ferry that took me across the Hudson River into New Jersey, I turned back and looked one more time at New York. I wondered what it would take to convince those people of the righteousness of the cause and bring them into the fold. For the rest of the day, I rode silently through the countryside of New Jersey, lost in my thoughts. I daydreamed about driving a sword through Auger's heart. By my calculations, I would be in Philadelphia the next day. My appointment was scheduled for the day after that.

The rest of the trip was uneventful, and after crossing the Delaware River into Pennsylvania, there were only twenty miles to go to get to Philadelphia. As I got to the outskirts of the large city, my spirits were lifted by being at the place where the new government resided. I increased the pace of the horse that had been such a good companion to me over the last week. It was all now a reality, and there was a good chance that my future would be decided for me the next day.

Chapter 60

Peter Smith

The Interview

I took a room as close to the State House, located on Chestnut Street, as possible. I rose early and had breakfast at the inn where I stayed. I struck up a conversation with the innkeeper, a man named Peters.

"Mr. Peters, this is my first time in Philadelphia. What can you tell me about the city?"

He was a kind, elderly man. "Well, young sir, it's the largest city in the colonies. Founded by the Quakers. So you will see a lot of churches." He had a mischievous smile.

"Is there anything that I should see while I'm here?"

"That depends on what you're looking for. Why are you visiting our fine city?"

I paused, my mind racing with the weight of my secret mission. I had to be careful announcing my intentions. "I'm here on business. I have some time to kill before my meetings."

"Then you should walk the streets to see the beauty of the city. I recommend going to the piers on the Delaware River to see all the ships.

My meeting was at two o'clock, and I had time to walk around the city to take in the sights Mr. Peters discussed. It was a beautiful city, with wide, cobblestoned streets lined with trees and shops. There were many public buildings and even a library. The architecture was very different from Boston. It was a busy seaport even though it was not on the coast. A large wharf stretched along the Delaware River crammed with all manner of shipping and commerce. The downfall that I noticed was the stench and sweltering summer heat that engulfed me. Peters didn't warn me about that. I was used to the cooler summers of Boston, which would take some getting used to.

When it was time for my meeting, I returned to Chestnut Street to find the Pennsylvania State House. The building was a large and impressive two-story red brick structure topped by an ornate clock tower cupola. As I walked up the steps to the structure, I saw two soldiers in uniform guarding the entrance. I strolled up to them and was challenged by one of the men.

"State your business here."

"I have a scheduled meeting with the Continental Navy board."

Both guards eyed me suspiciously. "Do you have any orders that can prove that?"

I reached into my coat jacket and pulled out my papers.

One of the soldiers reviewed the paperwork. "These look in order. Follow me."

I followed the soldier into the building. We walked past several offices where men were racing back and forth in a hurry. It was chaotic and confusing. I thought, "*Is this how the government is being run?*" At last, the guard stopped and pointed to a chair in the hallway near a closed door.

"Wait here. Someone will get you when the committee is ready."

I sat down and continued to watch the hustle and bustle. A few minutes past two, the door opened, and a small, bald, chubby man stepped out and addressed me. The man looked familiar.

"Mr. Smith, please follow me."

I followed the man into the room. It was a small office with a desk that two other men were sitting behind. The man that led me into the room pointed at a chair facing the other men.

"Thank you for coming on such short notice. My name is John Adams, and this is John Langdon from New Hampshire and Silas Deane from Connecticut." He pointed to the other men.

It was clear that Adams was in charge of this interview.

"We have been reviewing this letter sent by Colonel Prescott about you. He is very impressed by you, young man. It states that you were involved in the fighting around Lexington and on Breed's Hill. You were promoted to lieutenant and gallantly led your men during the battle. It also appears that you are a graduate of Harvard College. You do look familiar to me. I'm from Boston and also attended Harvard."

I was overwhelmed by where I was and what the colonel wrote. "Sir, I have seen you in Boston during the trouble with the British soldiers firing on the citizens and the issue of the tea being thrown overboard. I believe that you know my father, John Smith."

"Indeed, I do, young Mr. Smith."

The other two men quietly listened to the conversation until Mr. Deane asked, "Why does Colonel Prescott believe you would make a good naval officer?"

This was the question that I dreaded. I really wanted this appointment, but how much detail should I provide? "As a young boy in England, I was taken and made to serve on an English warship during the war with the French."

John Langdon then spoke up. "How does that qualify you, young man? What were your duties on the ship?"

I fidgeted in my seat as beads of sweat formed on my forehead. "Sir, I was a cabin boy responsible for helping the ship cook and care for the captain and senior officers. My duty station was on the gun deck, where I assisted the gunners."

Mr. Adams must have noticed my discomfort and tried relieving me. "Tell us, Mr. Smith, why do you want to serve in the Navy again?"

"Sir, America has been very kind to me, and I owe a debt for that kindness. I feel compelled to pay back that debt."

Mr. Deane asked, "How did you come to the colonies?"

"The ship I served on was sent to battle the French in Canada. After the battle, the ship went to Boston for repairs. During the great fire in Boston, I made my escape and was taken in by the Smiths."

Mr. Langdon continued the questioning, "Do you feel you would be a capable naval officer in the service of your country?"

I took my time to answer the question. I looked each man in the eye and said, with a resolute voice, "I strongly believe that my experience both at sea and in the militia has prepared me for this moment. You need experienced sailing men, and I am here to be that man."

All three men nodded their heads in unison.

Mr. Adams looked at his colleagues to see if they had any additional questions. They both twisted their heads back and forth.

"Mr. Smith, thank you for your time and cooperation through all our questions. As a side note, we are all very impressed by your record in the army and your demonstrated leadership skills. I also want to commend you for completing your studies at Harvard, which are challenging. We are interviewing many candidates and will send you the results of our findings."

"Am I free to return to Boston and be with my men?"

"Certainly, you can leave as soon as you see fit."

I stood up and gave a short bow to the men, then turned around and left the room. I glided back out of the building's entrance, feeling the euphoria of the moment. Still, I was unsure if I had done an adequate job convincing them. I decided to spend one more night in Philadelphia and return to Boston in the morning.

The trip back to Boston was uneventful as I retraced my steps along the same route. I was distracted by thoughts of the interview. I was conflicted about serving in the Navy again due to my bad memories. The upside was that it could provide me with the platform to gain my vengeance against those who wronged me. I was grateful for the opportunity to take the trip to Philadelphia. It gave me a different perspective about the colonies and how vast they were. How could we be stopped if they could all be united in the cause for independence from England?

Even though I didn't feel the same drive to complete my journey to Boston quickly, I still reached Cambridge in a week. I planned on calling Anne to update her on my adventures in Philadelphia. As I rode through the streets of Cambridge, everything was the same as it had been two weeks prior. The siege of the British troops in Boston was still ongoing. They must have been licking their wounds.

I was greeted warmly by Anne.

"Peter, I can't believe you are back so soon! You must tell me everything."

Weary from my travels, I smiled and said, "It was wonderful to see parts of the colonies I had not seen. New York was impressive but crowded with Tories. I especially enjoyed Philadelphia. It was grand and bustling with trade and commerce. It didn't appear the people were concerned about what was happening in Boston. They were going about their business as if nothing were happening."

"How was your meeting with Congress?"

"I met with three gentlemen. One was John Adams. Do you remember him?"

"I do. Adams is the famous attorney in Boston."

"Well, they asked me many questions to determine if I would be a good fit for the new Navy they are forming. I must admit that I was not very impressed with my answers."

"When are they going to tell you your fate?"

"They did not give a specified time to respond."

She had a hopeful look on her face. "What will you do now?"

I averted eye contact. "I need to report back to camp. I'm still in the militia." I briefly glanced to see a look of disappointment on her face.

"I hope you find what you're looking for."

Chapter 61

Captain Auger

Hurricane

I diligently updated the ship's logs. HMS Progress successfully patrolled the waters off the Massachusetts colony, capturing several ships smuggling goods into America. I felt pride but also concern. We stopped the shipment of vast war material from reaching the rebels. How much got through our blockade?

My officers reported that morale among the men had never been higher. Each sailor had received a portion of the value of the bounty, but due to patrolling along the coast, they had yet to get the opportunity to spend any of their prizes. Maybe I was getting soft in my old age, but they all got the chance to get some liberty with restrictions.

When we sailed back to Boston, we had new orders awaiting us. As a reward for our excellent work, the Admiralty ordered us to report to the British colony of Jamaica to add additional security for English interests in the area. This would allow me to authorize the crew a chance to get some time for rest and relaxation. Jamaica was an essential part of the British Empire, providing vast amounts of sugar from the plantations scattered across the island. There had been reports of unrest due to slave uprisings and the intrusion of other European nations into the area.

It took a couple of weeks to transit from New England to Jamaica. A few days before we reached our destination, a strange cloud formation was spotted off the starboard beam, and the sea began to churn and turn violent. I was called to the quarterdeck. I noticed it was a scorching day, and the sky darkened as the massive cloud moved toward us. I heard tales about these storms, but I had just faced one. I turned to the officer of the deck. "Mr. Jones, what action is being taken?"

The young man's vision was transfixed on the growing storm.

"Mr. Jones!"

He snapped out of his trance. "Sorry, sir. I ordered the crew to prepare the rigging, and we turned the ship to run parallel to the storm."

I went to the railing and scanned the horizon. I calculated the storm's speed, wondering if we could outrun it. I shook my head, realizing it was moving too fast. Just then, the outer bands of wind engulfed the ship and sent it listing to port. I had to grab the railing to prevent me from falling.

"Mr. Jones, call the men to quarters."

I watched intently as the crew quickly manned their duty stations and set to lower the sails and batten down the ship. My hope would be to ride the storm out without being swamped. The rotation of the storm and the ensuing winds battered the ship and knocked it off course. The storm started to draw the ship toward it as if in a vacuum. The rain drenched me, soaking every part of my body. I watched with dread as we were engulfed by the massive, destructive tempest. Seawater washed over the decks. There was a loud crashing noise that caught my attention. It was heard over the roaring sound of the storm. I squinted against the rain and wind to see that the main mast had sustained a fracture that threatened its integrity. This also snapped several rigging lines and sent two crewmembers overboard. The rest of the crew could only watch in horror as the two men floated away in the massive waves, never to be seen again.

The men worked heroically to save the ship from being swamped and sunk. Then, as quickly as the storm had appeared, it moved on. It was as if the squall had never been there. I barked out orders. "I need damage reports! Mr. Harris, take a muster of the crew to see if any other hands are missing." I spotted my second in command. "Mr. Crittenden, see if we can set the sails again without causing further damage." He nodded and ran off. I took some deep breaths of the humid air to calm my nerves.

Mr. Harris reported to me. "Sir, a muster of the crew determined that two men were missing, presumed dead, and eight others injured. The carpenter told me the ship sustained damage to the main mast and sails. Fortunately, the hull was not damaged, and the ship is seaworthy."

"Very well, Mr. Harris."

Temporary repairs were made at sea, but we still had to limp into port at Port Royal to make permanent repairs.

My God, how did we survive the fury of that storm?

Chapter 62

Peter Smith

Navy Duty

I settled back into my company lieutenant role upon returning from Philadelphia. I had been back with my men for over a month but couldn't forget my last conversation with Anne. I felt a deep regret for the way things ended. Was my sense of duty and shame more critical than having her in my life? She made it clear to me that our relationship was over. I don't know if I could ever mend the fence that I had broken. I was also restless, waiting for news about my possible appointment to the Continental Navy. I promised myself that I would stay the course and do my duty.

There continued to be a lull between the Colonial militia and the British troops in and around Boston. The men continued to drill and strengthen our lines. My fellow officers and I were challenged to keep the men occupied to prevent them from deserting and going home. Despite our best efforts to maintain morale, the men slipped away at night. I couldn't understand why they weren't as committed to our cause as much as I was. They had everything to lose, as I did.

I had yet to meet the new commanding general but had seen him riding the lines and inspecting the defenses erected to keep the English bottled up in Boston. There was some dissension among the troops when George Washington took command of the militias from men known to them. Those men commanded us through the fighting at Lexington and Concord and on Breed's Hill. Washington was an unknown and a Virginian to boot. He also appeared timid about bringing on any conflict with the British. The troops wondered what he was thinking or his strategy to win the war.

The day I had waited for came at last. I received notice to report to Colonel Prescott. My stomach lurched with turmoil as I strode toward headquarters. The news I would receive might set me on a collision course to gain revenge. I was nervous as I was led back to the Colonel.

"Lieutenant Smith, I have wonderful news. It appears that you made quite an impression in Philadelphia. I have your orders in my hands to report to Providence. You have been accepted to serve in the Navy. Congratulations." He held out his hand, and I grasped it firmly.

"Thank you, sir, I won't let you down."

I floated away as if walking on air. The orders in my hand stated that I had a week to report to Abraham Whipple, the commander of the Continental Navy. My thoughts turned to Anne. Should I go to her and let her know where I would go? I still cared deeply for her, and even if she refused to see me, I owed it to her.

I went back to camp to pack my things and say my goodbyes. The men who served with me had been through a lot. Our shared experiences left an indelible imprint on us. It was a bind that would last a lifetime. I found it extremely difficult to leave them when their future was still in doubt. I gathered them around.

"Men. It has been one of the greatest privileges of my life to serve with you." My voice faltered, and I saw tears in the eyes of men who had stared death in the eye. "This isn't goodbye. After all this is over, we shall meet again and raise a glass together."

Each man approached me, shook my hand, and wished me well.

I glanced over my shoulder to look at the sprawling camp behind me. I decided to go to Cambridge first. On the ride, I rehearsed what I would say to Anne. All of the words needed to be corrected. I was conflicted about my duty to Anne and my new country. There was such a heavy weight on my shoulders.

Hester met me at the door. She had a surprised look on her face.

"Peter, what are you doing here?"

"Is Anne available?"

She looked over her shoulder. "I'm not sure that she wants to see you."

Anne obviously told her mom about our last encounter. "Do you mind seeing if she will see me?"

She shrugged and left me standing there. A minute later, Anne appeared. She had her arms folded around her.

"What is it, Peter?"

"I came to let you know that I was accepted by the navy and will go to Providence to serve on a ship."

She stood there glaring at me and didn't respond.

"I wanted you to know that I never intended to hurt you. I promise that I will return to you once this is all over. I know you still have feelings for me." I glanced up at her, hoping for a response.

The stern look on her face melted somewhat. She dropped her arms to her sides. "Promise me you will be careful."

I took a step toward her, but she retreated.

"I promise. Can I write to you?"

She nodded.

As I turned to leave, I turned back. "If you see my parents, tell them where I will be?"

She pursed her lips and shrugged. Then she went inside and closed the door.

The journey to Providence took two days. I was familiar with the route, as I had made the trip multiple times during the smuggling enterprise I assisted in running for my father. Colonel Prescott told me that Congress was raising funds to establish an American fleet. My orders should have specified an individual ship for me to report to. This intrigued me. I knew firsthand about the might and strength of the British Navy. How would we be able to stand up to that power? I had to trust that every effort was being made to accomplish that feat.

When I entered the city of Providence, I rode down to the docks. My orders were to report directly to Abraham Whipple. As I walked along the wharf, I saw a bee hive of activity going on. Work was being done in the shipyard building, which appeared to be a man-of-war. There were also several foreign-flagged ships unloading cargo. I was surprised they had gotten through the British ships patrolling the area. I stopped a man who appeared to be a sailor and asked for directions. He pointed to the end of the pier. I felt an excitement I hadn't felt in several years to go to sea again. This time, I would have more control over my situation.

I found the headquarters of the fledgling American Navy and went directly to the commander's office. I knocked, entered the small office, and saw a large-bellied man sitting behind a desk. I came to attention. "Sir, Lieutenant Smith reporting for duty."

Whipple looked up at me. "At ease, young Lieutenant. Have a seat."

I handed over my orders. I watched silently while the older man read the papers.

He threw the orders on his desk. "You are to be a gunnery officer on one of our fighting ships. What experience do you have?"

"Sir, I served as a lad on the British man-of-war Progress during the war with the French. My duty station was the gunnery deck assisting the gunners."

"Is that so? How does that make you an officer in my Navy?"

I maintained a neutral face and replied with too much emphasis. "I served in the militia as an officer in the fighting on Breed's Hill. I have led men in battle, and I have experience as a sailor."

Whipple sat back in his chair, rubbing his enormous stomach, and smiled, "I like your spirit even if you are insubordinate. We need good officers to train and lead the men we recruit to man our ships. I need to be sure that you fit that description."

"What are my orders, sir?"

"Presently, I do not have a ship for you to report to. I need you to assist in recruiting more men while we build and confiscate additional ships to serve on. See my adjutant; he will explain the specifics and show you where you will be berthed."

I stood and saluted the man, then left the office.

I was provided temporary quarters in a repurposed warehouse on the pier. I received orders to go on a recruiting trip throughout the northeast. I had a small staff to travel with. We were to sign up and catalog any men interested in joining the Continental Navy. I had strict orders to meet quotas and do everything possible to meet those goals. I knew what that meant and was unwilling to impress men into service. No matter what. I also knew that I would not, under any circumstance, recruit young boys to serve. I was given a month to perform this duty and return to Providence when I would be assigned to a ship.

The orders explicitly directed my small group of recruiters toward the coast to find men who had sailing experience. We started traveling south along the Rhode Island coast and then west throughout Connecticut up to New York. We would stop in each town for a day and move to the next. My staff consisted of a lieutenant and two experienced seamen. We had been allotted money to entice the recruits with a bonus to sign up for one year of service. There was a lot of pressure put on this small group of men to find quality recruits in a short amount of time. It seemed like a sound plan, but like all plans, there were many hurdles to overcome.

Our first stop was in Warwick. We stopped our wagon in the main square. I directed the two sailors to hang up printed notices around town while we set up our stand. A pub was off to our right, and I noticed three disheveled men stumble out of the establishment. One of the drunks yelled out, "What have we here? It looks like the rebels are in town."

I watched them for any sign of trouble.

Another followed, "We don't need your kind here." Then, all three nearly fell over, shouting, "God save the King!"

The noise began to raise a crowd. The three men seemed harmless, but I turned to my charges. "Prepare yourself if they mean to attack." I drew my sword and stood tall. Some of the citizens came forward and forced the Tories to leave.

One of the men who came to our aid turned to me. "They are harmless. You are welcome here. This is a city loyal to your cause."

"Thank you, sir. We have important business here recruiting for the Navy."

He wished me luck and, along with most of the crowd, left the scene. A few men came forward to investigate what incentives there were to serve.

Overall, there was little interest. We only signed up two men that first day. Both were older men who had served in the British Navy but changed their allegiance like mine. It could have been a better start.

Over the next month, going from town to town, we recruited fifty-five men of different ages and abilities. We aimed to sign up one hundred men but needed more time. After we returned to Providence, I reported our results to Commander Whipple. He was less than pleased. Other recruiting parties sent out to the north had been more successful. I chalked the trip up to gaining more experience in administrative duties and getting to know more of the budding country.

I finally received orders to report to a ship called the Triumph. She was a frigate that had been converted into a fighting ship. The Triumph was armed with twenty guns and manned by a crew of over two hundred men and officers. The moment that I saw her, I was reminded of HMS Progress. The two ships were very similar. This bodes well for me. It had been fifteen years since I had been on a fighting ship, but the memories returned. The first time I went aboard the Progress as a young boy, I was scared but also fascinated. Now, I am determined. Below decks, it was cramped, and the smell was foul. That was something that I never got used to. Other than the memories of the abuse I sustained, it was good to be back to something familiar to me and be part of something bigger than myself.

I reported to the officer of the deck, a young lieutenant named Peterman. A sailor was directed to guide me to the Captain's cabin to meet the Captain. As I followed the sailor, I noticed the galley was eerily similar to the one I worked at on the Progress. The sailor knocked on the Captain's cabin door and entered. I came to attention before the Captain and handed him my orders.

"Lieutenant Smith, reporting for duty as ordered."

Captain Alfred Pullman was a middle-aged man who was short and rail thin. He had a chiseled face and deep-set eyes.

"Please sit, Lieutenant."

I sat looking around the cabin. It was tidier than Auger's. Captain Pullman reviewed my orders in silence.

"I see that you are to be my gunnery officer. Have you any experience navigating?"

"No sir, I served as a cabin boy, and my duty station was the gun deck."

Captain Pullman sighed and stood up. "I need experienced officers, and they send me you."

"My apologies, sir, but I have led men in battle and served aboard a British man-of-war during the war with France."

He looked as if trying to appraise me. "Don't get your feathers ruffled, young man. We face an experienced enemy and need every advantage we can find."

Pullman folded his arms across his chest. I could see that the older man was deep in thought. "You will also be my supply officer, and once we are at sea, you will learn how to navigate. I want my officers to be able to perform multiple duties."

"I understand, sir."

"Good. Get settled and come to my cabin for dinner tonight to meet the other officers. We will set sail in three days."

Chapter 63

Peter Smith

Sea Trials

The next three days were a whirlwind of preparations to set sail. I meticulously oversaw the loading and storage of provisions, a task I was well-acquainted with from my previous role as the cook's assistant. The operation went off without a hitch. I led by example, willingly pitching in to carry heavy loads below decks. Despite the disapproving looks from the other officers, I remained steadfast in my commitment. I couldn't change who I was, and I was determined to fulfill my duties to the best of my abilities.

More importantly, I took the time to familiarize myself with the gun crew. I put the men through rigorous practice sessions to load the big guns, knowing that our true test would come when we set sail. The crew, for the most part, was raw and inexperienced. I was eager to see how they would perform under pressure, but I knew that predicting their reactions in the heat of battle was a near-impossible task.

I was deeply impressed by the Captain and the other officers. Captain Pullman was a serious man, but he was fair. He commanded respect without resorting to corporal punishment for minor offenses, and the men responded to his leadership. I observed the crew's deference to the Captain when in his presence, a stark contrast to the fear I had experienced on the Progress. The other officers, too, were dedicated and committed. There was a good mix of experienced and novice sailors among them, and I felt a growing sense of confidence in our collective abilities.

I often thought about Anne. I missed her dearly. It had been impossible to take leave before departing, with all the work required to prepare the ship and crew. I wrote to Anne often and was surprised to receive a few letters in response. She was still angry with me, and no romantic language was included. I had to win her back. I was comforted that Anne would be safe in Cambridge. I heard from my father, who had reestablished his business in Cambridge, trading in black market goods. He used his prior connections to smuggle the goods into and out of the colony. He was especially intent on bringing in goods supplying the Continental Army. It was a patriotic thing to do, but it didn't hurt that he profited from his enterprises.

The Triumph received orders to depart Providence to expedite the training of the crew while seeking opportunities to engage British merchant ships between the coast of Massachusetts and the Carolinas. The orders didn't specify the length of the assignment but left it to the discretion of the Captain. It was a sullen and dreary morning when we got underway. I stayed on the quarterdeck while preparing the ship to sail until clearing the last set of small islands off the coast of Rhode Island. Determined to make good on my orders and learn the navigation aspect of working on a ship, I took the duties seriously. At any time during the confusion of battle, each crew member may be required to perform any role.

Hypnotized by the crew's handling of the lines and sails, I paid attention to all the orders the Captain gave the helmsman steering the ship through the maze of obstacles. I studied the charts used to navigate while familiarizing myself with the sextant, the device used to navigate by the stars. The device utilized two mirrors, measuring the angular distance between a fixed spot in the heavens and the horizon to plot an accurate course for the ship to travel. I liked challenges and spent every free moment mastering all these details.

As I tried to learn the other duties aboard the ship, my primary responsibility was supervising the gun crew. I retained a distant memory of working the guns on the Progress, but I read the manuals concerning gunnery actions before leaving shore. I was determined to be prepared once we were at sea. We worked diligently on loading and simulating firing the big cannons while in port. I got to know the gunners and learned how far I could push them when the time came. I was mature enough to realize that I could learn from the experienced members of the gun crews. Men who had served during the war. Now that we were at sea, we could practice and hone our skills. This included firing the guns.

The gun deck was located below the main decks and was cramped with cannons on both sides. I was always amazed at how low the overhead hung, and the men could not stand up straight as they made their way through the compartment. I inspected the space and ensured the guns were tied down and secured to the deck with ropes. My gaze ran up the ropes attached to pulleys so that they could be moved back and forth to load and fire. I knew the process was very labor intensive, and a well-trained crew could be the difference between life and death.

As we left the coastline behind, Captain Pullman finally allowed us to practice live fire. I smiled at the assembled crews and yelled out, "Men, to your stations."

Each sailor quickly took up his position at his assigned gun.

I looked at my pocket watch. "Load your guns."

I watched with an appraising eye as the three-man crew pulled the ropes that moved the cannon back away from the side of the ship to the loading position. Each cannon weighed nearly two tons, and the men strained to get them in place. I enjoyed watching the competition between the crews as each placed a cloth bag of gunpowder in the barrel and rammed it home using a rammer. The cannonball was then placed in the gun barrel, followed by another wad of cloth, which kept the cannonball from rolling out when it was hoisted back in place. The order to pull the gun into the firing position was barked out by each crew's Captain. The men could be heard grunting while pulling in unison to manhandle their guns back toward the opening in the ship's side. Wooden chocks allowed the barrel to protrude through the gun port. I walked down the aisle between the guns to observe each gun being primed to fire by pouring a small amount of gunpowder in the touch hole at the gun's breech. The gunlock or firing mechanism was set, and the gun was sighted.

After each gun captain motioned that their gun was prepared, I ordered. "Fire!"

Simultaneously, the gun captains pulled a lanyard, and all twenty guns fired. The ship shuddered, and the sound was deafening. The stench from the burnt gunpowder was overpowering—just like I remembered.

I rechecked my pocket watch. "Four minutes, gentlemen. We can do better than that."

I saw the resolve in all their faces. "Reload."

The process started again, but the cannon barrel was swabbed to remove any burning embers and gunpowder that could clog the next shot. I watched with nostalgia and anxiety as the powder boys brought more gunpowder from the ship's magazines to each gun. Having these boys on board the vessel wasn't my choice, but I would ensure they were protected.

The practice continued for another hour until the firing rate was down to three minutes. I saw the fatigue on the gun crew's faces, ordered them to clean up the space, and dismissed them for dinner. Impressed by the crew's improvement, I eagerly located the Captain on the quarterdeck to give my report.

"Sir, I have concluded the live fire exercise and would like to make my report."

Captain Pullman stoically looked at me and nodded.

"The gun crews have shown much improvement in their actions and are firing at a rate of one shot every three minutes."

The Captain thought about the report and answered, "Very well, Lieutenant, but I expect that to be under three minutes."

I excused myself and walked away a little dejected, but I understood the importance of gaining every advantage possible in the battle. Over the next week of constant drilling, the fire rate was reduced to under three minutes. The Captain was pleased with the progress, but tragedy occurred when there was an explosion from one of the guns. The crew had not adequately swabbed the barrel, and an ember sparked the loaded gunpowder bag. The resulting blast killed two of the gun crew and injured three others. There was also damage to the gun deck that needed to be repaired. I blamed myself for needing to be more thorough with my instructions. It was an essential reminder of the dangers we faced.

After two weeks at sea, the ship sailed back to Providence for repairs and refitting. The cruise had given the crew valuable time to practice their sailing and gunnery skills. However, we did not locate any British shipping, and the effort was considered to be a failure.

Chapter 64

Captain Auger

Repairs

We limped into Jamaica to make repairs and rest the crew. The storm we encountered was fierce, its howling winds threatening to tear our sails and its towering waves threatening to capsize us. I allowed a more liberal leave policy for the men to debark the ship for some time on the island. After our close call with the storm, I felt they deserved the respite. I paced the quarterdeck, waiting for the report from the ship's carpenter. I couldn't even look at the island paradise where we were anchored. When I saw the man come toward me, I knew it was bad news based on the look on his face.

He was visually dreading giving me his report. "Begging your pardon, Captain, a closer inspection showed that the damage to the main mast can't be repaired. It needs to be replaced."

I fought hard to control my rage. It was not this man's fault. The news was a blow, a setback we could ill afford. "Very well, Mr. Wilson. What do you recommend?" I asked, my voice steady despite the turmoil inside me.

He had removed his cap and was twirling it in his fingers. "Typically, pine or conifer trees are used to fashion a main mast. A large enough tree to make the mast in one piece is most desired. I don't know if these trees are here." He twisted his head toward the island.

I stood there, torn between the safety of my crew and the urgency of our situation. "Mr. Wilson, I want you to take a party of as many men as you need to go ashore and find a replacement," I finally commanded, my voice betraying my inner conflict.

"Yes, sir." He turned and started barking orders at the crewmen standing near him. The crew, though tired and disheartened, responded with renewed energy. They knew the task ahead was not an easy one, but they were ready to face it, their loyalty to the ship unwavering.

I watched from the ship as ten men, their faces etched with determination, set off with a confiscated team of oxen and wagons to bring back a new mast. Despite the scorching heat and the muggy air, they trudged into the island's interior, their spirits undeterred.

I busied myself in my cabin, completing paperwork. I suffered through the heat that I was not accustomed to. The melancholy that enveloped me could not be displaced by a dalliance with my latest cabin boy. News traveled slowly, and my thoughts returned to the American colonies' rebellion. We could be recalled anytime, but we were held hostage until a new mast was found. The crew read my mood and left me alone. So I sweltered alone, waiting for news. The silence was deafening, the weight of responsibility heavy on my shoulders.

Three days after I ordered the search party to find me a replacement mast, I heard a commotion on deck. I started to get up when there was a loud knock on my door.

"What is all the shouting about?"

The door opened, and Lieutenant Pressley poked his head in. "Captain, they have returned," he announced, his voice filled with a mix of relief and excitement.

I followed Pressley up to the quarterdeck. The crew had lined the side of the ship and were pointing. Out of the jungle emerged men who looked barely alive. They were guiding the oxen, which were dragging an enormous tree. The crew, watching this spectacle, started cheering, their voices echoing across the water. The search party waved back in acknowledgment, their tired faces breaking into smiles. I turned to Mr. Crittenden. "Supervise getting that enormous thing aboard and have Mr. Wilson report to my cabin."

He saluted and ran off, calling out orders.

I sat at my desk, fidgeting with the papers, anxiously waiting for the carpenter. A few minutes later, he appeared. I couldn't hide my shock at his appearance. He was filthy and looked like he lost twenty pounds he couldn't afford to lose. I got up and walked to him, guiding him to a chair. He genuinely appeared to appreciate my show of concern. I poured him a cup of water and sat across from him.

"Are you well, Mr. Wilson?"

"Yes, sir. Sorry for my appearance. It was a difficult journey."

"Drink up, and tell me everything."

He took a gulp of his water and looked at me with dead eyes. "We had been told by locals that the largest trees were silk cotton trees in the island's center. After more than eight hours of fighting the overgrown jungle, we came to a clearing and spotted a large tree with an unusual root system. To be of any use, the tree had to measure at least sixty feet high and be more than three feet in diameter. After careful consultation and measurements, we agreed that this was the tree we sought." He sat back, drained.

I put my elbows on my desk and let him have a minute. "Go on."

He took another drink and sat the cup down. "It was getting late by then, and the men were exhausted. We waited until the next morning to cut it down. It was hard and dangerous work cutting down the giant tree with the axes we brought. The men took turns chopping, and finally, after a few hours, the majestic tree fell to the ground. We removed all the branches and prepared to move the tree. The wagons were useless in the dense jungle. We used the ropes to attach the tree to the oxen."

"Anything else?"

He looked troubled. "Captain, we saw all sorts of animals we had never seen. There were colorful birds and deer. We came across the largest snake I had ever seen. It easily measured ten feet in length. This was when we slogged through a swampy area where we saw a monster with a long tail and a snout full of teeth sunning itself on a patch of dry land. I am amazed that we all returned alive."

I stood and held out my hand. Wilson focused on the outstretched hand, not sure what to do. Finally, he grasped it, and I helped him up.

"Mr. Wilson, you have done this ship and His Majesty a great service. Now, I ask that you complete the task of replacing the mast."

He gasped and nodded his head.

Nearly six weeks later, a packet arrived with a new set of orders. I had the officers assemble in my quarters.

"Gentlemen, it appears the Army had been forced to abandon Boston and relocate to New York. We have been ordered to return to the fleet to escort the Army to its new location. The rebels have proved to be more of a nuisance than we were led to believe. Prepare the ship to sail. We leave in the morning." The officers exchanged glances, their expressions a mix of concern and determination. They knew the task ahead was not an easy one, but they were ready to face it.

Chapter 65

Peter Smith

Harass the Enemy

There was shouting topside, and I went to investigate. Men were packed into small groups, chatting wildly. I snagged one of the sailors and asked, "What is all this about?"

He took notice of me and saluted. "Sir, there is news that the British have abandoned Boston."

I released him, and he went off to celebrate. I was elated by the news, but what did it mean? It seemed too good to be true. The crew was speculating that the British army would retreat back to England. I doubted it. King George would not allow his colonies to gain their independence that easily. I looked for the Captain to see if he had any information. He was up on the quarterdeck surrounded by the other officers. He noticed me as I joined the group.

"Mr. Smith. It appears that the British have done us a favor."

"Captain, do we know where they are going?"

"No. I told your fellow officers that we have been ordered back to sea."

I looked at the assembled staff, who were as elated as I was.

As we prepared again, word came that the British Army had repositioned to New York. We also received word about a document drafted by the

Continental Congress in Philadelphia. The document was titled "The Declaration of Independence," Captain Pullman assembled the whole crew and read it to us. From my vantage point behind the Captain, I could see those solemn words' impact on the men. This new concept was unheard of: "All men are created equal." Now, we shall see if these men can do their duty so we can live free by the immortal words written on the document.

The Triumph received orders to head south to harass British shipping, especially merchant ships supplying the army. We were to meet with other American warships to engage the British fleet. There was a sense of urgency as I directed the men to load the last supplies and prepare the ship to sail. It was a clear, warm day, and the winds were favorable for the sails to guide us through Rhode Island's maze of islands and out into open water. I could see excitement among the crew on their faces. I even noticed the Captain smiling, which he rarely did.

Once the ship was safely out to sea, the Captain called the crew together to read the official orders.

"Men, we have been ordered to rendezvous with Columbus and Cabot off the coast of Massachusetts. We are then to proceed south and harass any British shipping we encounter. We are to ultimately sail to the Bahamas and capture all stores aboard any British merchant ships. We have been given a great opportunity to show the British what we are made of. Good luck, and God bless."

The crew shouted three "huzzahs," and we were dismissed for assuming our duties.

I watched the crew as the orders were read and could tell from the severe expressions on all their faces that reality was setting in about the difficult job that lay ahead of us. I also felt confident that I had done everything I could to ensure we were prepared.

Chapter 66

Captain Auger
Crush the Rebels

We had been at sea for four days. I was pleased that the new main mast and the other repairs made in Jamaica were completed. I haven't shared the new orders with the crew yet. I wanted to ensure that the main mast would hold up first. With the stifling heat of Jamaica behind us, I assembled the crew. I kept an eye on the horizon, searching for any more of the storms that nearly destroyed us. It was a calm day at sea. The water returned to the deep blue color that I was used to. I looked up at the main mast, and it appeared strong and in tack. The sails were cradling the wind that propelled us through the water.

"Men, your conduct has been exemplary during the last few weeks. I applaud your hard work and loyalty to the ship. We have received new orders to sail to New York. We are to assist the main fleet in protecting the merchant ships supplying the army. Our other duty is to seek out and destroy any rebel shipping we encounter."

The crew was unaware that the colonists had any form of a navy. Their faces displayed their surprise.

"It's time for us to get back into the action. We have to prove to the Americans that they are making a drastic mistake, thinking they can rebel against the might of our army and navy. They are weak and ineffective. We shall show no quarter to them until the last of them surrender."

As the men were dismissed, I saw no signs of dissent.

I was pleased with how the ship and the crew had held up. It had been months since they had been home, but the men's morale was excellent, and this was the best crew I ever had. I needed to relax my discipline while we underwent repairs in Jamaica. Now that we were back at sea, I would resume strict adherence to all the rules and punishment for any infraction. It was important for the men to follow all orders without question since we were back at war. I saw this as my opportunity to finally make my mark and be recognized by the Admiralty. I smiled at the thought of receiving the promotion that I was destined for.

I met with my staff as we sailed north toward the American coast. I stared at the assembled group and waited until the room was silent. Standing with great deliberation, I grasped the lapels of my jacket and addressed them.

"Gentlemen, we have been given a great opportunity to crush the American rebellion." I paused for effect and watched for a reaction from the assembled officers. For their part, the group remained stoic, prepared for more information.

I deflated but recovered quickly and, striking my desk with a fist, continued, "I intentionally omitted part of our orders from you and the crew. Not only are we to protect British shipping supplying the army, but we have been ordered to seek out and destroy all shipping transporting goods to supply the rebels. There was also some mention of a navy the Americans have formed in Rhode Island that has been menacing our beloved fleet. I can think of nothing more absurd than the thought of an American navy."

There was a spattering of laughter from the gathered officers, and I smiled with uncontained pleasure.

"It shall be our honor to crush this so-called navy and bring the colonies to their knees. We must remain diligent and maintain strict discipline among the crew."

That statement garnered a few mumbles of dissent. *They have to understand the importance of tight control over the crew.*

I continued, "My plan is to sail to the coast of Rhode Island, where the rebel navy is reportedly based. We shall lay a trap for any ship sailing out of that area and destroy them. I want increased drills to prepare the crew for battle. You are dismissed."

I turned my back to the officers as they left the stateroom. Most of the men remained silent, but I heard one of the more senior officers say, "That man is going to get us all killed."

Chapter 67

John Smith

Samuel Adams

I heard that the British had abandoned Boston, and I dreamed that this day would come. I ran home to share the news with Amanda. I bolted through the door and surprised her. She looked at my face and gasped, "Is it news about Peter?"

I caught my breath and shook my head. "I have not heard from him in a while. I do have good news."

She tilted her head, waiting for me to go on.

"The British have abandoned Boston. Isn't that great news?"

She smiled timidly. "What does it mean, John? Is the war over?"

I didn't want to disappoint her. "I'm not sure. Time will tell."

I rebuilt my import business from our new home in Cambridge. I successfully re-established my contacts and formed smuggling routes to move the goods. It was a godsend when the British abandoned Boston. I also remained busy fulfilling my responsibilities to the Continental Congress to supply the American army with clothing, food, and, more importantly, armaments. This duty was curtailed by the continual presence of British warships off the coast attacking supply ships from France and the Netherlands. Lack of funding was another issue. I took my concerns directly to Samuel Adams to get relief and assistance from Congress.

I heard that Samuel was back in town while Congress was in recess. I hurried over to his office for an audience. When I arrived, a line of visitors stood outside, waiting to see the powerful man. I patiently waited my turn and was greeted warmly by my old friend.

"How are you, John? I heard you had a difficult time in Boston during the occupation."

My eyes wandered as I relived that tense time that seemed so hopeless. "It was indeed challenging to survive in that environment."

"Sit down. What brings you here today?"

To show the seriousness of my visit, I remained standing. "Samuel, the British Navy is playing havoc with the shipping sent from our European friends. When will we see any assistance in protecting the supply ships?"

He grinned while looking up at me. "John, you have to trust that everything possible is being done. Let Congress worry about it."

I calmed down from his words but stood there, wanting to say more.

"Is there something else?"

"Yes. There is also the matter of paying for the supplies we receive. I have used some of my resources to purchase the goods."

He sat back in his chair. "We have representatives in France right now negotiating loans to pay our debts and ensure a steady supply of the items we need to wage war."

I raised my eyebrows. "I had no idea."

"John, it is a process; you must be patient."

I left feeling better about my circumstances.

My other ongoing concern was Amanda's well-being. She was slowly adapting to our new home in Cambridge, sleeping better, and regaining her strength. She never brought up the subject of Robert, for which I was grateful. However, it was our other son who kept her from getting back to her old self. Amanda was shocked to hear from Anne about Peter joining the Navy. When Anne left our house after delivering the news, Amanda turned to me.

"John, why would he do that?"

I walked to her and embraced her in my arms. "Peter is doing what he thinks is best. He has experience. I can only imagine it will help our cause."

She pushed me away. "How can you be so cavalier about the fate of our son?"

I had to fight to maintain my anger. "Darling, I, too, am fearful for his safety. There are many families making sacrifices right now. Why should we be any different?"

She stormed out of the room. "I shall never forgive you if anything happens to Peter."

She barely spoke to me over the next few days. It was helpful that Peter wrote letters. His notes were upbeat, and he didn't want to worry his mother.

With my prodding, she became involved in local charities that raised money and donations to assist citizens displaced from Boston by the English occupation and the subsequent destruction of the city. Still, her words chilled me.

Chapter 68

Peter Smith

Rendezvous

I stood as the officer of the deck watch as the Triumph headed north, hugging the coastline of southern Massachusetts to rendezvous with our sister ships, Columbus and Cabot. The seas were rough and choppy as a cold gale blew from the north. I wondered about the upcoming challenge of meeting with the other two American ships. We would have to safely transit south toward New York in search of British shipping to engage. I shuddered while I watched the cold's effect on the crew who had to serve on the exposed decks of the ship. Then, I was directed to a crashing sound as ice dropped from the sails onto the deck.

I yelled, "Men, clear that ice off the deck!" Then, I looked at the coat of ice that had formed on the rigging. As I was about to resolve that issue, I heard the Captain.

"Clear off the rigging and the sails. Now is not the time to put the ship in peril."

I touched my hat in salute. "Sir, the weather is trying to get the best of us."

He was so calm. It was inspiring.

"Mr. Smith, we have no control over the conditions, but we must keep the ship seaworthy and protect the crew."

"Yes, sir."

I was below decks, trying to get some sleep in my hammock when word was passed that Columbus and Cabot were spotted. Off the coast of Cape Cod, the three ships maneuvered in a southerly direction with the senior Columbus vessel in the lead. I was climbing the ladder to the quarterdeck and heard Captain Pullman tell the assembled sailors on the quarterdeck that conditions should improve the further south we sailed. I pulled my coat tighter around me and hugged my sides. Then, I saw the magnificent sight of the other American warships.

I felt a hand on my shoulder and turned to see who it was. I saw the smiling face of the executive officer, Daniel Turnbury. "Quite a sight, Mr. Smith."

The older man was short and stout. He had the bluest eyes I had ever seen. He seemed to always be in a jolly mood, and it was infectious.

"It is, sir. Who would have ever thought that we would have a navy."

"Now we will see how American sailors fight." He patted me on my back and said, "Make sure that your men are ready when the time comes."

True to Captain Pullman's word, the seas settled significantly the further south we sailed. The three American ships traveled loosely in a vee formation, with Columbus in the lead, Cabot to Columbus's port side, and Triumph to the starboard. The Captain told us there had been no time to make detailed plans for attacking British shipping as we were still determining what we would face.

I walked among the sailors busy with their duties as the opportunity for battle loomed. Most of these men had never been in combat, and I wondered how they would react when the time came. I stood at the quarterdeck railing and stared at the rolling waves. My mind drifted back to the young boy I was when I first went to sea. I would look out at this same ocean all those years ago. I had been through my fair share of war and knew that I could count on myself to handle whatever I faced. I hoped it would be soon because the waiting was the worst part.

As the sun began to set, it didn't appear that we would see any British that night. I took one last look at the sea and went below decks to get some sleep. Maybe I won't have the dream tonight.

Chapter 69

Captain Auger

Swallowing My Pride

We entered the waters off the coast of New Jersey on our journey north. The seas were relatively calm, but there was a noticeable chill in the air, belaying the time of the season. The tension among the crew on the quarterdeck was noticeable. I did my best to hide my confidence and general disdain for the possible rebel navy. I was startled when the ship's lookout yelled, "Sails on the horizon off the starboard beam!"

I ran to the railing and took out my spyglass. As I tried to make out the details of the ship, I cried out, "Order the men to quarters!"

The crew mechanically scrambled to their duty stations as the ship came about to investigate the lone ship. My adrenaline surged as I strained to identify the phantom ship. As Progress neared the other ship, I saw the giant ship flying the Union Jack. It's British. I ordered the crew to stand down from quarters and had the helmsman take a course to come alongside the British man-of-war. As the two ships neared each other, lines were cast to tie them together. As the crew for both ships secured the lines, the sails were lowered to prevent damaging either ship. Captain Nigel Pritchett of HMS Amboy called, "We have orders to hunt down American ships that were reportedly heading toward New York. I am ordering you to sail with us to confront these ships."

I knew Pritchett only by reputation. He descended from royalty. I knew that I had to proceed cautiously. I calmed myself and tempered my response. "How did you come across this information?"

"We were informed that our spies in Rhode Island spotted two American frigates set sail with orders to engage British merchant shipping heading to New York."

Swallowing my pride, I considered this information and quickly decided that I could assist Amboy and still meet my personal goals. "We shall follow you at your discretion, Captain Pritchett."

I ordered the lines attaching the two ships together to be released, and the sails raised to follow HMS Amboy north to intercept the two American ships. I smiled at my good fortune. If the intelligence was accurate, this would be an uneven battle with upstart American ships against the might of the British Navy.

Chapter 70

Peter Smith

The Dream

I had a restless night of tossing and turning, intermixed with troubling dreams of seeing myself slowly sinking into deep water. In the dream, I was helpless as I slipped into the dark abyss, and a panic settled over me when I couldn't breathe. As I became aware of my surroundings and remembered where I was, I tried to make sense of the nightmare and find some meaning behind it. Soaked with sweat from head to toe, I climbed out of my hammock to prepare for the day. Walking through the berthing compartment, I noticed the other men coming to life. I hardly noticed the stench anymore. It was eerily quiet, and each man looked lost in their thoughts. I grabbed a stale biscuit to chew on as I went topside.

When I climbed out on the main deck, I felt the chill in the air. I could see the sun peek over the horizon, which was off the port side of the ship. It cast a dull orange glow in the cloudless sky. I reported to the deck officer as the ship's bell rang out, reporting the time and alerting the crew of the change of watch. Lieutenant Fulmer stood on the quarterdeck and tipped his hat at me as I neared.

I scanned the sea around Triumph and saw Columbus and Cabot nearby. "Any news from overnight, Fulmer?"

The lieutenant looked exhausted, stared at me, and responded, "No, sir. It was a quiet night. There was no sight of any British shipping."

"Very well, Lieutenant, you are relieved."

The young man handed over the looking glass saluted me, and headed below decks to get some sleep. I looked around at all the activity and other sailors relieving their shipmates as they took their watches. I smiled with admiration as the ship's crew progressed in their training. I continued to have the nagging thought, *"How would they fight when it came down to it?"* I raised the telescope to my right eye and scanned the horizon ahead. Nothing. I turned to the helmsman, an older man named Bixby. "Keep her at a southerly heading following Columbus and Cabot. I'll make my rounds now."

"Aye, sir."

I took a deep breath of the salty air, feeling invigorated and wide awake. I slowly walked around the top deck to check on the men and ensure the rigging and sails were correctly set. I also wanted to get a sense of the mood of the men. I need to stop doubting their resolve. As I passed, each sailor would tip his hat in salute, and we would exchange small talk. The men were nervous and apprehensive about the upcoming events that were to take place. I trembled thinking back to my dream. I hoped it wasn't a bad omen.

I was relieved from my duty on the quarterdeck four hours later. The watch was uneventful, with no sign of any other ships. It could be another day of sailing without coming in contact with the British. I decided to go down to the gun deck before eating. I still felt in my bones that something would happen today, and I wanted to ensure that everything was ready for any impending battle.

As I stepped down the ladder leading into the gun deck, I spotted one of the young powder boys, a lad named Arthur. I had been against any boys serving on the ship, but I was overruled by the Captain, who told me that it was tradition. I made every effort to protect Arthur and the other boy, named George, from any abuse. No one on the ship knew of my demons, and I intended to keep it that way. It didn't stop me from being vocal about how these young men were treated.

"Good morning, young Master Arthur."

The boy jumped at the sound of my voice. "I'm sorry, sir, I did not see you enter the compartment."

I held back a smile. "I didn't mean to startle you, Arthur. What are you doing?"

Arthur shyly looked up at me. "Sir, I am ensuring that each gun has the proper supply of powder and fuses for the upcoming battle you warned us about."

I looked at the boy and felt a swelling pride build up in my chest and choked at the lump in my throat. I had to maintain an air of authority, but I really wanted to go to the boy and give him a hug. "It looks like you have everything in order. I shall leave you to it."

I left the gun deck to get something to eat. The biscuit I had for breakfast sat unsettled on my stomach.

Chapter 71

Captain Auger

Enemy Sighted

I refused to abandon the quarterdeck as we sailed in a northerly direction toward a collision course with the American ships. The prevailing winds blowing off the coast of the American colonies tried to push the boat further out to sea, but we made good time hugging the coastline on our way north. I seethed about following the young and privileged Captain of the Amboy. Shaking my head and tightly gripping the rail, I was continually baffled by the decisions made by the British Admiralty on who they gave command. Once the battle was underway, I determined that each man would be on his own. This upcoming fight would be my opportunity to command something more formidable than the old and battered Progress where I had spent so many years of my life. I was confident that the crew was well-trained and ready for anything that the Americans could put up against us. Still, I had to maintain my facade of a stern taskmaster to instill fear in the men so they would do their duty. I strode around the deck, barking orders while keeping my eyes on the horizon as the sun continued its gradual ascent in the morning sky.

When it became clear that nothing would happen today, I went to my cabin. I was on edge, optimistic that we would find the American ships that day. As I waited in my cabin for my dinner to be served, my mind drifted over all the years I had spent at sea. There were some bright spots during my career, but it was mostly a wasted period. A knock at my cabin door shook me from my doldrums.

"Enter."

The newest cabin boy opened the door, holding a tray. I could see the fear and contempt on the boy's face. This usually emboldened me, and I would prey on the defenseless young man. Today, I wasn't in the mood for my extracurricular activities and only wanted to be left alone.

"Put the tray down and then leave me be."

The tension on the lad's face eased as he placed the tray on my desk. "Yes, sir."

As the door closed, I could hear a loud commotion outside my cabin. I stood quickly, knocking my lunch off the desk, and raced for the door. When I reached the quarterdeck, I saw utter confusion.

"What is the meaning of this?" I yelled out to no one in particular.

Ambrose Crittenden turned to me and calmly stated, "Captain, our lookouts have spotted three sets of sails on the horizon. I was about to call the crew to quarters."

I looked around at the chaos and steadied my breathing so that I could take charge. "Very well, Crittenden."

I scoured the northern horizon through the spyglass to identify the unknown ships. Unable to see any markings that would distinguish them, I slammed the spyglass shut. "There were only reported to be two rebel ships heading in this direction." I looked at Amboy and noted that she was coming about on a course to confront the ships directly. Maybe Pritchett could see something I could not. I ordered the helmsman to set a course to mirror Amboy. We would soon find out who we were facing.

On the quarterdeck of Progress, I kept watching the advancing ships. I had yet to engage any American naval vessels, and it was unclear what flag they flew. It didn't matter at this point because the three ships we faced were making offensive maneuvers and had to be considered enemy combatants. I noted that the two forward ships had made course corrections and were headed directly toward Amboy. I quickly changed my gaze to the Amboy to see if Pritchett was giving any direction for the upcoming battle. There wasn't any signal from the lead ship, but it turned from its northerly course to meet its immediate threat. *The fool is panicking and is leaving us behind.*

I smiled despite myself. It was clear what needed to be done. I then made my own command decision. I would attack the lone rebel ship, and when we dispatched it, we would go to bail out Amboy. I ordered the helmsman, "Come about to port to overtake the lone ship!" I pointed.

He followed my finger. "Aye, Captain."

I took time to scan the sails. A steady wind was blowing, which would aid us in overtaking our foe. The crew was well trained and in position for battle. My mind blocked out any distractions and focused entirely on the lone American ship that had foolishly chosen to confront me. It would indeed be a race to get in position first.

Chapter 72

Peter Smith

Load Your Cannons

The crew was called to "go to quarters." We were told that lookouts on Triumph spotted two British men-of-war on the horizon. The large Union Jack flying from the stern of the two boats quickly identified the ships. I knew the flag had a red background and included a smaller version of the British Union in the upper left corner. Our flag had thirteen red and white horizontal stripes with the same image of the British Union in the upper left corner.

I raced from the galley to the gun deck. I steadied myself as the ship made a wide arching turn to meet the threat. I knew being the first ship to get in position broadside to the enemy to get off the first volley was important. When the vessel steadied itself, I took off again to get to my station.

The entire gun crew was on the gun deck, ready for action. I silently nodded to each gunner as I saw that each cannon was manned in preparation for performing its deadly work. I slowly stepped among the crew, adding calming words to each man. As the ship made another abrupt turn to engage the enemy ship, the men on the gun deck had to reach for something solid to not be tossed about the crowded space. I quickly accounted for any injuries or damage when the boat steadied its course.

When I was content that all was well, I stuck my head out one of the gun ports on the starboard side of the ship to see if I could see any British vessels. Craning my neck for a better view, I spotted one of the ships heading directly toward Columbus and Cabot. I turned my head slightly to my right and spotted the other British ship directly ahead of us. It was turning toward the coast, trying to bring its portside guns to bear on us.

I quickly surmised that Captain Pullman was trying to position Triumph across the bow of the enemy ship so that the port batteries would have the first chance at damaging the English ship. I raced across the port side and barked orders for the gun crews.

"Men, load your cannons and prepare to fire on my command."

Just then, a messenger came down from the quarterdeck. "Lieutenant, the Captain orders you to prepare to fire your port guns when the British ship comes into range.

I narrowed my eyes as I looked at the messenger. "Tell the captain that we are prepared to fire."

I turned my attention back to the port gun crews and received notice from all ten gun captains that their guns were loaded and prepared to fire. I looked out a portside porthole and saw the British ship turn across our bow to present its portside guns to fire on us. I tried to calculate the distance between the two warships. I determined that we were about five hundred yards apart. It was an agonizingly slow wait for Triumph to be in position to fire. I knew the importance of getting off the first shots but couldn't rush my fire and miss the enemy entirely. My next consideration had to be where to aim the first volley. Should I aim for the mast to stop the vessel or fire at the hull, hoping to penetrate the two-foot-thick planks at the waterline, which could sink the ship? At the present distance, aiming at the main mast and rigging made more sense.

I turned toward the port gun crews with fire in my eyes. "Port gun captains, elevate your guns to fire at the mast and wait for my order to fire!"

I watched as each man went to work elevating their guns as ordered, and then they turned back toward me and nodded. Now, we wait for a few precious minutes more. Just then, the messenger returned and yelled out.

"Captain orders you to fire your guns!"

I looked at the British ship, which was still turning to present its port side. *Too soon.* My eyes pleaded with the messenger. Deflated, I turned toward the gun crews.

"Fire!"

There was a thundering blast as the guns fired in tandem. The ship shuddered and rolled toward the starboard side. Smoke obscured all vision on the port side as I stared helplessly, waiting for any sign we had damaged the other ship. The gun crews automatically went through the motions of reloading their guns to prepare for the next shot. When the smoke cleared, I was horrified when I saw little or no damage to the sails or mast. The ships had now closed to within two hundred yards, and I could see the British guns aimed directly at my guns.

I screamed. "Lower your elevations and fire!"

There was another thunderous blow followed by multiple explosions on the gun deck. I was thrown across the compartment, crashing into the starboard bulkhead. As I shook my head to clear the cobwebs, I looked around the compartment and saw the jumbled wreck of men and cannons strewn along the port side. The gun crews on the starboard side rushed to give aid and put out small fires ignited. It appeared that at least six of the guns were damaged beyond repair. I stumbled over to the four remaining guns with blood flowing down my face and ordered them to fire.

The guns fired in unison.

Chapter 73

Captain Auger

Still in the Fight

From the quarterdeck of HMS Progress, I watched with controlled pleasure as the first volley from the American ship went harmlessly by my boat. *The amateurs fired prematurely.* I noted some minor damage to one of the sails and part of the rigging, but the crew quickly repaired that. I ordered the gunnery officer to take out the American guns with the first volley. I then spread my feet apart on the deck and grabbed tightly onto the railing in preparation for the impending blast from the ship's port guns. As Progress came parallel to the rebel ship, the first volley rang out, and the boat rocked to the side. It was covered in smoke from the blasts, which made it hard to see.

I ran down the port side of the quarterdeck to get a good view of the damage. I could hardly contain my emotions as I saw the destruction caused by the expert shots from the gun crew. I knew the guns were reloaded for a second shot at the damaged vessel. My thoughts were to quickly sink this ship and join the fight already underway with the other two rebel ships. Then, unexpectedly, there was another volley from the crippled American vessel. The Progress shook violently, and the screams of men could be heard. I was knocked to the deck.

"How could that be?"

I pulled myself up and checked for injuries. The helmsman got my attention as I looked around to assess the damage.

He cried out as he tried desperately to turn the ship's wheel. "Captain, they must have damaged the rudder. I have no control."

As I went aft, the executive officer caught up with me. He bent over to catch his breath. I stood there impatiently, waiting for him to give his report.

"Captain, the Americans got off a lucky shot that damaged the steering and punched a sizable hole in the stern. We are taking on water."

My mouth hung open as I absorbed my second-in-command words. "Can the damage be repaired, Mr. Crittenden?"

Crittenden wiped a dirty hand across his brow and looked around. "The ship's carpenter is attempting to plug the hole, and we have some crew manning the pumps, but as you can see, we are dead in the water."

I looked around to see what he was talking about and noticed that the ship had nearly stopped for the first time, only rocking along with the waves. Looking up at the sails, I said, "We are not catching the wind." I then turned my gaze to the American ship, which had sailed past the Progress and looked to be coming around to turn its starboard guns to face us to try and finish us off.

"How could this be? I saw the damage caused by our first volley."

Mr. Crittenden only stood there silently, squinting his eyes and looking at me. "What are your orders, Captain?"

I pulled at my jacket and took a minute to compose myself. "We are not out of this fight yet. Go personally down to the gun deck and have the crew prepare to defend the ship when the American comes back into range. We shall tie up with the rebel ship and board her if needed."

"Yes, sir, I will see to it."

I returned to the quarterdeck, and as I looked back at my ship, I asked, "Why didn't the second volley get fired as I ordered? How did they get the best of me?"

Chapter 74

Peter Smith

Make Your Report

I could feel the rocking motion, showing that Triumph continued to sail. I wondered if the last volley did any damage to the British ship. Other crew members helped, and the ship's surgeon worked on the wounded survivors from the British volley. When I was confident that things were under control, I went to report directly to the quarterdeck. I had yet to learn how the battle was progressing. As I climbed the ladder up to the quarterdeck, I got my first look at the British ship we were battling. It appeared to be dead in the water as Triumph was sailing to come about to engage it again. I spotted the captain, who was vigorously barking out orders. Captain Pullman noticed me and motioned for me.

"That was some fine shooting, Lieutenant. Please make your report."

"Sir, we sustained severe damage to six of the guns on the port side with many casualties. There are still four operational guns. No damage to the starboard guns."

"Very well. I'm having the ship come about so our starboard guns can finish off the enemy ship."

"I need to get back to my men."

He waved his hand at me.

Before I went below decks to manage the guns, I watched as Triumph sailed around the stern of the British ship. I looked at the damage my guns did to the steering. There was a gaping hole at the waterline. I let out a shout and shook my fist. "That had to be the luckiest shots ever fired." Right before I turned to go down the ladder, something made me take one more look at the enemy vessel. The ship's name was printed in large letters on the stern and read, "PROGRESS." My knees gave out, and I sat on the deck, shaking my head in disbelief. How could I be facing my old ship?

This was my chance at redemption. I pulled myself off the deck and went to the gun deck, determined to finish the job.

Chapter 75

Captain Auger

Slowly Sinking

On the deck, under the scorching sun, I spotted Lieutenant Press-ley making his way towards the quarterdeck. His gaze was fixed on the wooden planks, avoiding any eye contact. Just as he was about to climb the ladder, I called out, "Mr. Pressley, what's the status of our repairs?"

He raised his head, and I could see the dread etched on his face. It was clear that the news he carried was grim.

"Captain, the effort to repair the damage to the hull is failing. The ship is taking on more water than the pumps can expel."

I looked at the stern and could tell that the aft section of the ship had started slowly sinking into the Atlantic's dark waters. I screamed at everyone around, shouting out confusing and disjointed orders. As the men worked to save the ship, I watched the American ship pass Progress's stern and make a wide sweeping turn to come about to fire her cannons. I was determined to get a volley off before the enemy could get in position for the kill shot. Before heading down to the gun deck, I noted that Mr. Crittenden had ordered all able men to be armed and prepared to board the American vessel if she came too close. I grunted with satisfaction and went below to personally command the guns.

When I entered the compartment, I could see the extent to which the ship listed toward the stern. I quickly scanned the guns, which were undamaged and still manned by their crews. The danger was that the cannons could tumble down the deck the lower the ship sank. I jerked my head toward the gunnery officer.

"I'm taking command of the guns. Go to the quarterdeck, watch the American, and yell down when she gets into range."

The bewildered lieutenant only shook his head and headed out of the compartment as ordered.

Turning to the starboard gun crews, I projected a sense of unwavering confidence. "Men, we will exact our revenge by decimating the rebel ship. Align your guns with their gun deck and await my order to fire."

The next few minutes went agonizingly slow. We couldn't do anything but wait for the Americans to make their final turn to come alongside Progress. We only hoped that the American captain would make a mistake and come in too closely. If that happened, I could take out their guns before they could get a shot. Then, we could tie up and board the American to capture her. I blocked everything else out of my mind as I waited for word from the quarterdeck that our prize was in range. Then suddenly I heard.

"Captain, the American ship is coming in close and is in range."

I smiled a devilish grin. "Fire!"

Chapter 76

Peter Smith

Not Again

I entered the gun deck, still reeling from what I had witnessed. I quickly assessed the damage done by the British initial volley. Most of the destroyed cannons had been removed, as had the wounded. The wooden deck was slippery with blood. I went to the starboard side batteries and explained what the captain had in mind to the crew.

"Men, this will be our chance to destroy the British ship. I want all of you to aim your guns at the waterline, and when we come alongside, I will give the order to fire."

I saw each man acknowledge my order with a determined look in their eyes. It was again a waiting game. I went to a starboard portal and saw that the ship was turning too close to the Progress. My mind panicked as I knew that we would be vulnerable to the British guns. My only choice was to fire my volley first, hoping it would incapacitate the enemy guns. As I turned my head and began to open my mouth, there was a deafening cacophony of noise and smoke engulfing the compartment. I felt myself being thrown through the air again and crashed in a heap against the bulkhead. As I tried to make sense of what happened, I could hear the screams of my men. *"Not again."*

I sat up and shook my head. I worked my jaw and was suddenly engulfed by a ringing noise in my ears. There was severe pain coming from my left arm. I hesitantly looked down at the arm and saw it was shattered. There was a bone protruding from my forearm, and a steady flow of blood ran from the wound. I looked around and found a rag lying near me. I cautiously wrapped the rag around my useless arm and slowly stood up.

I was enraged when I saw the damage to my cannons and crew. I was hardened by battle, but the sight of those mangled bodies made my stomach queasy. I had to hold it together. The ringing began to subside as I wondered what happened. Somehow, the British had gotten the drop on me again, and my guns never fired. This time, it appeared that all the guns on the starboard side were damaged, and the gun crews were either dead or seriously wounded.

I didn't have time to grieve and had to go topside to see what happened. I took one more look back, and as I ascended the ladder, there was another earth-shattering sound. I was knocked off my feet, landing on my injured arm.

The only sound I heard was my screams.

Chapter 77

Captain Auger

Start Boarding

As the smoke cleared, I tried to see what damage my guns did to the Americans. I looked around as the gun crews were busy reloading their weapons. I had to know. I raced to the ladder up to the quarterdeck. As I stepped onto the deck, the rebel ship crashed into Progress. Like every man on the boat, I was knocked off my feet and landed roughly on the deck. There was a god-awful screeching sound as the two ships scraped against each other, throwing debris everywhere. I realized we had only a few minutes to board the enemy ship before Progress was destroyed. I grabbed the side rail and drug myself up. Holding onto the railing, I scanned for my officers to take charge of the men. Spotting Crittenden, I yelled.

"Mr. Crittenden, have the men send over the lines and start boarding."

I watched Crittenden pull himself upright and bark orders to the two dozen men stationed along the railing. He rallied them to throw over lines attached to grappling hooks to tie the two ships together in preparation for boarding the American vessel. I knew this was dangerous because the rebel ship was still moving, as its sails were still set. The enemy was pushing the

Progress in a circle, and eventually, it would sink her. The men would need to capture the quarterdeck to prevent that from happening.

I cheered as half a dozen lines were jettisoned to the American ship. I scanned the enemy ship as sailors were being rounded up to defend their ship. Four of the six lines sent over had taken a firm grip and were pulled taut. Then, as the vessel continued to move as if in a dance, the two dozen men started to climb over the line onto the American ship.

The rebels responded, and it was only a matter of time before my men were outnumbered. As the hand-to-hand battle ensued on board the American vessel, I ran down to rally more men to join the battle.

It was another race against time to see who would be victorious, and I was not going to lose.

Chapter 78

Peter Smith

Redemption

I partially recovered from being thrown off my feet again and climbed slowly up to the main deck. I could see that Triumph and Progress were bound together in a deadly embrace. Out of the corner of my eye, I saw the lines being cast from Progress. *They are meant to board us.* I looked up on the quarterdeck and saw the Captain desperately trying to save the ship by maneuvering away from the British. I understood the immediate threat from the boarding party coming onto Triumph. I spotted the master-at-arms bringing up armloads of muskets and sabers to hand out to the men to defend our ship. I looked down at my useless left arm, shrugged, and ran to get a weapon.

Grabbing a saber tightly in my right hand, I looked around at the other sailors around me. I raised the saber over my head and yelled at the top of my lungs, "Who will follow me!"

Without looking back, I ran to enter the melee. Other sailors took up my call, armed themselves, and followed. As we neared the fighting, there were shots from marksmen on the Progress who were picking my men off before they could get into the fight. I couldn't be concerned with them and continued to lead my men. As we reached the battle sight, we clashed with the invaders. We slowly drove them back to the edge of the ship. I slashed my saber at one of the British sailors, knocking him to the deck with a ghastly wound. I was driven by my demons. I had yet to exorcize them and fought like a wildman.

It was a war of attrition, and the crew of Triumph outnumbered our foes. There was blood and bodies everywhere, littering the deck. There was no let-up, and the fighting became more desperate.

As we looked to take the advantage, I spotted more men from Progress attempting to enter the battle. I was exhausted but determined. Taking a deep breath, I turned to the men around me and pointed the sword at the new threat. Their eyes showed the hatred they felt for the enemy. I knew it would be enough to carry the day. As we started to meet the British, there was a loud series of bangs, and I saw more than a dozen British sailors drop. Confused, I turned back and saw that a line of American sailors armed with muskets had come to our aid and stopped the threat. Slowly, the British started to retreat back to their ship.

Without receiving orders, I again raised my sword and ran to cross over and board my old ship. I didn't care if anyone was following me. It wouldn't have mattered anyway, as I was on a mission. It was eerie setting foot on the place that gave me so much grief. I gained a second wind as I slashed at each man in my view. Everything was a blur as I was engaged in a duel with an officer I did not recognize. I felt intense pain on my left shoulder where an unseen British sailor had slashed me with his sword. I ignored the pain and ran the officer through with my blade. I was possessed, and I turned to confront the other threat. Before I could engage him, the man fell to his knees with a horrible wound to his head. Confused, I looked up to see more than a dozen men from the Triumph who had followed my lead and boarded Progress. I barely noticed the blood that flowed profusely from the wound to my shoulder. I would not be deterred.

Looking around for my next victim, I spied an older, overweight man I instantly recognized. "Cook."

The man stood there staring at me. He was trying to remember who I was. After a few seconds, I could see the old cook's face contorted as he realized who was standing before him.

"Is that you, lad?"

"Why didn't you protect me all those years ago?" I yelled.

With the battle raging around us, the old man dropped to his knees and started to weep. Somehow, I felt pity and not contempt for the cook. I decided I had more important matters to attend to and walked off, leaving the shattered man where he knelt.

I had tunnel vision and ignored everything around me. I had to settle this once and for all. I was driven to find the man who took away my innocence. There were so many dead and dying men around me, and I panicked that someone else had finished off the sadistic tyrant. I frantically searched for the man that fueled my anger. When I was sure he wasn't topside, I knew where the coward would be in his cabin.

I carefully went down the ladder, going aft toward the scene of many of my nightmares. I looked around every corner to make sure there weren't any surprises or ambushes. Safely reaching the cabin door, my right hand shook as I went to open it. Tightly gripping the sword under my arm, I slowly pushed the door open. There was a loud clapping sound as a musket ball flew within inches of my head. I was startled by the sound of the gun and jumped back. When I realized I wasn't harmed, I entered the room and faced Captain Auger. The deranged old man was trying desperately to reload his weapon. I took a few seconds to look around the room, which had been damaged by my cannons. A calmness came over me as I slowly approached the Captain's desk and gently placed the sword down. I then reached out and took the musket from the bewildered and shaking man. Tossing the gun behind me, I bent down and looked into Auger's eyes.

"Do you remember me, old man?"

His face had an ashen tint as he stared back at me. Then, after a minute or two, the old man gasped, and his eyes opened as wide as they could go.

"Beale."

"That's right, Captain, your cabin boy is back to avenge his childhood."

The old man fell to his knees and began to blubber. As spittle ran down his chin, he began to beg. "That was so long ago. You don't understand the pressure that I am under. Please spare my life."

I tried to feel pity for the man as I did for the cook, but I couldn't find any. My face contorted into a scowl as I looked down at the man. Slowly reaching over, I grabbed the sword off the desk with my right hand. Then, standing above the pathetic shell of a man, I violently drove it deep into Auger's chest. I stood there watching the life run out of the man, and when it was done, I sat down on the desk.

Holding my head with my right hand, I sobbed and uttered, "Please let this be the end of it."

Chapter 79

Peter Smith

Aftermath

I didn't know how long I sat there in Auger's cabin. My head spun as I tried to focus on the room around me. Faintly, I became aware of a quake in the ship's hull. The room appeared to be tilting at an odd angle. Trying to understand what was happening, I slowly twisted my eyes toward my useless left arm. I gasped loudly when I got my first good look at the extent of the damage. Trying to stand, my eyes rolled back into my head as I was overcome by nausea and crashed to the deck. Weak from the loss of blood sustained from my shoulder wound, my body was shutting down, and I shivered uncontrollably, spiraling into shock.

My eyelids fluttered rapidly as I dreamed of rising above the Earth, looking down at a vast, rolling body of water. I had the sense of being free, and it comforted me, but something still nagged at my soul. What could it be? Then suddenly, I started to hurl back toward Earth, and when it seemed that I would crash into the water -- my eyes opened. I gasped, trying to take in a breath of air. I panicked and jerked my head from side to side, trying to determine where I was. I could feel my clothing was soaked with sweat, and I began shivering. I noticed that I was rocking ever so gently from side to side, and I was in a dark space that smelled like death and decay. I let out a groan as loud as I could muster.

"Mr. Smith. We weren't sure that you were going to make it."

I looked up into the eyes of a familiar face. Why can't I remember anything?

"How are you feeling?"

Squinting my eyes and tilting my head, I suddenly remembered the man. "Doctor Tyler. Where am I?"

The ship's surgeon smiled warmly. "You are on the Triumph. You sustained some serious wounds in the battle, and we were concerned that you might leave us."

"What wounds? What happened in the battle?"

I could see the change of expression on the doctor's face, and the man broke eye contact with me.

"Well, you had a severe saber wound to your shoulder that had to be stitched. You lost a lot of blood, and we found you very weak and barely alive."

I stared at the man and realized the doctor struggled to tell me more.

Slowly, Doctor Tyler looked into my eyes. "You also had serious damage done to your left arm. The arm became infected, and I -- um, had to remove the arm."

My eyes pleaded with the doctor, "No, it can't be true!" I moved my right hand to feel for the left arm -- gone. My mind raced, trying to remember what happened. Then, like being struck by a lightning bolt, I saw the image of myself running the sword through Auger, killing him. I laid back in the hammock and looked at the doctor. "It will be fine."

The doctor looked concerned over the sudden change in my demeanor. "You need to eat something. I will send someone to let the Captain know you are awake. He would like to talk to you."

After picking at some stew, I saw Captain Pullman come toward me.

"Lieutenant Smith, it's good to see you up and about."

I could see through the Captain's smile and the concern in his eyes. "What happened, sir?"

Captain Pullman looked around the cramped compartment. "Do you feel up to getting some fresh air?"

I nodded and put the spoon down next to my uneaten meal. I slowly got to my feet, standing on unsteady legs. After a few seconds of trying to ensure I wouldn't fall down, I followed the Captain to the ladder to the main deck. As I started to climb the ladder, I felt the steadying arms of Doctor Tyler helping me with the climb. Stepping onto the deck, I took my first deep breath of fresh air. The chilly salt air had a regenerative effect on me. I saw that the Captain had walked over to the port side railing. I took slow, steady paces and noticed that the other crewmen around me were staring with awed looks on their faces. Each man removed his cap in respect. When I reached the railing, I saw the Captain staring out at the horizon where land could be seen.

"Where are we, Captain?"

"That is the coast of Massachusetts. We are to go to Boston to undergo repairs."

I looked back at the Captain. "What happened?"

The Captain leaned on the railing and turned toward me. "Young man, you are a hero. I witnessed you lead men to engage the enemy crew in a hand-to-hand battle. You took the fight to the British ship. I also received word that you killed the British Captain."

I looked down at my feet, not feeling particularly proud of myself. "What happened to the Progress?"

"We captured the crew and transferred some of their store of supplies before we cut her loose. She sank to the bottom of the Atlantic."

I slowly nodded my head as I let the news sink in. "What happened to Columbus and Cabot?"

"They engaged the other British vessel. Cabot was badly damaged, and the enemy ship was able to escape."

I looked down to where my left arm should be and asked. "What is to become of me?"

Captain Pullman grabbed my shoulders. "Son, I wanted to talk to you about that."

As the Captain looked intently into my eyes, I stood as straight as possible, waiting for news of my fate.

"Lieutenant, it has been the greatest honor of my life to serve with you, but you have done your part. When we reach Boston, you will be released from your service. Go home and take care of your family. You have nothing else to prove."

I sank and began to sob uncontrollably. Captain Pullman had to catch me to keep me from falling. He grasped me firmly and had tears in his eyes.

Chapter 80

Peter Smith

Departure

I stood on deck and watched as we entered Boston Harbor and sailed to the drydock in Charlestown. I let out a slight snicker at the irony of going back to the place where I first came to America as a young boy. It was a bittersweet moment for me to be going home. The war with England was still in its infancy, and there was much more to do. I had toured the gun deck to see for myself the damage that was sustained in the fight. It was horrific, with all but three of the ship's cannons destroyed. How the boat wasn't blown to pieces from all the gunpowder that was stored near the guns was something I couldn't answer. I could still see bloodstains from the dead and injured sailors whom I commanded. The experience was one that I would never forget for the rest of my life. *Why was I allowed to survive?*

Before entering port, I took a tour below decks to where the British prisoners were locked up. I hoped it would give me some closure by seeing the men I served with as a boy. The hold was cramped and dark. The smell of human waste was overpowering. I squinted to get my bearings, and the only sound was the creaking of the boat as it cut through the water. When my eyes adjusted, I looked for any signs of recognition from the captured sailors. The men were utterly defeated. Most would not look up at me as I meandered through them. I thought how embarrassing it must be for a lowly American ship to be bested by one of the King's warships. I recognized only a few faces, but those sailors would not return my gaze. When I was about to leave the compartment, I saw a large man in the corner trying to hide from my view. I smirked as I instantly knew that I finally found the old cook. Striding next to the pathetic old man, I looked down at him and said, "I see that you survived, old man."

The cook raised his head. He stared at me with hate in his eyes. "Why didn't you kill me, boy?"

"I showed you more compassion than you ever did for me."

The destroyed man couldn't hold his gaze.

My face contorted, and an evil grin crossed my face. "I wanted you to know that it was me that you bumped into in Boston as you were stumbling around drunk. I also am the one that killed Auger."

As I turned to leave, the old cook could only look at me in disbelief. Then it hit me. What about Charles? I swiveled back toward the prisoners. I desperately hoped that he survived. After a few minutes of scanning the room, I gave up. He is in a better place.

Captain Pullman ordered an official ceremony for my departure. As the ship was towed into the drydock and the lines were set, the ship's crew was called to the weather deck. They were dressed in their best uniforms and lined up for me to review them. I joined the Captain on the quarterdeck and fought hard to control my emotions. I was lost in my thoughts as the Captain addressed the crew and made some kind comments about my service and sacrifices. When the crew cheered, I seemed to snap back to reality. I tried my best to smile. I could only muster a wave at the assembled men. I followed the Captain down the ladder and slowly stepped past each man. They tried to control their emotions, but a few were visibly shaken. Without looking directly at them, I nodded as I passed. This was harder than I thought it would be. Upon reaching the gangplank, the Captain stood before me, handed me a ceremonial sword, and then saluted. My eyes welled with tears as I looked at the sword tightly grasped in my right hand. I made a short bow to the Captain and turned to walk down the gangplank.

As I walked on solid ground for the first time in a few weeks, I was directed to a waiting carriage. I noted that the driver was a soldier who had already loaded my belongings. The young man saluted and helped me climb into my seat.

"Sir, I have been ordered to take you to Cambridge."

I looked at the stripe on the man's sleeve, "Thank you, Corporal. That would be fine."

As we traveled down the familiar roads leading to Cambridge, I looked around, amazed that I didn't see any signs of the British or the damage they had caused.

I wasn't sure what my future held.

Chapter 81

Peter Smith

Reunion

"Sir, we are nearing your parents' home."

My heart thumped outside my chest as I looked around. Somehow, the driver knew where to go. I had never been there before. The increased blood pressure made my wounds throb. I wiped the palm of my right hand on my pants. It seemed like a hundred years since I had seen my parents. What I really longed for was to see Anne.

The driver pulled off to the side of the street in front of a nicely adorned, two-story brick home. I looked for any sign of activity and turned to the driver. "Is this the place?"

He cocked his head toward me. "Yes, sir. I was told to bring you here."

Gathering myself, I climbed down from the carriage and stood there, unsure what to do. I turned to the driver. "Do they know I'm coming home?"

He only shrugged.

I felt the empty jacket sleeve with my right hand. *What would my mother think about my injuries?* Taking a deep breath, I strode up to the front door and, hesitating for a few seconds, knocked. I heard footsteps coming to the door, and I was nauseous with anticipation. Suddenly, the door opened, and standing right in front of me was the most beautiful sight that I had ever seen.

Anne shrieked, "Peter, is that really you?"

I couldn't stop staring at her. I was speechless. My knees began to wobble, and I was about to drop when Anne ran to me and hugged me tightly. I felt her tense up as she released her hold on me and took a step back. I could see the worried look on her face as she frantically felt my empty left sleeve.

"My God, Peter, what happened?"

No longer able to stand, I slumped down on the steps at the front door. Anne quickly knelt by my side and grabbed my head to look into my eyes. She called out, "Mrs. Smith, it's Peter. Come quick."

Amanda came to the door and screamed at the sight of me. "Peter, you have come home to me!"

Anne grabbed Amanda's arm. "There is something wrong with him. We need to get him inside."

With the help of the soldier, they carried me into the parlor and laid me on a couch. I saw the concern on my mother's face as she smothered me with kisses.

"Peter, we had no idea you were coming home." She then looked at the empty sleeve. "My God, what happened to you?"

I recovered some strength and tried to sit up. The room began to spin and I slumped. Slowly raising my head, I looked at both women. "Anne, what are you doing here?"

She turned to look at Amanda. "I came to see your parents to get news about you." She grabbed one of Amanda's hands. "Your mother is so kind to me."

Amanda interrupted Anne. "Peter, you must tell me what happened to you."

I was exhausted and didn't want to talk about it.

"Mum, your son is a hero."

We all turned to the sound of the voice. The soldier was standing at the doorway holding my belongings.

"What is he talking about?" Amanda pleaded.

I shrugged my shoulders.

"He almost single-handedly captured a British ship."

I shook my head. "That's absurd. It was the crew that won the battle."

The two women looked at me and then back to the soldier.

"That's not the way I heard it told."

Amanda looked at him for more. "Why are you here, young man?"

"I was ordered to take the lieutenant to your home in Cambridge."

"Please put his things down there." She said, pointing. "We will take care of him now."

I scanned the room. "Where is Father?"

Amanda started to remove my jacket. "He is at his office. I will send someone to fetch him."

I winced as she pulled the jacket off my injured shoulder. She gasped when she saw the blood-soaked shirt. She turned to Anne. "Go get the doctor."

After a few minutes, Anne returned with the doctor in tow. The doctor removed the bandage around my shoulder. I let out a groan.

"I'm sorry. I need to inspect your wound."

I heard footsteps. I turned, and there was my father. He was panting, trying to catch his breath.

"Peter, it really is you." He watched the doctor inspect my wound. "Will he recover, doctor?"

The studious man stopped what he was doing. He had a stern look on his face. He turned toward John. "He is very fortunate to have survived his injuries." He then turned toward Amanda and Anne. You need to replace these bandages every day while keeping the wound clean." He then looked at me. Son, you need to rest and not put a strain on yourself for a few weeks."

After the doctor finished, he walked to the door with my father. They spoke in hushed tones, and I couldn't hear them.

Over the next few weeks, I slept as much as possible. The dreams remained to haunt me, but they were more about the horrors I witnessed during the battle. I seemed to be over Auger and his hold on me. My parents seemed to respect my need not to talk about what took place. Anne visited me every day. There were a number of times that I wanted to tell her everything, but it never seemed to be the right time.

I woke to the sun shining brightly through my bedroom window. The dust in the air danced among the sun's rays. I sat up and gingerly stretched my back and shoulder. There was no pain. It was a beautiful spring morning, and I felt reinvigorated. Today would be the day.

When Anne arrived at her usual time, I took her aside. "I'm ready to talk."

She initially looked confused, but after she realized what I was saying, she beamed.

"Let's take a walk."

She grabbed my arm, and we started down the street. We walked silently for a while, and I could feel tension growing out of anticipation. When we reached a small park, I directed her to a bench. We sat there, and I tried to think of how to start. I took a deep breath and faced her. "Anne, you were right about me needing to tell you everything."

She sat there without talking.

"This is very hard for me."

She reached out and squeezed my hand.

"You know that I came from England. You don't know that my family was destitute, and I had to steal to help my mother feed my brothers and sisters."

She continued to listen.

"I was in prison when the sailors took me away to the ship. I was so young and didn't understand what was happening." I stopped and looked down. I took another deep breath. "While on the ship, I had to serve the captain his meals. Sometimes, when we were alone, he would molest me." I stopped, wanting to see her reaction.

She sat back and released my hand. I could see her trying to process what I told her. "That is why you didn't want to tell me about your past."

I nodded.

She leaned closer and hugged me. "I'm so sorry that you had to go through that."

While she held me, I whispered. "I killed that horrible man." I then started to sob. We sat there and rocked while I released my emotions.

On the walk back home, she stopped. "I think it is time that we get married."

I hadn't expected that. "I am a cripple. What kind of husband could I possibly be?"

"You are perfect to me. Before we can get married, you have to get my father's permission." She hesitated. I could tell she was considering something. Staring directly into my eyes. "You can never tell him what happened to you. He would never understand."

"I don't plan on telling anyone other than you."

Chapter 82

Peter Smith

The Wedding

Anne planned a dinner at her parents' house and invited my parents. We sat around the table and passed small talk. Both sets of parents acted as if they knew why we were gathered. It didn't make my task any easier. I was relieved to not have to talk about my experiences in the Navy. There was enough news going around the colony about that battle. I shied away from the celebrity and avoided the admiration my fellow citizens tried to bestow.

After dinner, I asked Abraham if I could speak privately with him. He looked like he was expecting this, and we retired to his office. After he shut the door, my mind raced, thinking this situation was more troubling than facing the British. I rehearsed what I would say but needed help to remember everything I practiced. He must have seen the fear on my face and said, "Please sit down, Peter, and tell me what it is you want to say."

I sat down, and Abraham took a seat behind his desk.

"Sir, as you know, I care very deeply for your daughter. The times are uncertain, but I want your permission to marry Anne."

Abraham sat quietly with his hands held together in front of his face as if in prayer. He stared at me for what seemed like an eternity. "I was wondering when we were going to have this conversation. You are correct that I know how you feel about my daughter. I have always been very impressed with you and the respect that you have shown for me, Hester, and Anne. Before I answer, what are your plans for your future?"

I sat up straight and looked directly at him. "As you can see, my fighting days are over." I looked over at my missing left arm. "I plan to work for my father and eventually take over the family business." I narrowed my eyes.

"I have a question for you, sir. Where exactly do your loyalties rest concerning the British?"

Abraham didn't seem surprised by the question. "A man in my position must be cautious in expressing political opinions. I hold sway over many people, and my duty lies directly in religion and saving souls."

"That still doesn't answer my question."

"You are correct, it doesn't. Let me say this, I would not be opposed to the colonies gaining their independence from England."

There were a few moments of silence between us.

Finally, Abraham broke the silence. "Mr. Smith, I give you my blessing to marry my daughter. Please do not make me regret it."

"Thank you, sir, she will be very pleased."

"It looks like we have a wedding to plan. Shall we let everyone know?"

We both shared the news with Anne, Hester, and the Smiths. Everyone was excited that the two families would unite, even in these troubled times.

It was a bright, clear summer day. A gentle breeze meandered through the trees, having a calming effect, along with the chirping of birds. Cambridge seemed to be a million miles away from the war and all the events going on in the world. The ceremony was to be held at ten o'clock in the morning at the church, and the reception was to follow at the home of the Proctors. We decided to make the affair more personal, and a limited number of guests were invited.

My mother assisted Anne and her mother with the preparations. Anne's dress was a lovely combination of bright colors made from wool. I was persuaded to wear my naval uniform and looked very regal. The ceremony, officiated by Reverend Proctor, was a somber sermon about the sacrifices and responsibilities required. I considered that it had more to do with the man losing his daughter than with some enlightened commentary of the times. I swooned when I first laid eyes on the beauty of Anne in her wedding dress. My knees were knocked together, and I had trouble standing. I realized that I made the right decision to wed Anne and could not help but stare deeply into her eyes during the sermon.

After the ceremony, everyone was invited to the Proctors' house for the reception. A line was formed, and we greeted each person. I was polite, but my mind was on Anne and our first night together as man and wife. They probably took the smile on my face as joy from the ceremony. If only they knew.

Anne grabbed my arm and led me into the house. I looked with amazement at all the food spread out on the table. There was fish, roasted pork, venison, potatoes, bread, and casseroles. To drink, there were spiced ciders and coffee, but no tea. There was a running ban on tea in the colony. The wedding cake was thick and rich, with dried fruits and nuts. In the middle of the cake was a piece of nutmeg. Folklore said it would give good luck to the person it served to.

We sat through many toasts, and the celebration went well into the late evening. My nerves were raw, sitting there with a smile plastered on my face, waiting for this to be over. I sensed Anne staring at me. She must have been concerned.

"Peter, what's wrong?"

"This is too much. I just want to be with you."

She got up and went to talk to her father. I don't know what she said, but he got up before everyone.

"Excuse me, everyone. It is late, and we need to let the newlywed couple get some rest. Thank you for sharing this day with us."

That night, we went to bed together for the first time. We were given our own room in the house. I was nervous with anticipation of what was to come. I could tell by how Anne avoided eye contact that she was equally apprehensive. We had agreed to stay chaste until we were married. This had been difficult for two young people who were madly in love with each other. The lovemaking was awkward, passionate, and tender. It was magical for us as we discovered each other's bodies and the pleasures we experienced. It had been a long and glorious day, and we fell asleep in each other's arms.

Chapter 83

Peter Smith

What's Next

"Peter, why are you alone again?"

I turned from my desk. I still couldn't believe how fortunate I was to have Anne in my life. She liked to surprise me at work with a visit every day. "I'm going over the ledger again. The numbers aren't adding up."

She had a coy look on her face. "You know what I'm talking about."

I let out a sigh. "What do you want me to say?"

"Husband, why are you so unhappy – distracted?"

I pulled at my pant leg and looked away. "The last few weeks have been the happiest days of my life."

She looked for more.

"The war is not going well. The Army is struggling to stay one step ahead of the British." My voice rose as I continued. "All I do is sit here and go over these ledgers!" I tossed the ledger across the room.

She stepped back in response to my outburst. I took a deep breath. "I'm so sorry. You didn't deserve that."

She came to me and held me. "What do you want to do?"

"I'm not sure."

"You have already given so much. Your place is here with me and your family."

"In my heart, I know you're right. Is there more I could have done?" I thought back to all the events of my life. "Maybe I still have things to prove to myself."

My words hung in the air.

She spoke with a hitch in her voice. "You told me yourself that killing that horrible man has made you forget your childhood nightmares."

I calculated my words carefully. "That's true to a point. I'm not giving that man any more thought. What I can't forget is all the men who have died serving with me against the British. Those deaths are still going on while I sit here in this cramped office, safe and sound."

She pulled back. "What can you do?"

"I'm not sure, but I intend to find out."

To find out the next chapter in Peter and Anne's journey, click on the link and purchase your copy of The Sacrifices of Men. https://www.ama zon.com/Sacrifices-Men-Tragic-Saga-Cabin-ebook/dp/B0CR8M8NQ8

About Author

Danny Bradbury is originally from Colorado. He is retired from a career in the insurance industry. He also served in the U.S. Navy. He has a life long interest in history. He currently lives in South Carolina with his wife Tricia. He has also published, A COMMON MAN, and FROM THE PLAINS TO THE SEA.

Please leave your review of THE SINS OF MEN on www.amazon.com, www.goodreads.com, and www.bookbub.com

Made in the USA
Middletown, DE
31 October 2024

63657547R00181